Encountering
the Book of Genesis

Encountering Biblical Studies
Walter A. Elwell, General Editor and New Testament Editor
Eugene H. Merrill, Old Testament Editor

Encountering the Book of Genesis

Bill T. Arnold

BakerBooks

A Division of Baker Book House Co
Grand Rapids, Michigan 49516

© 1998 by Bill T. Arnold

Published by Baker Academic
a division of Baker Book House Company
P.O. Box 6287, Grand Rapids, MI 49516-6287
www.bakeracademic.com

Printed in the United States of America

Library of Congress Cataloging-in-Publication
Data is on file at the Library of Congress,
Washington, D.C.

ISBN 0-8010-2638-5

Photo acknowledgments:
Alfred J. Hoerth: p. 127

Biblical Illustrator Photo/David Rogers/The
    British Museum, London, England: p. 47

Biblical Illustrator Photo/David Rogers/The
Louvre, Paris: p. 61

Biblical Illustrator Photo/James McLemore:
    pp. 59, 63

Chris Miller: pp. 22, 71, 80, 82 (2), 107, 183

Darwin Archive/Syndics of the Cambridge
    University Library: p. 26

Phoenix Data Systems: pp. 34, 38, 45, 79 (2), 85,
91, 108, 110, 111, 122, 153, 172, 177

For my parents
Reverend and Mrs. Walter L. Arnold
Who prove the truth of Wisdom's counsel:

Hear, my child, your father's instruction,
and do not reject your mother's teaching;
for they are a fair garland for your head,
and pendants for your neck.
—Prv 1:8–9

Contents in Brief

Contents

Editor's Preface

The strength of the church and the vitality of the individual Christian's life are directly related to the role Scripture plays in them. Early believers knew the importance of this and spent their time in fellowship, prayer, and the study of God's Word. The passing of two thousand years has not changed the need, but it has changed the accessibility of many of the Bible's ideas. Time has distanced us from those days, and we often need guidance back into the world of the Old and New Testaments.

To that end Baker Book House is producing two separate but related series of biblical textbooks. The design of these new series is to put us back into the world of the biblical text, so that we may understand it as those early believers did and at the same time see it from and for our own day, thus facilitating the application of its truths to our contemporary situation.

Encountering Biblical Studies consists of undergraduate-level texts, and two surveys treating the Old and New Testaments provide the foundation for this series. Accompanying these survey texts are two collateral volumes of readings, which illuminate the world surrounding the biblical text. Built on these basic survey texts are upper-level college texts covering the books of the Bible that are most frequently offered in the curriculum of Christian colleges.

A related series, titled Engaging Biblical Studies, provides graduate-level treatments for introduction and theology courses.

Complementing both levels of textbooks is a set of standard reference books that may be consulted for answers to specific questions or more in-depth study of biblical ideas. These reference books include *Baker Commentary on the Bible*, *Baker Topical Guide to the Bible*, *Baker Encyclopedia of the Bible*, *Baker Theological Dictionary of the Bible*, and *Evangelical Dictionary of Theology*.

Encountering and Engaging Biblical Studies series are written from an evangelical point of view, in the firm conviction that the Scripture is absolutely true and never misleads us. It is the sure foundation on which our faith and life may be built because it unerringly leads willing readers to Jesus Christ.

Walter A. Elwell
General Editor

Publisher's Preface

Bible courses must be considered the heart of the curriculum for Christian colleges and evangelical seminaries. For Christians the Bible constitutes the basis for both our spiritual and our intellectual lives—indeed for *all* of life. If these courses are fundamental to Christian education, then the textbooks used for these courses could not be more crucial.

Baker Book House is launching two separate but related series of volumes for college- and seminary-level Bible courses. Encountering Biblical Studies consists of undergraduate texts, while Engaging Biblical Studies represents graduate-level treatments.

Encountering the Book of Genesis is part of the college-level Encountering series, and it attempts to build on the basic survey text, *Encountering the Old Testament: A Christian Survey* (Bill T. Arnold and Bryan E. Beyer). While the survey text is written for college freshmen, this Genesis volume is intended primarily for upper-level collegians.

Rather than providing a sustained exegetical analysis of each verse in Genesis, this volume surveys the entire book with an emphasis on drawing out its theological message and its practical significance. It consists of appropriate introduction and survey material with the necessary historical, literary, hermeneutical, and background concerns woven within the exposition of the biblical text. For the most part, introductory critical issues are reserved for the end of the volume.

Guiding Principles

As part of the developing of this volume, the series editors, author, and publisher established the following principles:

1. It must reflect the finest in evangelical scholarship of our day.
2. It must be written at a level that most of today's students can understand.
3. It must be pedagogically sound.
4. It must include appropriate illustrative material such as photographs, maps, charts, graphs, figures, and sidebars.
5. It must seek to winsomely draw in the student by focusing on biblical teaching concerning crucial doctrinal and ethical matters.

Goals

The goals for *Encountering the Book of Genesis* fall into two categories: intellectual and attitudinal. The intellectual goals are to (1) present the factual content of each book of the Old Testament, (2) introduce historical, geographical, and cultural backgrounds, (3) outline primary hermeneutical principles, (4) touch on critical issues (e.g., why some people read the Bible differently), and (5) substantiate the Christian faith.

The attitudinal goals are also fivefold: (1) to make the Bible a part of students' lives, (2) to instill in students a love for the Scriptures, (3) to make them better people, (4) to enhance their piety, and (5) to stimulate their love for God. In short, if this text builds a foundation for a lifetime of Bible study, the author and publisher will be amply rewarded.

Overarching Themes

Controlling the writing of *Encountering the Book of Genesis* have been three essential theological themes: God, people, and the gospel as it relates to individuals. The notion that God is a person—one and three—and a transcendent and immanent Being has been woven throughout the text. Moreover, this God has created people in his image who are fallen but still the objects of his redemptive love. The gospel is the means, the active personal power that God uses to rescue people from darkness and death. But the gospel does more than rescue—it restores. It confers on otherwise hopeless sinners the resolve and strength to live lives that please God, because they walk in the love that comes from God.

Features

The publisher's aim has been to provide an exceptionally unique resource on the one hand but not merely trendy on the other. Some of the distinguishing features we hope will prove helpful to the professor and inspiring to the student include the following:

- Liberal use of illustrations—photographs, figures, tables, charts.
- Sidebars exploring ethical and theological issues of interest and concern to modern-day collegians.
- Chapter outline and objectives presented at the opening of each chapter.
- Study questions at the end of each chapter.
- A helpful glossary.

The publisher is convinced that this textbook should be as pedagogically sound as possible and that it should reflect the best insights from educational psychology. *Encountering the Book of Genesis* has benefited from the work of two educational specialists. Donald E. Ratcliff, Ph.D., prepared the chapter objectives and reviewed the study questions. Klaus Issler, Ph.D., developed the instructor's manual (with assistance from Dr. Ratcliff). The publisher extends heartfelt thanks to both.

To the Student

Encountering the Book of Genesis in a systematic way for the first time is an exciting experience. It can also be overwhelming because there is so much to learn. You need to learn not only the content of this book of beginnings but also important background information about the world in which the patriarchs lived.

The purpose of this textbook is to make that encounter a little less daunting. To accomplish this a number of learning aids have been incorporated into the text. We suggest you familiarize yourself with this textbook by reading the following introductory material, which explains what learning aids have been provided.

Sidebars

Sidebars isolate contemporary issues of concern and show how the Book of Genesis speaks to these pressing ethical and theological issues.

Chapter Outlines

At the beginning of each chapter is a brief outline of the chapter's contents. *Study Suggestion:* Before reading the chapter, take a few minutes to read the outline. Think of it as a road map, and remember that it is easier to reach your destination if you know where you are going.

Chapter Objectives

A brief list of objectives is placed at the outset of each chapter. These present the tasks you should be able to perform after reading the chapter. *Study Suggestions:* Read the objectives carefully before beginning to read the text. As you read the text, keep these objectives in mind and take notes to help you remember what you have read. After reading the chapter, return to the objectives and see if you can perform the tasks.

Key Terms and Glossary

Key terms have been identified throughout the text by the use of **boldface** type. This will alert you to important words or phrases you may not be familiar with. A definition of these words will be found at the end of the book in an alphabetical glossary. *Study Suggestion:* When you encounter a key term in the text, stop and read the definition before continuing through the chapter.

Study Questions

A few discussion questions have been provided at the end of each chapter, and these can be used to review for examinations. *Study Suggestion:* Write suitable answers to the study questions in preparation for tests.

Further Reading

A helpful bibliography for supplementary reading is presented at the end of the book. *Study Suggestion:* Use this list to explore areas of special interest.

Visual Aids

A host of illustrations in the form of photographs, maps, and charts have been included in this textbook. Each illustration has been carefully selected, and each is intended not only to make the text more aesthetically pleasing but also more easily mastered.

May your encounter of the Book of Genesis be an exciting adventure!

Author's Preface

This book has been designed from its inception as a textbook, which means that it differs in many ways from the standard genre of biblical commentaries. *Encountering the Book of Genesis* attempts to introduce the student to the major themes of the first book of the Bible, without commenting on every verse or passage. For this reason the volume has a selective feel to it. Professors using it for classes can supplement the contents with their own lectures, recapitulating certain themes and highlighting others that may have been omitted from the text. Also, the notes are replete with references to the best commentaries on Genesis, and all who are interested in pursuing more detail on individual passages should turn to the many excellent and recently published resources available. The book is intended to be read together with the text of Genesis in a modern translation. Students should read the selections from the Bible listed at the beginning of each chapter before continuing with the chapter itself.

I am grateful to the trustees and administration of Asbury Theological Seminary for a sabbatical in the spring of 1997, and for making it possible for me to spend three months at Tyndale House, Cambridge, in order to complete the manuscript. I am also indebted to the Warden of Tyndale House, Dr. Bruce Winter and his able staff for making my time there both enjoyable and productive.

My student assistant, Christopher F. Morgan, ably and expeditiously produced the study and review questions, and helped with the editorial process. I am grateful to the Old Testament series editor, Dr. Eugene H. Merrill, who improved the manuscript at several points with helpful suggestions. Jim Weaver and his staff at Baker Book House have been most efficient, as usual.

Finally, I would like to dedicate this volume to my parents, Rev. and Mrs. Walter L. Arnold, who have always been models of faith for me. The grace of God is evident in their lives, much as it was in the lives of the giants of faith portrayed in Genesis.

Before You Begin . . .

There are a couple of things you should know about the structure of the Book of Genesis before you begin. First, the book itself gives explicit guidelines for reading it. Few books of the Bible mark their individual units more clearly than does Genesis. The term *tôlĕdôt* ("generations") is used eleven times to mark the individual units, most often in the expression "these are the generations of. . . ." Each of these occurrences introduces the subject matter of either a genealogy or a narrative that follows.[1] If the following material is narrative, the phrase is typically translated something like "This is the account of X. . . ." If *tôlĕdôt* is introducing a genealogy, as happens five times, a translation such as "The descendants of X . . ." may be expected.

The *tôlĕdôt* occurrences serve as catchwords to arrange the book into eleven panels or sections. The creation account of Genesis 1 is the only panel not introduced with *tôlĕdôt*, and it serves as a prologue for the whole.

1:1–2:3	Prologue
2:4–4:26	*tôlĕdôt* of heaven and earth
5:1–6:8	*tôlĕdôt* of Adam's line
6:9–9:29	*tôlĕdôt* of Noah
10:1–11:9	*tôlĕdôt* of Noah's sons (Shem, Ham, and Japheth)
11:10–26	*tôlĕdôt* of Shem
11:27–25:11	*tôlĕdôt* of Terah (Abraham narrative)
25:12–18	*tôlĕdôt* of Ishmael

Abbreviations

Old Testament

Genesis	Gn
Exodus	Ex
Leviticus	Lv
Numbers	Nm
Deuteronomy	Dt
Joshua	Jos
Judges	Jgs
Ruth	Ru
1 Samuel	1 Sm
2 Samuel	2 Sm
1 Kings	1 Kgs
2 Kings	2 Kgs
1 Chronicles	1 Chr
2 Chronicles	2 Chr
Ezra	Ezr
Nehemiah	Neh
Esther	Est
Job	Jb
Psalms	Ps(s)
Proverbs	Prv
Ecclesiastes	Eccl
Song of Songs	Sg (Song)
Isaiah	Is
Jeremiah	Jer
Lamentations	Lam
Ezekiel	Ez
Daniel	Dn
Hosea	Hos
Joel	Jl
Amos	Am
Obadiah	Ob
Jonah	Jon
Micah	Mi
Nahum	Na
Habakkuk	Hb
Zephaniah	Zep
Haggai	Hg
Zechariah	Zec
Makachi	Mal

New Testament

Matthew	Mt
Mark	Mk
Luke	Lk
John	Jn
Acts of the Apostles	Acts
Romans	Rom
1 Corinthians	1 Cor
2 Corinthians	2 Cor
Galatians	Gal
Ephesians	Eph
Philippians	Phil
Colossians	Col
1 Thessalonians	1 Thes
2 Thessalonians	2 Thes
1 Timothy	1 Tm
2 Timothy	2 Tm
Titus	Ti
Philemon	Phlm
Hebrews	Heb
James	Jas
1 Peter	1 Pt
2 Peter	2 Pt
1 John	1 Jn
2 John	2 Jn
3 John	3 Jn
Jude	Jude
Revelation	Rv

25:19–35:29	*tôlĕdôt* of Isaac (Jacob narrative)
36:1–37:1	*tôlĕdôt* of Esau (used twice)[2]
37:2–50:26	*tôlĕdôt* of Jacob (Joseph narrative)

Notice the *tôlĕdôt* catchphrases as you move through Genesis. You might look at them as literary hinges for linking various types of material together.

The second thing you should keep in mind is that these eleven units in Genesis are grouped into four larger sections. The first five *tôlĕdôt* catchphrases have been collected together with the prologue into a section devoted to the history of the world from creation to the call of Abraham (1:1–11:26). This is often called the Primeval History, since it deals with the first ages prior to the appearance of Israel's **patriarchs**.

The remaining *tôlĕdôt* panels in Genesis are grouped according to patriarchal history.

1:1–11:26	Primeval History
11:27–25:18	Abraham
25:19–37:1	Abraham's Family: Isaac and Jacob
37:2–50:26	Joseph

I have followed this outline in the structure of this book.[3]

Part

1

Encountering
God's Creation

Genesis 1–11

The earth is the Lord's
and all that is in it.
—Ps 24:1

1 The Grandeur of God's Perfect Creation

Genesis 1:1–2:3

By the word of the LORD were the
   heavens made,
     their starry host by the breath of
     his mouth. . . .
For he spoke, and it came to be;
   he commanded, and it stood
   firm.

—Ps 33:6, 9

Supplemental Reading: Psalm 8:3–9

Outline

- **How Did It All Begin?**
- **Details of Genesis 1**
  The Recurring Creation Formula
  The Symmetry of Genesis 1
  The Role of Genesis 1:1–2
- **Significance of Genesis 1**
  Sovereignty of God
  Goodness of Creation
  Role of Humankind

Objectives

**After reading this chapter you should
be able to**

1. Compare the issues of process and products in the creation account, and how these relate to the theories of origins.
2. Outline two literary patterns in Genesis 1: the creation formula and the symmetry between the two units of three days each.
3. State several possible translations of Genesis 1:1 and how they impact the central issues conveyed in the chapter
4. Summarize the doctrine of God's sovereignty and the ways it is conveyed in Genesis 1.
5. Describe the implications of humans being created in God's image.

How often do you think about beginnings—the beginning of life, the beginning of the world, the beginning of civilization? Such questions were a constant source of speculation among all ancient peoples, including the Israelites. These questions have occupied the human mind since earliest civilization.

The Bible opens with a book of beginnings, Genesis. The word "genesis" itself is the Greek title of the book, meaning "origins." The Jews called it by the first Hebrew word, *bĕrēʾšît*, "In the beginning." As a book of beginnings, Genesis deals with the beginning of the world, the beginning of history, the beginning of sin, salvation, and God's people.

How Did It All Begin?

We humans have always been impressed, even awestruck, by this spectacular world around us. From the first primitive observations of celestial movements recorded by the ancient Babylonians to the remarkable photographs of earth taken by NASA's shuttles—all of us recognize the splendor of this universe.

It is surprising how little we actually know about the process of creation. After all, the Bible itself makes this one of the central issues of Christian thought. Here in the opening books of the Bible, creation is the foundation of Mosaic law. Later, creation becomes the psalmists' reason for praising God (Pss 19:1–6; 104:24–30) and Job's answer to the problem of evil (Jb 38). The grandeur of God's creation became the prophetic paradigm for restoration (Is 66:22–23) and the opening salvo in the Gospel of John (Jn 1:1–5).

Yet as important as creation is theologically, the precise details of the process of creation seem unimportant in the opening chapters of Genesis. As one author has put it, "The question, what was created, precedes the question, how did creation take place."[1]

Our lack of information leads to many controversies related to creation. Many Christians get caught up in debates about the "day-age theory," the "gap theory," or the ever troublesome question of evolution. If modern geologists are correct and the earth is 4.5 billion years old, did God suddenly create an earth that just appears

Genesis 1 puts the beauty and grandeur of creation in perspective.

The Day–Age Debate

Genesis 1 presents a perplexing question about the nature of the seven creation days, centering around the Hebrew word *yôm*, "day." Are the six days of creation literal, twenty-four-hour days, which describe an actual week in which God created the world? Or do the "days" represent ages of indeterminate length, the so-called day-age theory? Unfortunately the Hebrew term for "day" can be used in both ways, and the question cannot be resolved on the basis of the term itself. The expression "In the day that the Lord God made the earth and the heavens" in Genesis 2:4b (NRSV) is an example of "day" in the immediate context that certainly means an age of indefinite length.

The question of how the word is used in Genesis 1 is difficult enough. But to make matters worse, the issue is related to another controversial question. If one believes the days were twenty-four hours each, one must also accept the "young earth" theory, which must then be squared with the evidence of modern geology. Current geological evidence suggests the earth is around 4.5 billion years old. The day-age approach is easier to mesh with the geological evidence. But many Christians fear it opens the door to evolutionary theories.

We should not be too concerned with the issue of how long it took God to create the universe. Nor should this debate be used as a litmus test to determine who is really serious about Christ. This is not a faith issue. If it were important to know how long it took God to create the world, the Bible would have made it clear. The important lesson from Genesis 1 is that he did in fact create it, and that he made it orderly and good in every respect.

old, or is some form of theistic evolution appropriate? Can one accept an old earth while rejecting evolution? Though these questions are important and necessary to address, they are not the main concern of the biblical accounts of creation.

So why do we not have more information on the details of creation? Apparently the Bible is more concerned with something besides these controversial issues. We must conclude, as Christian readers, that God intends us to glean something else from these chapters, something more obvious. Though we will address these controverted questions briefly, our purpose will be to seek to determine the central messages of the Bible's accounts of creation.

Details of Genesis 1

Genesis 1 is the overture of what may well be called the world's greatest literary masterpiece. Its elevated style is more like poetry and the unit is unique when compared to the narrative sections you will read elsewhere in Genesis. We shall begin by looking at the recurring pattern and the symmetry of the chapter, and then ask how the first two verses relate to the whole.

The Recurring Creation Formula

As you read Genesis 1 (or, more specifically, Gn 1:1–2:3), you should note the recurring pattern that gives structure to the whole.[2] A characteristic feature of the chapter is the author's use of this literary pattern to introduce each day of creation.

1. Introduction: "And God said . . ."
2. Command: "Let there be/let it be gathered/let it bring forth"
3. Report: "And it was so"
4. Evaluation: "And God saw that it was good"
5. Time sequence: "And there was evening, and there was morning"

There is some degree of variation in the use of this recurring formula. But one constant is the divine evaluation that each element of God's creation is "good" (Hebrew *ṭôb*). In its use in chapter 1, the term does not seem to have moral or ethical connotations, as in "good" as opposed to

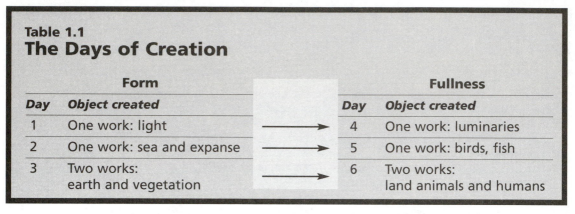

Table 1.1
The Days of Creation

Form				Fullness	
Day	**Object created**			**Day**	**Object created**
1	One work: light	→		4	One work: luminaries
2	One work: sea and expanse	→		5	One work: birds, fish
3	Two works: earth and vegetation	→		6	Two works: land animals and humans

"bad" or "evil," such as is the case in Genesis 2. Here the idea is approval and acceptance. The object created is just as it should be, with no flaws or blemishes. On each creation day, God is the gifted artist who steps back to admire and approve his own work. When God considers his handiwork, he is pleased with it.

The role of humankind in creation is emphasized by the activity of God on the sixth day of creation (1:24–31). This time the recurring formula includes the divine evaluation with a subtle change. When God inspects his creation of man and woman, he deems them not just "good," but "very good" (v. 31). The recurring formula gives the impression that humankind is the climactic moment of creation, and that God is more than well pleased with humans.

The Symmetry of Genesis 1

The use of the creative formula to introduce and conclude each day also creates an interesting symmetrical structure for Genesis 1.[3] The contents of the first three days of creation correspond to the last three days in a way that accentuates the third and sixth days. Days three and six correspond because they both contain two acts of creation: earth and vegetation on day three (vv. 9–13) and land animals and humans on day six (vv. 24–31). This correspondence of content is matched by literary form, since key elements of the creation formula are repeated for days three and six: the introduction ("And God said," vv. 9, 11, 24, 26) and the divine evaluation (using *ṭôb*, vv. 10, 12, 25, 31).

Similar correspondences of content pair each of the other days of creation. The luminaries of day four correspond to the creation of light on day one. The birds and fish created on day five match the sky of day two. Furthermore, it may be that each set of three days was God's response to the chaos and disorder of verse 2 ("formless and empty"), providing form and fullness. The first three days gave the earth shape and the last three filled it. If so, God's blessing to animals and humans ("be fruitful and increase in number," vv. 22 and 28) are ways in which we are to continue his creative activity. The "formless and empty" stage of creation simply means the earth was bare, an uninhabited place that now is to be populated and inhabited by humankind and the animals God has created.[4]

The recurrence of the creation formula and the symmetrical structure of the days of creation highlight the uniqueness of day seven (2:1–3). As the climax of creation, God's Sabbath rest is not what we normally think of as "rest," as though God needed a break from an exhausting job. Rather, the term fundamentally means "cessation," and implies also the celebration and completion of an accomplishment. The concept became important for national Israel, and still holds hope for the Christian believer, since the creation story builds to this point and testifies that "with the living God there is rest."[5] God pronounced the activity of each of the other days of creation as good, but this one he sanctified: "And God blessed the seventh day and made it holy" (2:3).

The Role of Genesis 1:1–2

As the important seventh day stands outside the purview of the creation formula, so do the first two verses of Genesis. These opening words of the Bible pose two in-

Semitic

creatio ex nihilo

terconnected questions, resulting in two mutually exclusive interpretations. First, we have to deal with the meaning of the first word of verse 1, *bĕrēʾšît*, traditionally translated "in the beginning." Second, the answer to this question will impact how the first three verses relate to each other.

The issues involved in interpreting *bĕrēʾšît* are complicated and require some knowledge of Hebrew to understand fully.[6] In sum, the noun has a prefixed preposition in a form that would often take a definite article, especially for a phrase such as "in *the* beginning." Without the definite article, this particular spelling of the word would normally occur in a bound or construct form with a following noun, a genitive. However, in Genesis 1:1 there is neither a definite article nor another noun bound to it as we would expect. For this reason, some scholars have argued the term is a dependent temporal clause: "In the beginning when God created. . . ," or "When God began to create . . ." In this case, verse 1 would be dependent on the main clause of verse 2: "When God began to create . . . , the earth was formless and empty . . ." Another possibility is that verse 1 is dependent on verse 3, assuming verse 2 is parenthetical: "When God began to create . . . (now the earth was formless and empty . . .), God said . . ." In either case, God set to work with preexistent, primordial substance. He created the world out of preexistent matter.

Though these translations are possible, they are not *required* by the rules of Hebrew grammar. There are other examples in the Old Testament of similar temporal designations without the definite article, and there is no need to take the first word as a dependent clause at all. Instead, all the ancient translations of the Old Testament and the vast majority of contemporary translations and commentaries assume the traditional understanding of the opening words as an independent main clause: "In the beginning God created the heavens and the earth." But that is far from the end of the matter.

Of those who assume this traditional understanding of verse 1, there is further variety. Some have taken verse 1 as describing an original, perfect creation. Between verses 1 and 2, the fall of Satan occurred, resulting in the contamination of God's creation. Verse 2 thus describes the condition of earth as a result of Satan's fall. Verse 3 then begins a description of God's "re-creation" or reconstruction of the chaotic world. This is commonly referred to as the "gap theory," since verse 2 describes a gap of an indeterminable period of time. Many who hold this view place dinosaurs and pre-*Homo sapien* anthropoids in this nebulous gap of time.

However, the gap theory does literary and linguistic injustice to the text of Genesis 1:1–3.[7] A more balanced approach takes verse 1 as an independent main clause summarizing the events of verses 2–31.[8] Verse 1 is a title or superscription for the entire chapter. The expression "the heavens and the earth" is **Semitic** merismus, a rhetorical device expressing totality (like alpha and omega, and everything between). Verse 1 then explains that everything that exists does so as a result of God's creative activity about to be described in the chapter. Verse 2 describes the situation prior to creation, the preexisting chaos. Though this interpretation presupposes the prior existence of chaotic matter, it does not necessarily portray chaos that is beyond God's control or antagonistic to his creative processes. Elsewhere in the Bible, it is clear that God created the universe from nothing and did so without taxing his powers or energy (Pss 33:6, 9; 148:5; Heb 11:3).

In addition to taking the first verse as a superscription, it is also possible to see it as describing the first act of creation.[9] This would also take verse 1 as an independent main clause, and has the advantage of being the most ancient and traditional way of reading Genesis 1:1–3. This approach interprets the first three verses synchronically: verse 1 is the first creative act, verse 2 is the consequence of verse 1, and verse 3 is the first creative word. This interpretation has the support of ancient translations and modern scholars, and is most compatible with the biblical teaching of *creatio ex nihilo* (that is, the teaching that God created the universe from nothing and did so effortlessly).

Regardless of our interpretation of Genesis 1:1–3, the importance of the preexistence of God is central. As we shall see, other ancient peoples had an interest not

mythology

sovereignty

magic

fiat

omnipotence

only in the creation of the world, but also in the creation of the gods! By contrast, Israel never tried to explain the origins of God. God always has been, and before he created, he was alone. He simply spoke and the rest of the universe came into existence. This was a radical and new concept in the ancient Near East, as it is for modern believers. Indeed, this is the first step in our journey of faith. If we can accept this great biblical truth, the rest will be easy.

Significance of Genesis 1

As we said at the outset of this chapter, questions about the beginnings of life and the world have constantly occupied the human mind since history began. As we shall illustrate in chapter 3 below, all other ancient cultures used **mythology** to justify whatever seemed essential to human life and society by relating it to some primordial, foundational act.[10] But the Bible's answers to such questions are different. Already in Genesis 1, we see that the Israelites were uninterested in mythological explanations of what seemed important. Rather, the essentials for human

Charles Darwin's theory of evolution offers a scientific explanation of origins.

life were determined by a sovereign, creator God.

We have also called the Book of Genesis the "world's greatest literary masterpiece." Yet Christian readers for two thousand years have recognized in it more than literary artistry. It is also God's Word for contemporary believers. As such, the theological significance of Genesis 1 can hardly be overemphasized. Our reading of the rest of the Bible would be impoverished, indeed impossible, without first learning the lessons of creation. Of the many important concepts here, I will highlight just three: the **sovereignty** of God, the goodness of his creation, and the role of humankind in creation.

Sovereignty of God

Other ancient cultures of the Old Testament period had creation accounts (see ch. 3, below). These various depictions of creation shared at least two features. First, the god(s) created the world with great difficulty. Typically, the creation of the universe was the result of some great cosmic struggle, and often a deity used **magic** to create. Second, the creating deity always began with some preexistent matter.

The early church recognized the importance of the creation formula's command: "Let there be light." The Latin translation of that phrase (*fiat lux*) gave rise to the expression "creation by **fiat**," emphasizing God's method of creating by divine order or decree. The implication is that creation did not require a great deal of effort on God's part. He simply spoke, and things happened. This doctrine of creation by fiat teaches God's **omnipotence** and sovereignty.

Though the precise significance of the first three verses of Genesis 1 is uncertain, the implication of the word "created" in verse 1 is interesting.[12] Throughout the Old Testament, the God of Israel is always the subject of this Hebrew verb (*bārāʾ*), never pagan deities or humans. Furthermore, the object of this verb never refers to the materials used in creation, but to the object of creation itself. Though this verb itself could not prove the doctrine of *creatio ex nihilo* ("creation out of nothing"), it certainly implies God's free-

Did God Use Evolution to Create the World?

How does the Genesis account of human origins relate to modern science, specifically, the theory of evolution? This question has been answered in different ways since Charles Darwin's publication of *The Origin of Species* in 1859.[11] I offer a brief overview of three positions here.

1. "Theistic evolutionists" believe the Bible is trustworthy and accept the biblical teaching that God created the world. But Genesis explains only *who* created, not *how* he did it. Theistic evolutionists also accept the processes defined by modern science as the means God used to create human beings. They accept concepts such as organic evolution (from molecule to human) and macroevolution (from ape to human) as explanations for the origin of life. Most theistic evolutionists view Genesis 1 as an allegorical or figurative explanation of humankind's dependence on the creator God.

Though the theistic evolutionary approach is possible, it is difficult to harmonize Genesis 1–2 with certain evolutionary ideas. The theory of evolution teaches that humans resulted from chance events, the outcome of natural selection and the survival of the fittest. On the other hand, Genesis portrays a first human couple as parents of the whole human race. Adam and Eve were intentionally created by God in his image. This important doctrine, which is confirmed elsewhere in Scripture, is difficult to harmonize with the randomness of evolution.

The still poorly attested theory of organic evolution (the development from molecule to human) creates even greater problems for the theistic evolutionists. Genesis 2:7 seems to convey a special creation from inorganic material rather than through some previously existing life form: "the LORD God formed the man from the dust of the ground."

2. In reaction to evolutionary theories, some accept a view that may be called "instantaneous creationism" (otherwise known as "fiat creationism"). This view accepts a literal interpretation of twenty-four-hour days in Genesis 1, which requires a young earth. Most geologists believe the earth is around 4.5 to 5 billion years old. But instantaneous creationists question the conclusions of modern dating techniques. Assuming the genealogies of Genesis 5 and 11 are intended to be used for precise chronology, instantaneous creationists adopt essentially the chronology of Archbishop James Ussher (1581–1656), in which case the earth is no more than ten thousand years old. A universal flood accounts for the sedimentary deposits and fossils, giving a partial explanation for the appearance of the earth's great age.

3. Another option is "progressive creationism." This view recognizes the problems of using the biblical genealogies for precise chronology. In light of the overwhelming evidence in support of the antiquity of the earth, progressive creationists accept the tradi-

tional day-age interpretation of the creation days in Genesis 1, assigning the days to various geological periods. In this way, progressive creationists emphasize the complementarity between Genesis and modern science.

Though there are several varieties of progressive creationists, all accept an old earth and some degree of microevolutionary theory. In other words, differences among biological species are explained as mutations involving natural selection over a long period of time. Such microevolution explains present-day varieties of organisms from the prototypes created by God "according to their various kinds" (Gn 1:11). But progressive creationists reject macroevolution and organic evolution because of a lack of scientific evidence.

The Bible does not discuss evolution. Modern science attempts to explain the origin of life with a "how" question, while the Bible begins by answering the "who" and "what" questions. Genesis begins with a personal God who deliberately created the universe and made humankind in his own image. Human beings are not the result of blind chance and natural selection. The Bible and objective science are never in conflict with each other. But any scientific approach that denies God's Creator role quickly finds itself in conflict with the Bible and those who hold it as trustworthy.

covenant

dom and power and his effortless sovereignty in creating. It must be left to other passages of the Bible to prove that God created the universe without the benefit of preexistent substance (Pss 33:6, 9; 148:5; Heb 11:3).[13]

The opening verse of Genesis establishes the theological foundations for all true biblical religion. Yahweh, Israel's Lord of the **covenant**, is also the sovereign God of creation. This is the opening assertion of Scripture, and serves to complement Israel's later assertions that Yahweh is the God of salvation.[14]

Goodness of Creation

As we have seen, God evaluated each element of creation and pronounced it "good." The recurring creation formula built to a climax on day six, when God created the humans and gave them vegetation to eat. When God saw everything that he had made, he was pleased ("it was very good"). At this juncture in the biblical account, there has been no mention of anything bad, or evil. There existed only the goodness of God and his creation.

As will become clear soon enough, God's creation was contaminated by the actions of the humans. The rest of the biblical story is one of redemption from sin and brokenness. But through it all, the message of Genesis 1 is the conviction that God's creation is innately good, and that sin and evil have somehow invaded where they do not belong and are unwelcome guests.

The Trinity in Genesis 1?

On the climactic day six, God created humankind (1:26–27). The divine decree of that day was unlike the others, in which God addressed the earth or some part of it: "Let the water . . . be gathered . . . ," "Let the land produce . . . ," and "Let the water teem . . ." Rather, on day six, God used first-person plural pronouns "Let us make humankind in our image, according to our likeness" (1:26 NRSV). This unique manner of divine speech emphasizes the exalted position of human beings over all of creation.

There are at least six possibilities for understanding the plural pronouns in 1:26.[15] First, some have argued the verse refers to other gods, and is a remnant of the author's polytheistic and mythological sources. Second, the plurals may refer to a heavenly court, comprised of an angelic host. Third, God is speaking to

something he has recently created, most likely the earth. Fourth, the plurals are the "plural of majesty," most commonly used by kings. The lack of a Hebrew plural of majesty used with verbs and pronouns has led most scholars to abandon this argument. Fifth, the pronouns may be an example of the "plural of deliberation," in which an individual speaks to himself or herself with the determination to take action. An example is said to be the divine speech of Genesis 11:7: "Come, let us go down . . ." Sixth, the plurals may be a "plural of fullness," in which God speaks to the Spirit, mentioned in 1:2. The Spirit then, becomes a partner with God in creation.

We should be careful about reading trinitarian theology into the plural pronouns used here and elsewhere in divine speech (see also Gn 3:22; 11:7; Is 6:8). On the other hand,

Genesis is sophisticated enough to deal with the concept of plurality within unity. The very next verse (1:27) portrays the singular human being created as a plurality, "male and female" (see also Gn 5:1–2a). The divine plurality of 1:26 anticipates and prepares for the human plurality of 1:27.[16] Just as the one God created from an expression of his plurality, human beings exist in their plurality. In this sense, the relationship between man and woman reflects the role of how God relates to himself.

Though we should not turn to Genesis to prove the existence of the Trinity, neither is this passage contradictory to a Christian understanding of the Triune God. That which appeared only as suggestion and inkling in Genesis had to wait for mature expression until "the time had fully come" (Gal 4:4).

Study Questions

1. How could one say that God's six days of creative activity relate to the statement in verse 2 that the earth was "formless and empty"?

2. Explain two possible understandings of the first Hebrew word in Genesis, and indicate the theological implications of each of these understandings.

3. In what ways does the creation account in Genesis differ from the creation accounts of other ancient cultures?

4. Explain the significance of the statement that "humans are created in the image of God."

5. Describe three ways of interpreting Genesis 1 in light of the claims of modern science.

6. Explain several possibilities regarding the use of the first-person plural pronoun "us" in Genesis 1:26.

7. Identify two definitions for the Hebrew word *yôm* (translated "day") and discuss how these definitions impact the interpretation of Genesis 1.

imago Dei

Role of Humankind

At the climax of this creation account, the dignity of humankind and the importance of the first human couple are highlighted: "Let us make humankind in our image, according to our likeness" (1:26 NRSV).

It is impossible to overstate the theological significance of being created in God's image (in the *imago Dei*, in the words of the early church). There are at least three implications. First, the command to be fruitful and multiply surely implies the humans are to continue the creative activity of God (1:28). They are to carry on what he has begun. Second, humanity was to have dominion over all creation as a result of bearing God's image (1:26). Adam and Eve were the visible representatives of God in creation. Third, being created as divine image-bearers also implies that humans were created specifically for relationship with God. Unlike the rest of creation, human life is not an end in itself. It bears the privilege of relating to God.[17]

This first chapter of the Book of Genesis is crucial for establishing who God is, who we are, and how we relate to the world around us. Your study of this chapter should lead you to join the hosts of creation in praising God, "for he commanded and they were created" (Ps 148:5).

Key Terms

Semitic
creatio ex nihilo
mythology
sovereignty
magic
fiat
omnipotence
covenant
imago Dei

2 The History of the First Human Family

Genesis 2:4–4:26

After the first blush of sin comes its indifference.

—Henry David Thoreau
(1817–62)[1]

Supplemental Reading: James 1:12–15

Outline

- **What's Different about Genesis 2–4?**
- **Events inside the Garden of Eden (2–3)**

  Adam and Eve in the Garden (2)
  - Historicity of Adam and Eve
  - Sex as a Gift of God

  Adam and Eve Expelled from the Garden (3)
  - What Is the Origin of Satan's Evil?
  - Are Women Supposed to Be Subservient to Men?

- **Events outside the Garden of Eden (4)**

Objectives

After reading this chapter you should be able to

1. Contrast the literary style of chapter 1 with the style in chapters 2–4.
2. Describe the significance of the change in terms used to designate God.
3. From Genesis 2, list the distinctions between God's creation of humans and the rest of his creation.
4. Summarize the moral implications of Adam and Eve eating the forbidden fruit.
5. Identify the characteristics of temptation from Genesis 2.
6. Specify the pattern of falling into sin and the consequences of that fall that are illustrated in Adam and Eve's transgression.
7. State the possible motivation for the first murder, and the significance of God's interactions with Cain.

All was bright and beautiful in Genesis 1. God began by bringing light onto the scene, and continued by speaking into existence a flawless and perfect world. This ideal world was capped off with a human couple made in his image and living in perfect harmony with him. But how quickly the Bible moves to the tragic turnaround! This next unit of Genesis is just as dark and dismal as Genesis 1 was bright and beautiful.

What's Different about Genesis 2–4?

As you read these chapters, you may have noticed some big differences compared to Genesis 1. Gone are the tight symmetry and the recurring formulas. Gone, too, is the elevated prose style, with its almost poetic quality. Instead, we find a narrative style that is down to earth, almost folksy. This narrative now tells the story of what happened to God's "good" creation, with special attention given to the zenith of his creation, human life. Humankind becomes "the pivot of the story, as in chapter 1 he was the climax."[2]

You will also notice that the universal, panoramic view of Genesis 1 is now replaced by the description of a specific garden. Instead of detailing the creation of the universe and everything in it, Genesis 2 relates the loving construction of the Garden of Eden, including its rivers and trees. The grand universal scene of Genesis 1 is replaced in Genesis 2 with a smaller stage, where an important drama is about to unfold. So, too, the tempo slows down. Chapter 1 took us through six days of creation in breathtaking rapidity. Now the pace slows dramatically in chapter 2, and even more in chapter 3 as the author relates the intimate details of a chat between Eve and her unwelcome conversant. It should be obvious that the details of this conversation, and the events that are about to follow, are of great interest to the author. In fact, we may conclude that God is more concerned that we learn from the tragic human choices made in the Garden of Eden than he is that we understand the details of how he created the universe. Apparently, our response to a crisis of temp-

tation is more important than arguing over the day-age theory or theistic evolution.

Events inside the Garden of Eden (2–3)

As I said in the prologue, the Book of Genesis has eleven occurrences of the *tôlědôt*-expression, "These are the generations of . . ." You will notice the first of these in 2:4, usually translated something like "This is the account of the creation of the heavens and the earth" (NLT). The next occurrence is in 5:1, tying together chapters 2–4 as a literary unit on the first human family.[3] Genesis 2 describes the creation of the family in their paradisaical garden, and Genesis 3 tells of its ruin.

Chapters 2 and 3 are further linked by a sudden shift in the way the author refers to God. In Genesis 1:1–2:3, we encountered the designation "God" when the author wanted to describe the majestic God who simply spoke the world into existence. But Genesis 2 and 3 suddenly use "the LORD God" (or Yahweh God), which curiously occurs only once more in the **Pentateuch** (Ex 9:30).[4] The author has combined the word for God with the more personal, intimate name of God ("Yahweh") in Genesis 2–3 probably because he wanted to reveal that the majestic, sovereign creator is the same personal, loving God who speaks directly to Adam and Eve and seems to have such an intimate relationship with them. This use of divine names in Genesis 1–3 has also played a major role in modern scholarly discussions about the authorship of Genesis, as we will see in chapter 14 below.

Adam and Eve in the Garden (2)

Genesis 2 (actually 2:4–25) has often been taken as a second creation account. It is true that the lofty creation of humankind in Genesis 1:27 is mirrored by the intimate, personal details of Genesis 2:7, and there are other parallels between these chapters. But in reality, this passage has a much different scope and function than Genesis 1. The Bible moves quickly from the universal creation to a garden in the east (2:8).

Historicity of Adam and Eve

The names used in this narrative for the first human couple and their garden-home have symbolic significance.[7] "Adam" is both a proper name *and* the generic term for "humankind." In the opening chapters of Genesis it may not be a personal name at all, but may refer to the creation of humanity collectively. Old Testament authors often used paronomasia (or wordplay), and the expression "the LORD God formed the man [ʾādām] from the dust of the ground [ʾădāmâ]" emphasizes humanity's relationship to the land (Gn 2:7). There is grammatical evidence for reading "Adam" as a personal name for the first time in Genesis 4:25–26 (or perhaps 5:1–2).[8]

Likewise, the names "Eve" and "Eden" have symbolic significance for our narrator. "Eve" (ḥawwâ) is a wordplay on the verb for "live," and therefore explains the man's comment that she would "become the mother of all the living" (Gn 3:20). The garden's name "Eden" should be associated with the Hebrew word "pleasure" or "delight." It is also likely that other names in the Genesis narrative, such as Cain and Abel, have symbolic significance.

The obvious symbolism intended by these names and certain other features have led many to assume the events described here are not historical. It is often asserted that the narrative is a metaphorical account of humankind's origins and a paradigm of the effects of sin in human life. In this sense, Adam and Eve represent humanity in general, but they were not historical figures in a literal place called the Garden of Eden. Furthermore, many deny that humans descended from a single set of parents or a first human couple (monogenism). They believe instead that humans emerged gradually from perhaps several beginning points (polygenesis).

But there are several problems with this approach. There is no doubt that a garden of God in the east named Eden was symbolic of God's presence in a perfect environment. But the mention of the Tigris and Euphrates rivers by name, and other details of the description of the garden (Gn 2:10–14), demonstrate that the narrator saw it as a real and historical place, probably located in Mesopotamia. Our inability to locate the garden today is not a reason to doubt its ancient reality.

Furthermore, the Garden of Eden episode (Gn 2:4–4:26) is linked by its *tôlĕdôt* introduction ("This is the *account* of the heavens and the earth," 2:4a) to those of Adam's line (5:1–6:8), Noah's (6:9–9:29), and so forth, all the way to Abraham, Isaac, and Jacob's sons, the ancestors of the twelve tribes of national Israel. In other words, the text of the Bible uses genealogies and narratives to draw a straight line from Adam to Moses and the Israelites, and to the rest of the figures of Old Testament history. At what point along this continuum would key individuals suddenly become mythical or metaphorical? Answering this question would require a subjective imposition on the text. The biblical text has no indication that these individuals are anything but historical figures.

The narratives of Genesis 1–11 are written with great literary artistry, and this is the likely source for the symbolism and wordplays. There is no basis for assuming the narrator saw the characters as anything but historical. It is more likely that the symbolic names and wordplays are intended for the telling—a result of the narrator's literary skill. Thus the account *is* a paradigm of the nature of sin and its consequences. But it is also a historical account of our first parents and the consequences of their rebellion.[9]

In the opening scene, the world is a total desert (2:5). The problem was that God was not yet sending rain, and there were no humans to care for the earth. But then, the Lord God "formed" the man as a gifted potter lovingly forms a new jar. The Lord took the lifeless body of the man and "breathed" his own breath into his lungs, which distinguishes the man from all the other creatures. Humankind is much more than a God-shaped piece of earth.[5] He has within him the gift of life, which is a gift of God himself. The act of breathing life into the clay creature has the face-to-face

This twelfth-century sculpture depicts Adam and Eve.

intimacy of a kiss, and portrays the personal intimacy of relationship between humans and God.[6] All of us were created to live in peaceful and loving harmony with our Maker.

The passage then describes the garden prepared by God for the first human couple (2:8–14). The beautiful garden was a perfect place, with pleasurable trees and four productive rivers. The garden was in a place called Eden, which should be associated with the Hebrew word for "pleasure" or "delight." God provided all Adam's needs for an ultimate, ideal life. This included a tree in the middle of the garden, which was the source of life itself—the "tree of life" (2:9). Adam and Eve will quickly learn that they are not the center of their universe and that life does not revolve around them. Even in an ideal world where all is paradise and God has provided all things necessary for blissful life, humans must learn that God and his gifts of life and his own personal presence are at the center.

A second tree is provided, "the tree of the knowledge of good and evil" (2:9).[10] Everything we know about God's creation has been "good," as was emphasized by Genesis 1. Now for the first time, we hear of the possibility of "evil." The precise meaning of the knowledge one attains by eating this fruit has attracted much scholarly attention.[11] It appears the significance of the tree of knowledge has to do with moral autonomy, or deciding what is right without regard for God's will. The command not to eat of this fruit is a prohibition against deciding on one's own what is best for one's future. Any human endeavor that determines a course of action without any God-given frame of reference or moral guidelines is moral mutiny, a usurpation of God's authority.

All that Adam and Eve really *needed* to know was the command, "you must not eat from the tree of the knowledge of good and evil" (2:17). The law of God (his Word to them) was sufficient knowledge for an abundant life in the Garden of Eden. God's own knowledge of good and evil is absolute and independent, like a doctor who understands a terrible disease without actually contracting it. A human does not necessarily have to encounter evil in order to understand it. We only have to accept God's Word about the nature of evil. Jesus was the world's greatest expert on sin, though he himself never committed it. This is the kind of life-giving knowledge our first human parents acquired by hearing and obeying God's command, accepting his Word regarding what was in their own best interest.

Eating the forbidden fruit provided another kind of knowledge altogether. Human knowledge of good and evil is relative and dependent. Once God's Word regarding what is best for us is rejected, we are left to our own devices. We take and eat for ourselves, and suddenly, to our dismay, we have acquired a wholly different kind of knowledge of evil. When a human being attempts to decide for himself or herself what is right, independent of God's revealed knowledge, that person is trying to replace the role of God in his or her life; trying to replace God. God's

Sex as a Gift of God

The first human couple was created in the image of God as "male and female" (Gn 1:27). These terms emphasize their sexuality in a way the phrase "man and woman" would not. Notice that the image of God was stamped on them both; neither is more in the image of God than the other. This divine image distinguishes Adam and Eve from the rest of the animals of God's creation. The contrast between the human couple and the animals is heightened when we realize the Genesis account makes no mention of sexuality among the land animals, as in the phrase "male and female." They were each created "according to its kind" (1:24), but no particular mention is made of their gendered sexuality, as with the humans.

This distinction implies that human sexuality is of a different sort from animal procreation. Human sexuality is not merely a God-given mechanism for reproduction, or even a means for expressing human passion. It is all of this, and more. Human sexuality in

God's order becomes an instrument for covenantal blessing, both in one's relationship with God and with one's partner.[12] For humans, unlike for the animals of creation, sex is more than an intrinsically physical act for reproduction and sensual enjoyment. In Genesis, sex is elevated to an expression of love and commitment between a man and a woman who are mutually and exclusively devoted to each other.

Marriage was instituted by God as the bond that brought the man and woman together in a singular solidarity (Gn 2:24). They were perfectly suited for each other, and in marriage they took responsibility to work for each other's welfare in exclusive devotion to one another. Sex was God's gift to Adam and Eve, and is intended for their mutual enjoyment (Prv 5:18–20).

Though eating the forbidden fruit was not a sexual act (as some have suggested), sex has been one way in which humans have most often attempted to usurp God's authority. Outside marriage, sex

destroys relationships. Within marriage, it is God's joyous way of building relationships (1 Cor 7:3–5). Sexual temptations are difficult to withstand because they appeal to our normal and natural God-given desires. But God has assured us we will not be tempted beyond our ability to resist, with the help of his Holy Spirit (1 Cor 10:13).

Today, God wants Christians to enjoy sex within the confines of marriage. Sex remains part of God's good creation, as a blessing for those who live in faithful, monogamous relationships. We might think of it as God's special wedding gift.

But as with any of God's gifts, sexuality becomes tainted if we misuse it. The Bible's guidelines on sex are meant to protect us from misusing God's gift and abusing each other. Premarital and extramarital sex hurt us and continue the effects of sin in our lives. God's grace can forgive and heal, but the consequences of sexual sin can last a lifetime.

word for such rebellion was clear: "when you eat of it you will surely die" (2:17).

The Garden of Eden is not only about the paradisaical place where God lives in perfect harmony with humans. It is also about the way humans relate to each other. The Lord God intended the man to enjoy loving companionship in the garden as well. But no suitable companion was found among the creatures of the garden (2:18–20).

God has created the man to be a social being. The garden where he lives is not really the Garden of *Eden* until he learns to love. The man has a need to give himself to someone of his own standing in creation, to someone of equal status. The expression "I will make a helper suitable for him" (NIV) in no way implies the woman is somehow subservient to the man; rather, she is a corresponding equal to the man in contrast to the inferior animals of creation. The sexes are complementary and share full and equal partnership in the garden.

Genesis 2 ends on a profound statement about marriage and innocence (vv. 24–25). These equal partners are bound to each other in a permanent relationship (they become "one flesh"). In the future, this marriage relationship will transcend every couple's immediate childhood families. They are in perfect harmony and peace with each other sexually, and have no reason for shame. This portrayal of Paradise is a foil that illustrates just how much was lost when our first human parents lost the garden. Yet it also reminds us of what is possible in our relationships with God and with each other through his restoring and redeeming grace.

Adam and Eve Expelled from the Garden (3)

Any of us who have ever felt a sense of guilt for something we should not have done will understand the events of Genesis 3. This chapter relates how sin entered the world and ruined the perfect Paradise God had provided in the Garden of Eden.

The opening paragraph (3:1–5) reveals much about the serpent. This creature was more subtle and crafty than any other in creation. His leading question ("Did God really say . . .") is not an innocent conversation starter. This is a malicious challenge

to God's authority. The serpent begins by calling into question the good intentions of God. Yet the remainder of the question stops short of actually accusing God of wrongdoing, and leaves it to Eve to draw her own conclusions: "Did God really say, 'You must not eat from any tree in the garden'?"

Eve's answer indicates that she clearly understood God's prohibition stated in 2:17. She cannot plead ignorance. It also indicates naiveté, for it assumes the serpent did not already know the answer. Though her response seems to cast her vote for God, she adds something to the prohibition ("you must not touch it" is not in God's original command), which shows that she had already contemplated the prospects of eating the forbidden fruit. Her actions were premeditated. Many have followed in her footsteps!

The serpent's next statement reveals his motives and teaches us how Satan works: "You will not surely die . . . for God knows that when you eat of it your eyes will be opened, and you will be like God, knowing good and evil" (3:4–5). This is an arrogant lie, substantiated by a distorted truth. First, it is a lie because it certainly contradicts what God said in 2:17. One of Satan's methods is to boldly and confidently challenge the truthfulness of God's Word (Jn 8:44). He will consistently rise up to challenge God's truth, and try to make us believe a lie. Second, his statement is a partial truth because, in a sense, Adam and Eve *did* discover good and evil. In the serpent's twisted logic, this discovery made them more like God.

In one of the great ironies of the Bible, the serpent claimed to be watching out for Adam and Eve while challenging God's true intentions. He wanted them to question whether God was actually holding something back from them, preventing them from attaining what was rightfully theirs. At the same time, he wanted them to believe that he, the serpent, had their best interests at heart. In a sense, his question, "Did God really say . . . ?" echoes through time as the serpent's voice can be heard throughout the rest of the Bible, and indeed, the rest of history. This is also the choice all who read the Bible must face: the authority of God versus the challenge of the world as sponsored by Satan.

The use of half-truths was his most dev-

What Is the Origin of Satan's Evil?

The problem of evil is a difficult and complex philosophical question. Evil is extraneous to God's perfect creation, which we are told repeatedly is "good" (*tôb*, Gn 1). Evil was a foreign invader into God's perfect Paradise of Genesis 2, since it does not originate with God. So the sin of Genesis 3 always raises the questions, "Where did evil come from?" and "Why did evil make an appearance in the Garden of Eden at all?"

The narrative of Genesis 3 makes no attempt to explain the origin of evil, since this is not its purpose. But it does illustrate the universal human problem of sin. The narrator wants only to explain the origin of human sin, so that he speaks "not of evil invading, as though it had its own existence, but of creatures rebelling."[13]

The presence of demonic sin in the Garden of Eden preceded human sin and provided the occasion for human transgression. Christian theology speaks of a fall of the angels prior to the fall of Adam and Eve. Like the first human sin, this fall of the angels is attributed to the abuse of the divine gift of freedom.[14] The concept of fallen angels is based on passages like Isaiah 14:12–14, though the biblical evidence is far from conclusive. For many, the pride of Satan, which led to his own downfall, explains the evil we experience on earth today (Lk 10:18–19).

Unfortunately, the Bible does not offer a definitive answer to the question of the origin of evil. But it does offer two observations helpful to this discussion. First, we begin with the perfection of God's creation. We can find refuge in the infinite wisdom of God and affirm the flawlessness of his creation. In a way difficult for us to understand, the world would have been less perfect and ideal for human life and relationship with God without the possibility of evil. It is a mystery. But evil had to be a potentiality in order for this to be the best of all possible worlds.

Second, we can emphasize the nature of human commitment. Relationship between God and humans requires a certain degree of free moral agency for humans. That is not to say that humans can simply choose or reject God's grace any time they want. Free will is not self-governing or absolute freedom. But to coerce human beings to act morally would be to override our free will, and thereby limit the nature of love and relationship.

astating method. In a sense the serpent was right![15] Adam and Eve did not die immediately, and their eyes *were* opened. They attained knowledge that belonged naturally to God. However, the serpent neglected to tell the whole story. While he cleverly extolled all that Eve would gain, he failed to mention what she would lose. He did not explain that this new knowledge, so illegitimately acquired, is not what she really wanted. Though Adam and Eve did not die immediately, they were expelled from the garden, which was the beginning of the death process. And their newly opened eyes revealed only their own shame and guilt.

Though the Old Testament is not explicit about the identity of the serpent, the New Testament leaves no doubt. Jesus refers to the Garden of Eden, where the serpent is the "devil" and "a murderer from the be-

ginning" (Jn 8:44), and the Book of Revelation foretells his ultimate destruction and defeat (12:8; 20:2, 10). In the meantime, Satan is still active in the world, looking for people to deceive about God's truth (1 Pt 5:8–9), and throwing "flaming arrows" at God's people (Eph 6:18). He particularly preys on young believers who are new to the faith or spiritually weak, or on those who are not regularly linked to other believers. But this evil purpose is doomed to failure and Christians have no need to fear Satan, though they should be aware of his tactics.

The pattern of sin was simple: Eve saw, took, ate, and gave (Gn 3:6–7). She learned what all of us know. Sin is not the temptation itself or the natural desire for something good, but sin begins with the deliberate and calculated look, the nurtured desire for something forbidden (Jas

etiology

1:13–15). Sin is also contagious. It tends to pollute those around you, as Adam partook of Eve's sinful act of rebellion. Indeed, this is the first step in what will become a major theme in Genesis 4–11: the rapid spread of sin, like a wildfire out of control.

The results were immediate and devastating, and we still live with them. Suddenly the man and his wife were no longer comfortable with each other, which anticipates the nature of human relationships for generations to follow (3:7). Not only so, but now Adam and Eve are uncomfortable in God's presence as well (3:8). Where once they were at ease with the Creator, now they feel compelled to hide from him. When God confronts them with their sin, they begin the same recrimination that all of us recognize, for it has become a common way of dealing with guilt: "The woman you put here with me—she gave . . . ," "The serpent deceived me" (3:12–13).

The first human couple choose their

As a result of their sin, Adam and Eve were expelled from the Garden of Eden.

course of action. Now it is God's turn. The sin of Genesis 3 results in divine judgment on Adam, Eve, and the serpent (vv. 14–19). These pronouncements carefully correspond to the nature of the crime, and therefore illustrate God's grace and mercy. As a holy and just God, he could not allow sin to go unpunished. Yet he also limits the punishment to fit the crime.

These punishments are etiologies, which means they explain why things are the way they are now.[16] Snakes are unpleasant and are frequent enemies of humans; women must endure pain in childbirth; and men must work the soil for their subsistence. This is not to assume the events in the Garden of Eden are not true or are unhistorical, as is often the case. Rather, for the ancient Israelite, **etiology** was an important historical explanation for the current order of life. As we shall see, there are several such etiological events recorded in Genesis.

The sin of the Garden of Eden explains why the serpent is detestable among the animals. The serpent was "more crafty than any of the wild animals the Lord God had made" (3:1). But after the serpent's role in causing Adam and Eve to sin, he is cursed more than any animal (3:14). More important, God establishes an adversarial role for the serpent with the children of Eve, between the serpent's offspring and hers: "he will crush your head, and you will strike his heel" (3:15). It would not be strictly accurate to say that the details of this verse *require* a christological identification of the woman's seed, who defeats the serpent. The word "seed" (NIV's "offspring") may simply mean the human race in general, since Eve is the mother of the race (3:20). On the other hand, such an understanding is not precluded by the details of this verse, and the question becomes, Who is the descendent of Eve who may be said to be victorious over the serpent?

The question must be answered by the history of the human race.[17] Eve had three sons. But the entire human family was saved from a flood only by the faithful line of Seth through his descendant Noah, as we shall soon see. Noah had three sons. But only through Shem, the ancestor of Abraham, were all nations to be blessed. This spiritual seed culminated historically and physically in Jesus of Nazareth, and in this sense Jesus is the seed of the woman. He has trampled Satan underfoot and has done so as a representative of all Eve's descendants, as a second Adam (Rom 5:18; 16:20). Therefore it is appropriate that Christian scholars since the second century A.D. have deemed Genesis 3:15 as the *protevangelium*, the first glimmer of the gospel.

Neither the woman nor the man was cursed, as was the serpent (3:14). Rather, their punishment involved a disruption of their God-given roles in the created order. The woman was created as an equal partner with the man and as the mother of children. These roles as mother and wife were the most important and most cherished functions for a woman in the ancient Near East. Yet after sin entered the world, both roles were marred.

Likewise, the man was created for abun-

Are Women Supposed to Be Subservient to Men?

Eve's judgment in Genesis 3:16 has come under intense scrutiny from many interpreters, with widely divergent results.[18] Modern feminism has motivated Christians to reconsider the role of women in home, church, and society. The church has debated this verse vigorously in recent years because of its important implications.

Eve, as a representative of all women, received a twofold punishment in Genesis 3:16:

I will greatly increase your
    pains in childbearing;
with pain you will give birth
    to children.
Your desire will be for your
    husband,
    and he will rule over you.

First, Eve will experience painful labor in childbirth. The very point at which she receives her greatest sense of fulfillment in life according to Old Testament conventions will also be a point of suffering. But this punishment also has a positive side, since it will be through her pain and childbirth that God will provide salvation for the world (3:15).

Second, Eve's relationship with her husband will be marred because of sin. Some have taken this verse to be **prescriptive**, or pronouncing a divine decree that women should or must remain submissive to their husbands. But this is an unfortunate misunderstanding of the words used in the verse.

The terms "desire" and "rule" in 3:16b are found again in tandem in Genesis 4:7b (*tĕšûqâ* and *māšal*, respectively). Sin is like an animal that "desires" to control and dominate Cain, but God challenged Cain to "rule" the unrestrained desire of sin. If, as seems likely, the author of Genesis intends us to read these verses together, the desire of Eve for her husband corresponds to sin's desire to pounce on Cain. It is a desire to break the relationship of equality established at creation and transform it into a relationship of domination and servitude. "To love and to cherish" has degenerated into "To desire and to dominate."[19]

We must not read Genesis 3:16b as God's decree for women to be subservient to men any more than we would take 3:16a as God's will for women to suffer as much pain as possible in childbirth. In other words, this passage is not **prescriptive**, but **descriptive**. It explains both *why* women have pain in childbirth and *how* marriage, this most beautiful of human relationships, also holds potential for great abuse. But it in no way should be used to justify male tyranny in marriage.

The rest of the Bible seeks to hold these consequences of sin in check. Though Old Testament culture was chiefly patriarchal, it valued women highly and provided important safeguards to protect them from immoral men. In addition, some women held important offices or leadership roles in ancient Israel, with kingship and the priesthood being the only restricted offices. Likewise, the New Testament established certain defenses to protect women from unchecked domination. The apostle Paul encouraged mutual submission within marriage (Eph 5:22–33). Women in the New Testament period served in many positions of spiritual leadership, except elder or bishop.

dant life in the garden. Now he must work to sustain himself, though he will ultimately fail, returning to the dust from which he was formed (3:16–19).

You and I, and every human being who ever lived with the exception of our Lord Jesus, sin because of the tendency toward evil set in motion by Adam and Eve. Every child of Adam inherits a nature marred by sin. Christian theologians have discussed the various implications of Adam as a representative of the whole human race. This is often called the doctrine of original sin.[20] Many object because they feel this implies we are condemned for someone else's sin. But all of us have confirmed our solidarity with Adam and Eve by our own sins. In Romans 5:12–21, the apostle Paul contrasts the obedience of Christ with the *dis*obedience of Adam in order to show the universal effectiveness of Christ's death on the cross. Just as sin and death entered the world by one man, so salvation and life came into the world through one righteous man, Jesus Christ.

Events outside the Garden of Eden (4)

The forgiving grace of God made life possible after the loss of the Garden of Eden. Their enlightened eyes revealed to Adam and Eve their shame and disgrace.

Their primitive "fig leaves" were inadequate for the cruelties of their new harsh life outside the garden (3:7). But God graciously clothed Adam and Eve in suitable garments (3:21), and they were permitted to continue life elsewhere.

The tragic events of Genesis 4 illustrate the harsh realities of the life Adam and Eve must now shape for themselves outside the Garden of Eden. More important, the chapter illustrates for us the realities of sin and its contagious nature. Here we begin to see its rampant and unrestrained spread, in terms of both breadth and depth in the human heart. How quickly sin in the human heart grows! In the first family, sin evolved in a single generation from the neglect of God's word to murdering a brother.

Conflict arises among the children of Adam and Eve. Details of this conflict are vague, but in the context of worship, it appears that Cain had an arrogant spirit. Abel offered the best of his flock, but Cain's actions were motivated by evil (1 Jn 3:12). The result was the world's first murder (Gn 4:8).

Eve had been talked into her sin. Cain could not be talked out of his, even by God himself.[21] God offers Cain a second chance and an opportunity to repent for his attitudinal sin: "If you do what is right, will you not be accepted?" (4:7). In a graphic verse that you should memorize, God warns Cain that if he refuses to do what

Study Questions

1. Describe the significance of the "tree of the knowledge of good and evil."

2. Explain the importance of God breathing life into the human creature.

3. What do the serpent's question and the woman's response tell the reader about each respectively?

4. For what reason did early Christian scholars term Genesis 3:15 the *protevangelium*?

5. What changes take place with regard to the roles of the man and the woman following their sin?

6. Give three examples of paronomasia (wordplay) in Genesis 2–4.

7. Offer reasons for viewing Adam and Eve as historical figures.

Key Terms

Pentateuch
etiology

is right, "sin is crouching at the door; it desires to have you, but you must master it" (4:7). Sin is personified as a wild animal, "lurking" at the door, perhaps the animal's resting place, ready to pounce on its victim if provoked. Sin is temporarily under control, but dangerously ready if induced. God warns Cain to "master" the creature, and not allow sin to grow further in his darkened heart. Indeed, sin can pervade every aspect of our lives, and left unchecked by God's grace, will certainly enslave us (Rom 1:18–32).

The failure of Cain to master sin illus-trates the full growth-cycle of sin (Jas 1:14–15). All of us are enticed by our own evil desire. After desire is conceived in our hearts, it gives birth to sin and sin gives birth to death. However, the story of faith that begins to unfold in Genesis is good news. We learn that by God's grace we do not have to remain enslaved to our evil desires (Jas 1:12). With his help we can resist temptation. But the picture of sin in the Bible is like that of a swimmer in the rapids of a large river, miles upstream from a mammoth waterfalls. The swimmer can easily get out of the water, but as the rapids get rougher and he gets closer to the falls, it becomes more and more difficult to be free of the currents and the force of the water. The safest and best time to resist temptation is before it is too strong or powerful to resist. The rising doubt or evil thought quickly becomes sin when we dwell on it and allow it to take up residence in our hearts.

3 What's Wrong with This Picture?

The LORD our God said to us at Horeb, "You have stayed long enough at this mountain. Break camp and advance into the hill country of the Amorites; go to all the neighboring peoples in the Arabah, in the mountains, in the western foothills, in the Negev and along the coast, to the land of the Canaanites and to Lebanon, as far as the great river, the Euphrates. See, I have given you this land."

—Dt 1:6–8a

Primary Readings: Excerpts from the Epic of Atrahasis, the Enuma Elish, the Memphis Creation Story (RANE[1])

Outline

- **Who Were Israel's Neighbors?**
  The Mesopotamians
  The Egyptians
  Peoples of Syria-Palestine
- **Ancient Theories of Creation and Early Human History**
  Ancient Near Eastern Parallels to Genesis 1
    Egypt
    Mesopotamia
  Ancient Near Eastern Parallels to the Themes of Genesis 2–4
- **Israel: A Picture, a Mirror, or a Window?**
- **Significance for Modern Christians**

Objectives

After reading this chapter you should be able to

1. List the cultural characteristics of Israel's neighbors, the Mesopotamians, the Egyptians, and other cultural groups in the area.
2. Compare the creation myths and the accounts of the first humans in ancient literature with the biblical account of creation.
3. List seven aspects of the biblical account of early history that clearly distinguish and oppose the legends of the surrounding culture.
4. Summarize how the worldview represented in the Bible contrasts with more commonly held ancient and modern views of life.

Have you ever felt alone in a crowd, or out of step with a group of peers? That is how Israel must have felt among her ancient neighbors.

When the other nations of the ancient world looked at Israel, they might have asked a question like, "What's wrong with this picture?" Israel would have seemed unusually different in many ways. The truth is, the nations of ancient Mesopotamia and Egypt had their own creation accounts and other stories with motifs and themes similar to those of Genesis 1–4. The precise relationship between these ancient Near Eastern literatures and the Old Testament is a constant source of scholarly speculation.

Who Were Israel's Neighbors?

We will begin by surveying the various peoples who surrounded Israel. The Book of Genesis, like the rest of the Old Testament, has numerous references to other people groups who lived in Mesopotamia, Egypt, and Syria–Palestine in ancient times.[2] Israel was a relatively small nation among many in an area known today as the Middle East. In Old Testament studies, we refer to this area as the "ancient Near East." This area comprised most of western Asia: from modern Iran, Iraq, and Kuwait in the east to Egypt in the southwest, along the northern coast of Africa.[3]

The Mesopotamians

The area known as Mesopotamia (Greek, "between the rivers") is a great stretch of land between the Euphrates and the Tigris rivers. Mesopotamia extends from the mouth of the Persian Gulf northwestward along the bend in the Euphrates and reaches eastward to the Tigris at the foot of the Zagros Mountains. Historians have long recognized Mesopotamia as the birthplace of human civilization.

For over three thousand years of ancient Near Eastern history, Mesopotamia was a melting pot for many different ethnic and cultural groups. The most important were

The Ancient Near East

the Sumerians and the various Semitic groups that succeeded them. At the dawn of human history, the Sumerians apparently invented writing in southern Mesopotamia. We are unable to determine with assurance the origins of these people or their ethnic kinship to other ancient groups.[4] The importance of the Sumerians and their influence on subsequent cultural developments in ancient history cannot be overestimated. They and the Semitic groups that followed them in Mesopotamia established the cultural infrastructure for the Old Testament world.

The Sumerians were followed by a long succession of Semitic groups of various nationalities. Near the end of the third millennium B.C., the first group of Semites, the Akkadians, had risen to power and occupied southern Mesopotamia together with the Sumerians. By the turn of the millennium, another Semitic group known as the Amorites began to arrive in enormous numbers, and dominated the next thousand years of Mesopotamian history. The Amorites eventually established major centers of power at Babylon on the Euphrates and at Assur and Nineveh farther north along the Tigris. The Babylonians in the south and the Assyrians in the north were two of the most important groups in

Mesopotamia and played a significant role in Old Testament history. Many scholars believe that Abraham was an Amorite from Mesopotamia.

The Egyptians

The northeastern coast of Africa is geographically dominated by the majestic Nile River. This imposing river stretches nearly 3,500 miles from the highland regions of East Central Africa through the northeastern deserts of the continent to the Mediterranean Sea. Ancient Egyptians treasured the great muddy river, which they recognized as the source of life-giving water and soil. One ancient historian fittingly described Egypt as the gift of the Nile.[5]

Unlike Mesopotamia, Egypt enjoyed relative seclusion and isolation from the outside world. The great desert borders and the Mediterranean Sea to the north provided natural geographical boundaries, and meant Egypt suffered fewer incidents of foreign aggression in its history. Consequently, Egypt did not encounter the large number of ethnic and cultural infiltrations that were so characteristic of Mesopotamian history.

Rather than a history of constant power changes and new people groups, the story

The livelihood of Egypt has always been interconnected with the Nile River.

Sea Peoples

of Egypt is one of the rise and fall of mostly native Egyptian dynasties. Some of these dynasties saw Egypt develop large empires with international significance in ancient Near Eastern history, such as Old Kingdom Egypt (dynasties 3–6, approximately 2700–2200 B.C.), Middle Kingdom Egypt (dynasties 11–13, approximately 2000–1700 B.C.), and New Kingdom Egypt (dynasties 18–20, approximately 1550–1100 B.C.). The Egypt we shall encounter as we read the patriarchal narratives of Genesis is probably Middle Kingdom Egypt, though the Bible does not provide enough detail to be certain. The Joseph narrative should probably be placed between the Middle Kingdom and the New Kingdom.

Syria–Palestine

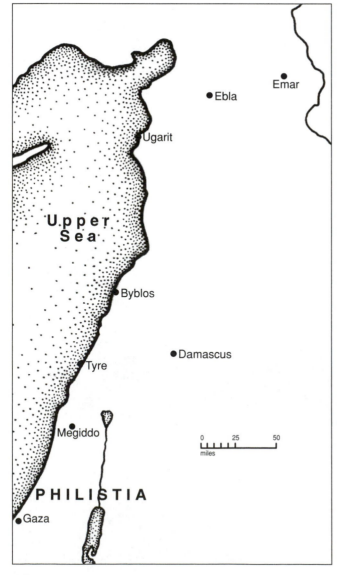

Peoples of Syria–Palestine

Syria–Palestine is the area from the northern bend of the Euphrates River along the Mediterranean coast, southward to the Sinai desert. Israel was the southernmost section of Syria–Palestine. In contrast to Egypt and Mesopotamia, Syria–Palestine was not the site of advanced civilization and national empires early in history. Rather, its political importance was a result of its role as a land bridge connecting Mesopotamia and Egypt, as well as Asia Minor and Europe. Throughout ancient history, the empires of Mesopotamia and Egypt sought to control access to Syria–Palestine for both economic and military-political reasons.

Like Mesopotamia, this region was a melting pot for many ancient people groups. The Canaanites and Amorites were prominent nationalities early in Syro-Palestinian history.[6] Of the important city-states established by these groups, those of Ugarit and Emar (see MAP) have provided the most interesting written materials for Old Testament scholars. Around 1200 B.C., another Semitic group known as Arameans began appearing in large numbers in the area. This people established important city-states, such as at Damascus, and played a large role in later Old Testament history. Likewise, around 1200 B.C., a variety of peoples presumably from the mainland of Greece and called the **Sea Peoples** began to appear all along the Mediterranean coast. One group of these Sea Peoples, known from Egyptian sources as "Peleset," settled on the southwest coastal plains of Syria–Palestine. They are known in the Old Testament as "Philistines," a term that also gave us the word "Palestine."

Ancient Theories of Creation and Early Human History

We may presume that all of the peoples surrounding Israel had their own traditions, myths, and legends to explain how the world came into existence. But only the great riverine cultures of Mesopotamia and Egypt have preserved details of those traditions. These great early civilizations first

cosmogony

used writing in a significant way to preserve the theological speculations of humankind. This literature was lost when the first great empires disappeared and lay buried beneath the sands of time for thousands of years. But in the nineteenth and twentieth centuries, archaeologists have discovered, deciphered, and translated Egyptian and Mesopotamian accounts of creation and the flood. This relatively recent development has obviously led to a greater understanding of Israel's view of God, the world, and humankind.

There are many possible comparisons that could be made, and this discussion is necessarily selective.

Ancient Near Eastern Parallels to Genesis 1[7]

Egypt

The most extensive account of creation coming from Egypt is the so-called Memphite Theology. This account draws on other creation texts, mostly the Pyramid Texts, but heightens the role of the god of Memphis, Ptah.[8] There are no other creation accounts as such, though there are separate works embedded in larger literary works, which give an account of how the world began.

The characteristic of these Egyptian creation accounts is diversity. Yet beneath the variety is a consistent **cosmogony** (creation of the cosmos). Creation begins with watery chaos (the god Nun), who is nevertheless not a creator god. In the Memphite theology, Ptah is the creator god, but elsewhere it is usually Atum. Ptah becomes identified with the substance of the primal waters; he becomes all. Starting with this chaotic matter he has subsumed, he then uses magic to create the world by divine decree. Like the Genesis account, the creative act is by fiat, but there is no *creatio ex nihilo* here since the chaotic primal matter had actually become part of the creator god.

Mesopotamia

The greatest expression of the Mesopotamian worldview is the creation story known by its Akkadian title, *Enuma Elish* (the first words of the composition meaning "when on high"). Since its discovery in the nineteenth century, the *Enuma Elish* has attracted the attention of scholars and amateurs alike because of its close parallels with the Genesis account. The story tells of a cosmic battle between the leading deities, in which the young and daring Marduk kills the monstrous Tiamat, mother goddess personifying the primeval ocean. Marduk split her corpse in two, making heaven from one half and earth from the other. Using the blood of her co-conspirator, Kingu, Marduk and his father created humankind to do the hard labor of the universe, leaving the deities free from work. The account continues by telling of the founding of the city of Babylon and a great feast in Marduk's new temple there, among other things.

Similarities with the Genesis account have frequently been cited. But in reality, the similarities are few and center around the role of Tiamat, the mother goddess. Marduk began the process of creating by splitting her cadaver into two separate spheres of water—obvious parallels with

The *Enuma Elish* is a Mesopotamian creation story that shares several parallels with the Genesis account.

the waters of the firmament on the second day of creation (Gn 1:6–8). Also, her name, Tiamat, has obvious similarities with the Hebrew word for deep in Genesis 1:2, *tĕhôm*. Many have argued over the years that there is a formal connection between the two and that Genesis is at least a polemical attack on the role of Tiamat in creation. This view is now, however, widely refuted.

Perhaps more pertinent for comparison with Genesis is the older document known as the "Epic of Atrahasis." This epic is the oldest Near Eastern primeval history in nearly complete form.[9] It presents in historical sequence both the creation of humankind and their near extinction in the flood in a similar sequence as in Genesis. The Atrahasis epic confirms at least that the basic plot of Genesis 1–11 was well known throughout the ancient Near East.

Ancient Near Eastern Parallels to the Themes of Genesis 2–4

The Atrahasis epic also depicts a fascinating account of the creation of humankind. In Mesopotamian myths, human origins usually involve a mixture of the blood from a slain god and clay material. In the Atrahasis epic, the flesh and blood of a minor deity are mixed with clay. After other deities spit on the mixture, the mother goddess (Nintu) mixes god and human thoroughly together in the clay. From this playdough mixture, Nintu uses magic to pinch off fourteen pieces, constituting seven males and seven females. The analogies with Genesis 2:7, where the first man is created of dust and given life by divine breath, are obvious.

In addition, the idea of a well-watered paradise is attested in both Sumerian and Ugaritic documents (Ugarit is a major port city in Syria–Palestine). But the Adapa myth from Mesopotamia has the most interesting comparisons.[10] The main character is Adapa, a priest known for his wisdom in early Mesopotamia, who lost his opportunity to gain immortality. His name is phonetically close to "Adam." In the myth, Adapa is called before the god of heaven to give an account for something he has done wrong. Ea, the god of magic, advises Adapa when he goes to the heaven god not to eat food and drink. He obeys Ea, but the food offered him was food of eternal life. Certain parallels with Adam and Eve are obvious. Both were tested by the deity based on something to eat; both failed their tests, missing the chance for immortality; and both failures brought consequences on humanity. But their respective narratives are emphasizing different things. Adam failed his test, while Adapa actually passed his. The similarities between Adapa and Adam are interesting, but they may not be more than that.

Israel: A Picture, a Mirror, or a Window?

Now that we have surveyed selected cosmological speculations of Israel's neighbors, you can understand why Israel looked quite unique to the neighboring nations. In our modern colloquialism, they might have looked at Israel and asked, "What is wrong with this picture?" They were accustomed to cultural, language, and sociological differences. But there were certain metaphysical assumptions that the ancient nations all seemed to share. In this regard, they mirrored each other. But when they looked at Israel, they did not see a mirror of their own culture. Israel was different; she was neither a mere picture nor a mirror. In reality, Israel offered a window on a completely different world, or at least, a completely different way of looking at the world. Israel was not a mirror that simply reflected the culture of the ancient Near East. Rather, Israel represented a window providing the ancient Near East with a different view on the world.

Indeed, Israel saw herself as unique as well. Old Testament scholars often debate the extent to which Israel was actually distinct from her neighbors. But the Old Testament itself contains many self-claims to distinctiveness, and these seem to be clearly centered in Israel's special relationship with God.[11] Her uniqueness can best be demonstrated by the singular "configuration of traits" that illustrates how she magnified certain ancient Near Eastern features while obliterating others.[12] Israel's unique cultural configuration had

monotheism

theogony

many features, but prominent among them was her **monotheism**, implied in the creation account of Genesis 1 but stated somewhat more clearly in Deuteronomy 4:35, 39, and 6:4. Flowing from monotheism was Israel's ban against making physical representations of God (that is, "idols"), the application of ancient treaties to the divine–human relationship (that is, the covenant), and the absence of sex and death in her descriptions of God.[13] All of these features were unique to Israel, and demonstrate how profoundly different she was from her neighbors.

Yet Israel's account of creation has certain similarities with those of her neighbors. So, for example, all ancient creation stories seem to begin with a watery chaos. And both Egypt and Mesopotamia imply a creation by decree, not unlike creation by fiat in Genesis 1. But the dissimilarities are more striking. The ancient Near Eastern creation accounts almost always involve **theogony**, or speculation about the birth of the gods. In contrast, Israel simply assumes God's preexistence ("In the beginning God . . ."), and offers no speculation on his beginnings. Likewise, the role of humankind in the created order is an example of dissimilarities between Israel and her neighbors. In all the ancient Near Eastern accounts, humans play a relatively insignificant role. They are created almost as an afterthought. But in Genesis 1–2, Adam and Eve are the crowning achievement of God, the central theme of his creative masterpiece.

We shall now analyze in more detail how these differences were expressed in Genesis 1–4 compared to the ancient Near Eastern cosmologies we have surveyed. The worldview expressed in Genesis 1–4 is not just *different* from its counterpart in the literature of the ancient world; it is *opposed* to it. Israel was not just offering an alternate opinion. Her understanding of first things and the nature of the world was mutually exclusive, and could not be squared with ancient Near Eastern philosophy. This alternate view of reality may be summarized in seven steps, which are logically sequential.[14]

First, everything that is unique to ancient Israel may be traced to her express monotheism. Some peoples of the ancient world believed in dozens, even hundreds, of deities, as many as there are natural and social forces in the world. Israel assumes the existence of one God who created the other forces of the world (Gn 1:1). All else flows logically and inexorably from this remarkable concept, which was so foreign and new in a thoroughly polytheistic world. Scholars debate vigorously whether Israel was actually monotheistic, or whether later authors of the exilic period altered the record to make her appear so.[15] But the evidence clearly suggests that Israel was monotheistic, though her creed was implicit because she lacked the analytic logic necessary to formulate it.[16]

The second feature of the ancient Israelite worldview flows logically from her monotheistic creation theology. This creator God is transcendent. He is not continuous with the world he has created.[17] This was likewise a remarkable and new concept. The prevalent worldview accepted the immanence of the deities. The gods were correspondent to, or continuous with, all other things that existed. There were no rigid distinctions in creation. This may be illustrated as in Diagram 3.1.

The circle represents a closed world system, with nothing beyond it. Everything that exists is contained therein, since all things are continuous with each other, including the deities. Even within the three realms of the cosmos, there is no real quintessential difference of being. The distinc-

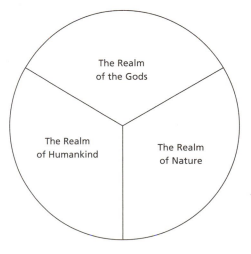

Diagram 3.1
The Closed World System
of Ancient Near Eastern Thought
(The Law of Correspondence)

tion between these realms is porous. The roles of the gods and humans are different, but they are not different in their essential natures. Thus, in the ancient Near Eastern creation accounts, the deities were portrayed much like humans: living in families, expressing jealousy, fear, envy, and other emotions.[18]

The contrast with Genesis 1–4 and the Israelite concept of divine transcendence is unmistakable and determinative for the rest of the Bible. The alternate view of reality offered in Genesis has profound implications for every other feature of Israel's worldview.

In contrast to everyone around her, Israel believed in a God who stands outside the created order (see Diagram 3.2). He has easy access to all of the universe's parts, since he created all that is. But he is not bound by its structures or contained in its cycles. He transcends the world, standing above and beyond our present reality.

The third distinguishing feature of Israel's worldview is her total disinterest in the origins of God. As you noticed, the other creation accounts from the ancient Near East were fascinated by the origins of the deities, including divine birth stories (or "theogonies"). In addition to divine births, the ancients speculated about divine deaths. Absu, Tiamat, and Kingu among others met violent deaths in the *Enuma Elish*. Since the deities were seen as continuous and similar to humans, they must have the same experiences that hu-

mans have, such as birth, death, and many others.

But Genesis shows no interest in such questions. By opening with the words, "In the beginning God . . . ," Genesis anticipates and precludes the idea of a divine pedigree. God has no genealogy, no ancestors, no rivals. This opening verse invites readers of every generation to accept the fact that the universe and everything in it began as a thought in the mind of God, who has always been there. He himself has no beginning or end. Indeed, to believe this great truth is to prepare you for reading the rest of the Bible. If Genesis 1:1 is true, all the rest logically follows.

The fourth feature of Israel's alternate view of reality is obvious from our brief review of the *Enuma Elish* above. That is, God is a nonsexual being. In the parallel ancient Near Eastern accounts, the deities were sexual beings, who had children and families. Once again, the gods merely mirrored the realms of humankind and nature, where life itself resulted from sex. Therefore, the deities must also depend on sexual activity for reproduction.

In Genesis, sex is a facet of God's creation. He himself is nonsexual, though he created man and woman as sexual beings in his image ("male and female he created them," Gn 1:27). Both genders are elevated in the statement so that both are made in the image of God. And both sexes naturally reflect features of the personality of God. But God himself is not male or female, and has no consort or wife. This important distinction between Israel and her neighbors has ramifications for her history, related elsewhere in the Old Testament. Israel would eventually be exposed to the agriculturalist fertility cult of ancient Syria–Palestine, in which divine sexual intercourse (especially between Baal and Asherah) was believed to guarantee fertility of crops and family. This ultimately presented an ideological challenge for Israel and is behind the prophetic reforms of Elijah and Elisha (1 Kings 17–2 Kings 13).

The fifth characteristic of Israel's worldview is her unique ban on magic.[19] All other nations of the ancient Near East believed in and practiced a wide variety of magical arts. They believed formulaic recitations and imitative acts could ma-

God

Diagram 3.2
The Israelite Worldview
(The Law of Transcendence)

eschatology

genre

canon

nipulate and exploit the powers of the divine and natural realms. Through these means, the ancients believed they could attain benefits for the human realm that were otherwise impossible. In this way, nature and the gods were seen as subservient to supernatural forces beyond their control.

Israel's monotheism and concept of transcendence made this an impossibility. The creator God is not subservient to any supernatural force beyond his control, and cannot be manipulated under any circumstances. Israel's theology simply forbade the use of magic. As monotheists, the biblical authors did not believe magic was connected to other gods, but depended on self-operating forces. They attributed a reality to magical power that was independent of the gods, though they seldom attempted a more specific definition of that power. Magic, therefore, was tantamount to human rebellion that unlocked divine secrets, making humanity equal with God.[20]

The implications of all this with regard to history is the sixth feature of Israel's distinctive worldview. The ancient Near Eastern worldview devalued history.[21] Although the gods intervened in history, there was no concept among the ancient peoples of a God who was Lord of history and who had an overarching plan for history. The pagan gods were reflections of the human realm. The gods were concerned with the cycles of nature, which were reflections of the genuinely important events happening in the mythical realm. Significant events took place outside of time and space, and therefore history was not important.

Israel, on the other hand, elevated history to an entirely new level in the ancient world. As the only God, the creator transcends nature. Israel attached importance to the beginning of time and space (creation), and to the beginning of the nation Israel (the Mosaic covenant). The rest of Israel's history had both a backward- and forward-looking perspective (the theologians refer to *Urzeit* and *Endzeit*, "origin-time" and "end-time"). For the first time in human history, there was an interest in the unique historical events because they revealed God's will for his people. And also for the first time, there was a definite divine plan in history, which had a specific terminus point. The Israelites were the only ones in the ancient world to have an **eschatology** (a doctrine of last things). For Israel, the conclusion of history is implied in its beginning.

The seventh and final feature of Israel's distinctive view of reality is an outgrowth of this unique view of history. Whereas the ancient Near Eastern peoples expressed their theology in the form of myths and legends, Israel was primarily interested in the writing of history. She believed God had revealed himself in the events of Israel's national history, especially the Mosaic covenant at Sinai. But the historical events of the covenant are also tied to the events of the patriarchs, the flood, the Garden of Eden, and the creation of time and space itself. Rather than myths, Israel elevated a little-used **genre** of literature to new heights: historiography. The Old Testament begins with nine books of history (first nine books of the Jewish **canon**),[22] often called the Primary History, and large sections of the prophets are also historical narrative. Such a role for historical narrative was radically new in the ancient Near East. In fact, it would be more natural to call the Hebrew authors of the Old Testament the parents of history rather than Herodotus, the fifth-century B.C. Greek historian who is often referred to as the "Father of History."

In sum, Genesis teaches that God created humans in his image and after his likeness. This is divinely revealed truth about God and the role of humans in his created order. We were created to worship and enjoy him forever. Wherever and whenever the revealed truth of God is rejected or neglected, human beings will replace God with gods made in their own image. The object of human adoration, if not the God of the Bible, will be a tawdry image of humankind. Idolatry is when we make gods of ourselves, or try to remake God in our image.

Significance for Modern Christians

Israel's worldview presented a dramatically different view of reality than was

Key Terms

Sea Peoples
cosmogony
monotheism
theogony
eschatology
genre
canon

then current in the ancient Near East. These contrasting worldviews have numerous implications for modern believers. But there are two I would especially like you to remember as we continue our walk through Genesis.

First, you and I are so familiar with the truths of Genesis 1–4 that we fail to realize how truly revolutionary these ideas were. Our modern culture does not accept much of what the Bible teaches. But at least the ideas of monotheism, creation, and the great value intrinsic to human life are *familiar* to most people in our society. Not

so in the ancient Near East! Genesis 1–4, and indeed the rest of the Bible, were unique and radically different answers to the most important questions of life. By inspiring the Israelite worldview, God was offering the world an alternate view of reality. As a result, the nation Israel formed a counter-culture in the world. The Christian church is likewise called to be a counterculture ("light" and "salt," Mt 5:13–16) in the world, and to present modern people with this alternate view of truth.

Second, these two views of truth, the biblical and the nonbiblical, are the only two available. Whenever and wherever biblical revelation is rejected, humankind will resort to some worldview related to what we have called the ancient Near Eastern view. But the human mind is limited in possibilities. Though the particulars change, the basic philosophical tenets are the same. In modern American culture, one of the prevalent new influences is the so-called New Age movement. This is really just a blend of Eastern mysticism and modern pop culture, resulting in "channeling," "centering," and the like. But if we examine the so-called New Age movement closely, we would see that it is not

Study Questions

1. Why was Egypt isolated from much of the ancient world, and how did this affect her political history?

2. What are the similarities between Genesis 2–4 and the Adapa myth from Mesopotamia? How are these two accounts different?

3. Discuss several ways that Israel may be said to represent a window providing the ancient Near East with a different view of the world.

4. Explain in some detail the significance of Israel's monotheism for her religion.

5. Compare and contrast Israel's view of history with that of her neighbors.

6. List and comment briefly on each of the seven ways that Israel's worldview may be said to be opposed to that of neighboring nations.

7. Having considered the ancient Near Eastern worldview, can you think of ways the New Age movement shares some of the same assumptions as Israel's neighbors thousands of years ago? Describe ways in which the biblical worldview is at odds with popular worldviews today.

new at all, but really just the same old lie. Biblical revelation is the only answer to such new winds of doctrine. Whenever the true God is rejected, people will seek ways to fulfill the serpent's insidious promise, "your eyes will be opened, and you will be like God" (Gn 3:5). Without God's grace and truth, we are incapable of getting past the Garden of Eden's failure.

4 Sin's Contamination of Creation

Genesis 5:1–11:26

> And where th'offence is, let the
> great axe fall
>
> —Claudius, *Hamlet,* act 4, sc. 5

**Supplemental Readings: Ps 14:1–3,
Matt 15:19, Romans 3:23**

Outline

- **So, What Happened Next? The
  Children of Adam and Eve (5:1–6:8)**
- **The Flood (6:9–9:29)**
  Review of the Narrative
  Parallels with Ancient Literature
  Problems after the flood (9:18–29)
- **Where Did All These Nations Come
  From?**
- **Shem Again?**
- **Postscript on Genesis 1–11**

Objectives

**After reading this chapter you should
be able to**

1. Identify the significant contributions of
   genealogies to biblical literature.

2. Contrast the degradation leading to the
   flood with the hope of new beginnings
   illustrated in Noah.
3. Compare and contrast the biblical
   account of Noah and the flood with
   ancient Babylonian flood stories.
4. Trace the effects of Ham's curse to sinful
   behavior among his descendants, the
   Canaanites.
5. Using the biblical account of Noah's
   family and the tower of Babel episode,
   describe the genesis of human diversity
   and the commonalities of humankind.
6. State the central purposes of the second
   account of Shem's genealogy.
7. Summarize and apply the three-phase
   progression of blessing, sin, and grace
   found in the structure of the early
   chapters of Genesis.

Borrowing the line from Claudius, we might say Genesis 5–11 is about the falling of the great axe because the offense of sin is everywhere.

Genesis 3–4 expressed powerfully the theme of sin's contagious nature and its effects on the first human family. Now this theme dominates Genesis 5–11 (more precisely, 5:1–11:26) to show sin's effects on all of creation. As the human family grew and nations began to emerge, the destructive nature of sin in the human heart became apparent. Just as sin had moved quickly from neglect of God's Word (Adam and Eve) to murder (Cain and

Abel), it then spread like an infectious disease out of control to pollute all of humankind. To use a musical metaphor, this unit is about the crescendo of sin.

As we said in the prologue, the *tôlĕdôt* catchphrases in Genesis are hinge devices for linking various types of materials together, like beads on a string. In chapters 5–11, there are four such units linked by their *tôlĕdôt* expressions.

1. The *tôlĕdôt* of Adam's line (5:1–6:8)
2. The *tôlĕdôt* of Noah (6:9–9:29)
3. The *tôlĕdôt* of Noah's sons (10:1–11:9)
4. The *tôlĕdôt* of Shem (11:10–26)

Life-Spans of the Pre-Flood Family of Adam (Gn 5)

The individuals in Adam's genealogy are said to have lived incredibly long lives: Adam lived 930 years, Seth 912 years, Methuselah 969 years. The average life-span of the antediluvian patriarchs listed in Genesis 5 was about 900 years! After the flood, the expected life-span dropped drastically. The descendants of Shem lived an average of 344 years (11:10–32). Average life-spans then began to level off gradually. Abraham lived 175 years, Jacob 147, and Joseph 110.

How could the pre-flood patriarchs have lived so long? Several attempts to explain such longevity have been offered. Some have suggested the names in Genesis 5 refer to both the individual and his tribal heritage. Each name has two numbers listed: the first number refers to the person's actual life-span, while the second is to the family he established. So Adam, for example, lived 130 years (total of his actual life-span). After Seth's birth, Adam symbolically lived

another 800 years (his family dynasty) for a total of 930 years (5:3–5). The problem here is that Enoch and Noah are two individuals who appear to have lived 365 and 950 years respectively (5:23; 9:29), regardless of the length of their family dynasties.

Others have suggested the words for time units may have meant something entirely different in the earlier period. Perhaps the word for "year" in Genesis 5 meant a period much shorter than our 365 days. But the specific chronology of the flood narrative implies the years of Genesis 6–9 were approximately 360 days (7:11, 12; 8:4, 5, 13, 14).

We should admit the possibility that these pre-flood patriarchs actually lived such long lives. Our difficulty here is with *our* expected life-span, which is the only standard by which we can conceive ancient lives. But other ancient peoples also have traditions of remarkably long-lived ancestors in primitive antiquity.[1] Is it

possible that Genesis 5 reflects an authentic memory of earliest human families stretching back as far as humankind can reason? Another consideration is the gradual nature in which the forces of decay and disease took effect in humanity. These early descendants of Adam and Eve were genetically pure and less affected by the deteriorating results of sin.

Furthermore, we have no perception of what earth's atmosphere may have been like before the flood. It is possible the earth had never had rainfall, and the effect of cosmic rays and environmental factors may have been drastically different from our current surroundings. Theologically, it is possible God granted these long life-spans in order for humans to "be fruitful and increase in number" according to his instructions (Gn 1:28). In the end, we may have to be satisfied with an incomplete understanding of the nature of these long life-spans.[2]

Messiah

We shall treat these together in this chapter to show the way Genesis traces mounting sin. Adam's sons had children of their own, whose sin eventually led to cataclysmic human destruction (the flood). Noah's children were no better. Their renewed sin after the flood ultimately led to human disharmony and geographical dispersion (the tower of Babel). However, we will also hope to show that through it all—through worldwide devastation and tragedy—there runs a thin line of hope. Genesis 5–11 is exacting in its description of the effects of sin on humankind and the world. But there is also a glimmer of hope that penetrates the whole.

So, What Happened Next? The Children of Adam and Eve (5:1–6:8)

When we left the story of Genesis 4, the first human family was in trouble. They had lost the beautiful Garden of Eden because of sin. Cain had murdered Abel, his brother, and had been punished severely. Cain's own children were apparently getting worse instead of better. Another killing had occurred, and this time with no remorse (4:23–24). Violence had followed Cain's family and his line seemed to have no regard for human life at all.

As a transition to the next part of our story (that is, the flood), the Bible decides to use a different kind of literature: genealogy. This is the *tôlĕdôt* of Adam's line (5:1–6:8). How do you feel about reading genealogies in the Bible? We may sometimes be tempted to brush over them too quickly or skip them altogether. But we miss an important part of the Bible's message when we neglect the genealogies. Every part of the inspired Scriptures contributes to the whole.

Genealogies play an important role in several books of the Bible (1 Chr 1–9; Ruth 4:18–22; Mt 1:1–17; Lk 3:23–38). In every case, they make significant theological points. Genealogies were important in ancient tribal societies, where they provided a skeletal outline of a nation's history. God inspired his people Israel to use this feature of their culture to show that he was at work in their history. By studying the various genealogies in the Bible, we learn that God has preserved his faithful promises to create and bless through the family of Adam to Abraham to David and ultimately, through his **Messiah**, Jesus Christ. Though Genesis 5–11 traces the devastating effects of human sin on God's creation, the genealogies in the unit remind us that God was still at work. While humans were headed for destruction, his grace was preparing a way for escape.

The first two verses of Genesis 5 tell again the story of God's creation of Adam and Eve. These verses reiterate that Adam and Eve were made in the "likeness of God" and were blessed by him, a point that needed reemphasizing after their sin and subsequent loss of Paradise. Much has been forfeited. But much is still possible because Adam and Eve still bear the privilege of relating to God (see discussion of *imago Dei* in ch. 1, above).

The genealogy serves to highlight the consequences of sin by its incessant chorus, "Adam lived 930 years, *and then he died*" (5:5); "Seth lived 912 years, *and then he died*" (5:8, and see 5:11b, 14b, etc.). Even in the Garden of Eden, God had warned about death as the unavoidable consequence of sin ("when you eat of it you will surely die," Gn 2:17). That process had begun when they were expelled from the garden and its tree of life. Now we read that Adam did in fact die, but not before having a son (Seth) "in his own likeness, in his own image" (5:3). Adam was still blessed by God with long life and a son to whom he passed along the divine image. But he also passed along to Seth the mark of sin and death (read Rom 5:12).

Each great member of Adam's lineage made a contribution to God's plan for humankind by leaving behind a child who bore the divine image and blessing for the next generation. But no single descendant achieved the full richness of God's blessing because death was the lot for all of them.

Enoch (5:21–24) is singled out as an exception. He "walked with God," a phrase repeated twice. This is a rare Old Testament way of saying that Enoch was a man of exceptional piety and devotion to God. He walked in special intimacy with God.

This is not to say the other members of Adam's family were godless people, but that Enoch was a remarkably bright spot in this already devout family. Enoch was one of only two (Elijah in 2 Kgs 2:11) against whom the gates of death did not prevail. This event anticipates and prepares for the truth that only righteousness of such magnitude will conquer death (1 Cor 15:54–57). Yet even Enoch did not entirely escape sin's consequences, since his son Methuselah also inherited the sentence of death (Gn 5:27).

In sum, Genesis 5 traces the faithful line of Seth, the "appointed" (4:25, NRSV), all the way to Noah, the deliverer (5:32). At the end of Genesis 4, where the results of sin and hatred had permeated Cain's family, there is the hopeful comment about Seth (vv. 25–26). Genesis 5 teaches that even before the flood, at the earliest stages of human history, there were two types of people: those who were faithful to the divine image conferred upon all of us, and those who were violent and godless (Seth's line versus Cain's).

In the Genesis time-scale, the genealogy of chapter 5 covers the longest period of history. Like a VCR fast-forwards a tape, genealogies move the narrative ahead rapidly. Genesis 5 links the early history of humankind to the appearance of Noah and the flood.

But before the flood narrative, Genesis includes the strange little paragraph about the "sons of God" and the "daughters of men" (6:1–4).[3] Though some have assumed the "sons of God" were fallen angels or demons who married human women, this is probably not the intent here.[4] The phrase may also refer to "godly sons," meaning members of Seth's faithful lineage, who intermarried with "worldly daughters," the evil descendants of Cain. Such intermarriages would have diluted the influences of the faithful line of Seth.

In light of the theological purpose of the Genesis storyline from the Garden of Eden to the tower of Babel (11:1–9), Genesis 6:1–4 makes an important contribution. Regardless of which interpretation we choose, this little paragraph is clear that a new stage has been reached in the spread of sin and evil in human history. Whether angels have intermarried with humans, or Sethites with Cainites, the point is that humankind has reached a veritable explosion of evil.

The last paragraph of Adam's *tôlĕdôt* section (6:5–8) relates God's angry sorrow at the widening evil afflicting the human family. Genesis 6:5 may be the most strongly worded verse in the entire Bible! It shows the shocking and dangerous degree to which sin and evil have overcome the human population. The first half of the verse reveals how *extensively* human evil had spread around the world: "The LORD saw that the wickedness of humankind was great in the earth . . ." (6:5a, NRSV). The last half emphasizes that sin had permeated *intensively,* deep into the heart of every single human: ". . . and that every inclination of the thoughts of their hearts was only evil continually" (6:5b, NRSV).[5] This is a theme verse for Genesis 5–11. The full extent of human degradation resulted in the intense divine anger: "The LORD was sorry that he had made humankind on the earth, and it grieved him to his heart" (6:6, NRSV). This is no heartless regret, but the reaction of someone who loves deeply. God was sorry that he had created, and he vowed to wipe it all away, "people together with animals and creeping things and birds of the air" (6:7, NRSV).

Yet the unit ends with a glimmer of hope. One man, Noah, "found favor in the eyes of the LORD" (6:8). The *tôlĕdôt* of Adam has trekked through the ages, from creation to the verge of disaster. One righteous man stands in the way of creation's destruction.

The Flood (6:9–9:29)

As you read about Noah and the flood, you may have remembered childhood lessons about this important episode of biblical history. This narrative is not only graphic as an object lesson for children, but as a critical juncture in the biblical storyline and in human history.

Review of the Narrative

The now familiar expression "This is the account of Noah" (6:9) is the *tôlĕdôt* catchphrase that opens the unit running through 9:29. The details are well known.

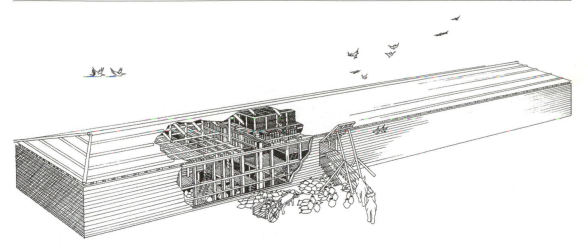

Modern depiction of Noah's ark.

The whole world had fallen so severely into sin that even the faithful line of Seth had disappeared, except for one righteous man, Noah. Noah was not just a good man in comparison with the bad generation in which he lived. Genesis emphasizes that he was righteous and blameless altogether, a man solely devoted to serving and pleasing God (6:9). The expression "among the people of his time" is a reminder that Noah stood alone with such commitments. You and I must remember that God's truth is not determined by majority vote. His people are frequently called to oppose the evil of the world, and to do so regardless of the company we keep.

God called Noah and warned of the impending doom. Noah was given specific instructions for building a ship large enough to save himself, his family, and enough animals to repopulate the earth after the flood. Remarkably, Noah obeyed God precisely. He built the ark to God's specifications, the length of one and a half football fields and taller than a three-story building. He likely did this far from any large body of water, totally dependent on the truth of God's Word.

God sent rain for forty days and forty nights. Noah and his family were confined to the ark for over a year while the flood waters rose and then receded. Noah used birds to gauge whether the waters were receding, and when God told him it was time to disembark, the eight humans and the animals left the ark. Noah built an altar to the Lord and offered sacrifices. The Lord commanded humans and animals alike to "Be fruitful and increase in number and fill the earth," reminiscent of the creation account (9:1). Noah and his family stepped into a world without human life. This was a new beginning. God then made a "covenant" or binding promise never to destroy the earth with such a flood again. The rainbow is God's sign for all times that he will be faithful to his Word.

Parallels with Ancient Literature

Like creation and early human history, the flood also has parallels in ancient Near Eastern literature. In fact, if one considers flood narratives from *all* early civilizations, including Greece and early Native Americans, there is no Old Testament passage with so many parallels as the flood.[7]

The closest parallels are those from ancient Babylonia in Mesopotamia. The most complete version is found in one of Babylonia's greatest literary masterpieces, the *Gilgamesh Epic*. This is the touching account of how Gilgamesh, an ancient king of southern Babylonia, rebelled against death when he lost his closest friend. On the eleventh of the twelve tablets, Gilgamesh meets Utnapishtim, who has been called the "Babylonian Noah." Utnapishtim relates how he achieved immortality when he was forewarned of a divine plan to flood the world. He survived the flood in a large reed boat accompanied by his family and pairs of all animals. But unfortunately for Gilgamesh, this event was not repeatable and gives him little hope for immortality. In defeat, Gilgamesh resigns himself to the inevitability of death and takes comfort in his achievements.

There are earlier versions of the flood

Was the Flood Local or Universal?

Christians have long debated whether the flood was local or universal. In other words, did the flood waters cover the entire globe, or only the portion of earth inhabited by humans at that time?

The language of Genesis 7 suggests a global flood. God sent the waters to wipe away every living creature from "the face of the earth," which can mean "the surface of the earth" (v. 4). As the waters rose, the text states "all the high mountains under the entire heavens were covered" (v. 19), and "the waters rose and covered the mountains to a depth of more than twenty feet" (v. 20). In addition, the inclusive nature of statements like "every living thing that moved on the earth perished" (v. 21), and "every living thing on the face of the earth was wiped out" (v. 23), supports the idea of a universal flood as punishment for unrepented evil.

On the other hand, the Hebrew words used in these passages do not decide the issue as quickly as one might think. Important to this debate is the word "earth" (ʾereṣ), which can and often does mean "land," "ground," or "country." In this light, Genesis 7:4 may mean "the surface of the land." The term "heaven" may indicate the amount of sky visible within one's own horizon (in which case it is often translated "sky," as in 1 Kgs 18:45).

Thus the details of the Genesis account can be used to support either a local or universal deluge. Likewise, scientists have often debated ideas such as geologic uniformitarianism versus catastrophist theories.[6] But the scientific arguments have also been inconclusive.

Though believers will continue to debate this issue, there can be no doubt that the flood was a real, historical event. We can also conclude that the flood waters covered *at least* the inhabited earth. The purpose of the flood was to destroy the earth's wickedness, and this of necessity means the flood waters covered all the earth inhabited at that time by human beings (Gn 6:7).

story from Babylonia, but they are much more fragmentary and incomplete. These are the Atrahasis epic and the Sumerian version.[8] The interesting point of these two is that each appears to place in historical sequence the creation of humanity and its near extinction in the flood in a manner similar to Genesis 1–9.

The similarities between Noah and Utnapishtim are fascinating.[9] Both men learn of the impending disaster from the deity and both are given specifics for constructing a boat coated with pitch. Both are told when to embark, and both preserve animals onboard. Both use birds to determine when the water is abating, and both ships land on a mountaintop. Both Noah and Utnapishtim offer sacrifices of thanksgiving.

But these striking similarities also serve to highlight the differences between Genesis 6–9 and the Babylonian traditions. Chief among them is the reason for the flood. No explanation is given in *Gilgamesh*, but the Atrahasis epic states that a human population explosion led to the divine decision to send the destruction. The noisy humans were disrupting divine sleep. The Bible, by contrast, consistently blames the flood on the rampant evil of humankind. And Noah was saved because of his intimate relationship with God, rather than through trickery. Though the Babylonian accounts are theological in essence, they have nothing of the high moral stature of Genesis. After the flood, when Utnapishtim makes his sacrifice, the starving deities swarm around the sacrifice like flies. The gods, for whom sacrifice served as food, had been without animal offerings during the flood, and they were famished!

In making comparisons between flood traditions from Genesis and Mesopotamia, I do not mean to imply the Bible's account was unmistakably borrowed from other ancient cultures. We simply do not have enough information to determine why there are so many similarities.[10] But regardless of the similarities, they simply

Problems after the Flood (9:18–29)

Although the flood had wiped out sinful people, the potential for sin remained in the heart of Noah and his children. Would they be more successful at avoiding sin? The answer comes quickly when Noah drinks too much wine and becomes inebriated. Genesis does not condemn Noah for his actions. But the Bible contains plenty of warnings against drunkenness, and there is a subtle displeasure implicit in this account.[12] Intoxication and self-exposure were serious indiscretions in that culture, and we have come a long way from the exalted description of Noah in 6:9: "blameless among the people of his time, and he walked with God."

Genesis is really more concerned about Ham's reaction. Noah is guilty of indecorous behavior, but Ham has committed a sin. His reaction shows clear disrespect for his father against all biblical and social prohibitions, not so much in seeing his father's nakedness, but in gossiping and publicizing the event: he "told his two brothers" (9:22). The honorable and righteous action would have been to quietly cover his father and mention it to no one. The actions of Shem and Japheth indicate the proper course of action (9:23).

Noah responds with a curse against Ham's son Canaan, and blessings for Japheth and Shem (9:24–27). This passage is unquestionably referring to the relationship between the later Israelites and their predecessors in the land of Canaan. The Canaanites were notorious in the Old Testament for illicit sexual practices, and were forced off the land that became Israel's "promised land" because of their wickedness (Gn 15:16; Lv 18:3). Canaan is "the lowest of slaves" because his descendants will be conquered by the Israelites in the conquest (see the Book of Joshua), which is a fulfillment of this curse.

Some have wrongly used this curse in 9:25 to argue that certain ethnic groups are superior to others. Groups like the Ku Klux Klan have based their racist ideologies on this passage, and have even argued that slavery is God's plan for inferior races. But this is totally wrong, and does an injustice to biblical truth. Noah's curse is not a matter of ethnicity, but of justice against the

A Neo-Assyrian depiction of Gilgamesh.

throw into bold relief the differences, which are more profound. One influential study done many years ago said it best: "The skeleton is the same in both cases, but the flesh and blood and, above all, the animating spirit are different."[11]

The Use of Birds by the Babylonian Noah

Utnapishtim, the flood hero of the *Gilgamesh Epic*, freed birds to find a resting place in a manner similar to Noah's raven and dove in Genesis 8:6–12.

When the seventh day arrived,
I sent forth and set free a dove.
The dove went forth, but came back;
Since no resting-place for it was visible, she turned round.
Then I sent forth and set free a swallow.
The swallow went forth, but came back;
Since no resting-place for it was visible, she turned round.
Then I sent forth and set free a raven.
The raven went forth and, seeing that the waters had diminished,
He eats, circles, caws, and turns not round.

Gilgamesh Epic XI, 145–54 (**ANET** 94–95)

Canaanite nation that would become the most wicked people of the ancient Near East. The Canaanites and Israelites were both descendants of Shem, and there can be no question that this passage is not condemning any race to an inferior position among the peoples of earth. Any attempt to use Genesis 9:24–27 in this way is anti-Christian, and is a "re-erecting of what God has demolished!"[13]

Where Did All These Nations Come From?

Genesis 10:1–11:9 gives an account of what happened to the descendants of Noah after the flood: "This is the account [*tôlĕdôt*] of Shem, Ham and Japheth . . ." (10:1). The unit has two sections; one teaching that all nations have their origin in one man, Noah (10:1–32), the other explaining the striking diversity and dispersion of the families of the earth (11:1–9).

The idea of the so-called Table of Nations (10:1–32) is the interrelatedness of the human family. We are all members of one human race by virtue of our descent from one family. Though we are of different languages, cultures, and geographical locations, we are all imprinted with the *imago Dei* and share in the dignity of human existence. An emphasis on our racial and cultural differences undermines this unity and runs counter to God's will for us. He basks in our rich cultural diversity and variety, which he has created. We need to learn to do the same.

The famous "tower of Babel" episode (11:1–9) closes this *tôlĕdôt* section, and explains the remarkable language diversity and dispersion of humankind. Though we humans are united by virtue of our common origins in Noah, we seem to be separated by a multitude of languages across the globe. This paragraph describes God's intervention against human pride and rebellion to scatter the peoples across the earth, disrupting their rebellious unity by making them use different languages. Though the tower of Babel episode follows the Table of Nations in the present arrangement of Genesis, the chronological order has been reversed for literary reasons.

The narrative emphasizes the scattering of humankind and the apparent hopeless nature of the sin problem. The sin of the people is not their desire to build a city, but their motivation: "Come, let us build ourselves a city, with a tower that reaches to the heavens, so that we may make a name for ourselves" (11:4). The Bible condemns Mesopotamian religion with its pyramids, temple-towers (or *ziggurats*) made of bricks and serving as mounds for temples. Genesis portrays this practice as a sacrilegious attempt to usurp God's authority. This prideful human achievement was at the same time a return to Adam and Eve's effort to become like God (Gn 3:5). If humankind remained unified in rebellion, there would be no end to evil in the world: "If as one people speaking the same language they have begun to do this, then nothing they plan to do will be impossible for them" (11:6). God decided that as good as unity and harmony are, division and separation are better than collective sin and apostasy.[14]

We have reached a literary summit with the tower of Babel. God has responded to sin in a number of ways in Genesis: curse and expulsion from the Garden of Eden, flood, and now dispersion of the human race. But still the problem of sin in the human heart goes on. As the literary apex

Modern depiction of an ancient Babylonian ziggurat.

of Genesis 1–11, the tower of Babel shows that "all human language has become a language of disobedience."[15]

Shem Again?

Genesis 11:10–26 is the last *tôlĕdôt* unit of Genesis 5–11. This paragraph returns to Shem's genealogy, which had been listed as part of the Table of Nations in 10:21–31. The list of Shem's descendants is included again in a different form in order to trace the faithful line of God's servants from Adam and Seth (Gn 5) through Shem and into the future.[16] Though the problem of sin has continued after the flood, God is not without representation in the world. God had blessed Adam and given him dominion over the earth. Even after the loss of the Garden of Eden, God had promised that Adam's seed would be victorious in a bruising conflict with evil. But with the continuing problem of sin after the flood, and now exacerbated by the tower of Babel, what hope could there be?

This genealogy demonstrates that the line of Shem was indeed blessed (read 9:26), and culminated in Terah's family, including obedient Abraham. Shem's genealogy brings us from the primeval world with its cosmic scope into the world of the patriarchs. We are about to enter a new section of Genesis in which we will read of individual patriarchs and their continuation of the divine promise. The call of Abraham was not arbitrary. He stood in a long line of those who received the blessing and promises of God: Adam, Seth, Enoch, Noah, Shem. If you come from a line of faithful and devoted Christians, you should pause now to give thanks for their influence on your life. Pray also that you will some day pass the torch of faith to others, who will also serve and please God.

Postscript on Genesis 1–11

Before we turn to the Abraham narrative, we should reconsider the theological theme of Genesis 1–11, and how it relates

Study Questions

1. Identify two understandings of "the sons of God" who marry "the daughters of men." What is the function of this paragraph in the narrative?

2. Compare and contrast the biblical flood tradition with the Mesopotamian flood tradition.

3. How does the reality of sin remain apparent even after the flood?

4. Describe what Genesis 10:1–11:9 teaches regarding both unity and diversity.

5. Why is Shem's genealogy presented twice, once in 10:21–31 and again in 11:10–26?

6. Comment on the exceedingly long life-spans recorded in Genesis 1–11.

7. What is meant by a "local" flood versus a "universal" flood? Why is the biblical evidence inconclusive in answering this question?

8. Trace the line of those receiving the blessing of God in Genesis 1–11. How does this line of blessing fit in the creation/uncreation/re-creation framework?

to the rest of Genesis and the Pentateuch as a whole.[17] As a way of tying all the various sections of Genesis 1–11 together, it is helpful to consider a "creation/uncreation/re-creation" theme. Human sin is so severe it comes to the brink of undoing God's good creation. But no matter how drastic sin becomes, God's grace preserves a means of saving humankind from the full consequences of sin. This theme culminates in the tower of Babel incident, since it does not *appear* to be followed by the usual "second chance," by which God preserves humankind. But then we encounter the *tôlĕdôt* section of Shem—again. It drives us relentlessly on until we arrive at Abram's family, the promised seed.

This idea of "blessing-sin-grace" is paralleled in the rest of the Genesis narratives. The patriarchs are blessed with covenantal promises, and in spite of their failures, God preserves the promises until they find

fulfillment in the nation Israel. Indeed, this theme is present broadly in the Pentateuch as a whole. For Moses and Israel are certainly the recipients of God's good blessings. But, as the Books of Exodus and Numbers explain, their sin and rebellion caused a forty-year delay in which they were forced to wander in the wilderness. Nevertheless, at the end of the Pentateuch Israel stood on the banks of the Jordan River, the Promised Land just beyond their grasp.

The sin problem in Genesis 1–11 is shown to be universal, so that all of us may understand our own personal problem with sin. None of us is exempt. But God's grace runs like an undercurrent throughout the whole. He has always preserved a means of escape. The promise to Adam and Eve that their offspring would confront and ultimately conquer the offspring of the serpent awaits fulfillment. As we continue through Genesis, we will learn the details of God's means of escape. Through the line of Shem and Terah, he prepared, at long last, for the Messiah and his triumph over sin and evil. And just as the sin problem is both universal and personal, so the solution, redemption through Jesus Christ, is the solution for your personal problem with sin.

In the next major portion of the Pentateuch, the Abraham narratives, we shall

Key Term

Messiah

read of a single individual whose exemplary faith became God's instrument of grace. The faith of Abraham is highlighted as the solution to the sin problem. He became the means of God's grace for saving the world, and all because he was obedient to God's Word. Throughout Scripture, God often uses the unexpected or the weak individual to accomplish some great purpose he has for his people. In doing so, God can claim glory for himself and demonstrate his own greatness. The apostle Paul was able to say he was proud of his weaknesses, so that Christ's power could rest on him (read 2 Cor 12:9–10). Never underestimate what God can do through you, or the contributions of your faithfulness to others around you.

Part
2

Encountering Abraham: God's Faithful Servant

Genesis 12–25

By faith Abraham obeyed . . .

—Heb 11:8

5 The Beginning of Our Faith Heritage

Genesis 11:27–14:24

> Our glorious God appeared to our ancestor Abraham in Mesopotamia before he moved to Haran.
>
> —Stephen, Acts 7:2b (NLT)

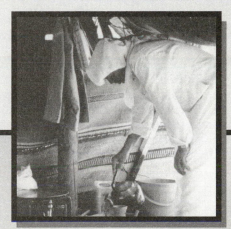

Supplemental Reading: Hebrews 11:8–10

Outline

- **Terah's Family (11:27–32)**
- **The Call of Abram and the Promises of God (12:1–9)**
- **Abram in Egypt (12:10–20)**
- **Trouble with Lot (13–14)**

Objectives

After reading this chapter you should be able to

1. Summarize the lineage of Terah, the move to Mesopotamia, and the opening comments about Abram and Sarai in Genesis 11.
2. Identify and apply key aspects of the call of God to Abram, including timing, the relational shift between Abram and God, what Abram was called from, and what he was called to.
3. List the promises God made and the significance of each to Abram and his descendants.
4. State the character weaknesses revealed during Abram's time in Egypt.
5. Contrast the choices made by Abram and Lot in chapter 13 and the consequences of those choices for each person.

You are about to embark on one of the most important journeys you will ever take. Reading and learning about Abram's call to follow God is more than an exercise in intellectual discipline. This is God's truth about saving faith, about establishing and maintaining a personal relationship with the Creator.

The story of Abraham (or "Abram" as he is known until Gn 17)[1] is one of the best known in world literature. Yet the Bible leaves out many details in its account of his life. For example, we really have no information about the first seventy-five years of Abram's life. This is because the story of Abram is more than just a biography of Israel's great patriarch. While leaving out much of the larger picture, Genesis portrays intimate details about the relationship Abram had with God. The Bible wants us to get this point: Abram became a righteous man because of his faith in God.

So in Genesis, Abram is the answer to the sin problem defined in chapters 1–11. At least he is the *beginning* of the solution to the sin problem. Through him, God raised up the nation Israel and eventually a Messiah. It is through the death of that Messiah that all who believe might be saved (Mk 10:45; 1 Pt 3:18).

Terah's Family (11:27–32)

The story of Abram's great faith is a continuation of the faithful line of believers traced by the genealogies of Genesis 1–11. After Cain murdered Abel and was driven from the Lord's presence (4:16), Genesis details the faithful line of Seth, in whose day people "began to call on the name of the LORD" (4:26). Seth's line is traced all the way to Noah, who had three sons, Shem, Ham, and Japheth. After the flood, it was Shem who was blessed by God (9:26). Shem's genealogy brings us to the faithful family of Terah, the father of Abram (11:27–32). In this way, Genesis illustrates that no matter how vile and evil the world seems, God always has his faithful band of believers through whom he is working to redeem the world (read God's response to Elijah in 1 Kgs 19:14–18).

Abram is the noted father of Israel's faith. But by starting with his father's genealogy, Genesis reminds us that he is also the son of Shem, and also of Seth and Adam. This paragraph links Abram to the Primeval History and places his call to follow God against a cosmic backdrop: the very same God who calls him to abandon everything and follow him to the Promised Land is the Creator and Sustainer of the universe in Genesis 1.[2]

The *tôlĕdôt* of Terah begins with the genealogy of 11:27–32, but is broadened to include the entire account of Abram's life (11:27–25:11). The beginning of this "account of Terah" is a brief genealogy that contains two important pieces of background information you will need to remember in order to understand the rest of the narrative on Abram. First, we are told in 11:27–28 that Abram's brother, Haran, died prematurely, leaving a son named Lot. Lot became the presumed heir of Abram's estate, and plays an important role in the drama to unfold. Second, 11:30 tells us emphatically that Abram's wife Sarai (whose name will also be changed later) was unable to have children. Barren women the ancient Near East were considered inadequate wives and often had no hope of future security.

Terah took his son, Abram, his daughter-in-law, Sarai, and his grandson, Lot, and left their home in southern Mesopotamia. They traveled to the edge of Canaan before stopping (11:31). It appears that God had called Abram (and perhaps Terah) prior to their departure from Ur (we will consider the chronological difficulties below). But we are not told why they stopped short of Canaan, whether due to ill health, weather, or fear. After Terah's death in Haran, Abram continued following God's call.

The Call of Abram and the Promises of God (12:1–9)

God's perfect creation had been ruined by human sin (1–11). His blessing had been turned into a curse. The attempt to reverse the tide of sin by destroying the human race and beginning over again with one righteous survivor (Noah) had not been successful. The curse of sin was too pervasive in the human heart. The call of Abram and the events of his life are the first step in a new way of salvation. God would bless Abram's family and the nation Israel was the result of his blessing. The rest of the Bible is really about this way of salvation, the means of victory over sin and death.

The precise timing between the genealogy of 11:27–32 and this call to forsake all and follow God is not certain.[3] Stephen's speech in the New Testament (Acts 7:2–4) states that Abram received the call while he was still in Ur, before he lived in Haran. This may imply he was honoring his father's wishes and waiting for God's timing before he entered Canaan. Often God's will for our lives is revealed gradually, and the most difficult part of obedience can be waiting. But obedience during the transition periods, while we wait, is the best preparation for serving him when we reach our destination in his timing.

It is a fascinating fact that Genesis devotes only two chapters to the creation of the world, one to the fall of Adam and Eve from sinless Paradise, but over thirteen chapters to the account of Abram.[4] This proportioning indicates something about the purpose and function of Scripture. The Bible seems much more interested in how individuals relate to God and the world around them than to the intricacies of how the world was created. Genesis is not a philosophical treatise, but a theological guidebook. It presents a bare-bones account of otherwise important issues on its way to explaining how we can find peace with God, and live peacefully with each other.

The account of Abram opens with divine speech: "Now the LORD said to Abram . . ." (Gn 12:1, NRSV). Just as God was the subject of the first verb of the Bible ("In the beginning God created"), so now the Lord is the subject of a new revelation. As God spoke the world into existence, so now he speaks in revelation of a new plan of salvation. As he is the subject of the first verb of this new relationship, initiating a new phase in the Bible's storyline, so he is the subject of the entire subsequent history of salvation.[5]

God's divine imperative ("Leave your country . . . ," 12:1) fell on the shoulders of a descendant from the line of Seth, Noah, and Shem. He was the heir to a great tradition of faithfulness, a tradition that prepared him to stand before God and take his turn in following God's command.

Nomads are still common in the Middle East.

Now God's plan was to take Abram into a deeper and more personal level of relationship, and to use him as an instrument of his own divine purpose for humankind. Righteous parentage is both a privilege and a responsibility.

The famous call of Abram in Genesis 12:1 was a command to go *away* from three things and *unto* one thing: "Leave your country, your people and your father's household and go to the land I will show you." The three things God called Abram to forsake were natural sources of security for any ancient Near Eastern nomad. God lists the three in rapid succession, each succeeding item narrowing the base of personal support and security. (1) His country (or "land") was his nationality and was the largest group in which Abram moved. (2) His people (or "clan") was smaller than his tribe, but larger than his immediate family. Such groups in ancient tribal societies provided personal identity and security. (3) His father's household referred probably to a call to give up his right of inheritance in his extended family. To abandon his father's house would certainly involve giving up his economic security. In a sense, God was calling Abram to go backpacking. God removed anything that might weigh him down or prove to be unnecessary for a trek through the woods. This illustrates Christian discipleship in several ways. God's claim on our lives always beckons us to leave certain things behind at the same time we are taking up a new journey following him: "At once they left their nets and followed him" (Mk 1:18, and see v. 20).

Five "I Will's" of Genesis

I will make you into a great nation, and

I will bless you;

I will make your name great, . . .

I will bless those who bless you,
  and whoever curses you

I will curse.

God called Abram to forsake everything in his life that typically provided security and comfort for ancient Near Eastern people. Not only did God ask Abram to forsake these three things; he called him *unto* one thing: "the land I will show you." It was startling enough to abandon everything, but how could Abram accept a mission so vaguely stated? Abram could only accept the fact that "the land"[6] was specific in God's mind, even if not in Abram's. The only thing he really understood about the one thing, the land, was that God would make it clear later. God was setting him on a path to follow, though Abram did not know where it led (Heb 11:8). The great patriarch was on a special road whose design and purpose was not of human origin.

God did not leave Abram completely without guidance or hope. He replaced the three things Abram had to abandon with something else—a set of promises. In Genesis 12:2–3, God gave Abram promises that become central for the rest of the patriarchal narratives of Genesis, and indeed, for the rest of the Bible. On the heels of the imperative "Go!" God makes five "I will" statements. The promises of Genesis 12:1–3 are basically three: land, descendants, and blessing.

These three promises are central to the meaning of Genesis. They are connected both to the creation account that preceded and to the rest of the patriarchal story to follow. These promises were introduced thematically in the Primeval History of Genesis 1–11. God created the land (*'ereṣ*, "land," is the same word here as in Gn 1:1). He also promised "blessing" and "seed," or progeny, to the first couple in the Garden of Eden. In this way, God's plan for the individual patriarch was also his benevolent design for all humankind. As we progress through the rest of Genesis, we will see how each of these promises is elaborated and broadened in meaning. As the Bible's message unfolds, these promises constitute the purpose of God for his chosen people.

The promises are a catalogue of what we all crave, even if only subconsciously. This is especially so for a landless, wandering Semitic nomad in the ancient world, like Abram. The promise of land spoke directly to Abram's immediate

Threefold Promise

Genesis 12:1a	Genesis 12:1b–3
country/land (ʾereṣ)	land (ʾereṣ)
people/clan/ family	descendants/ great nation
father's house	blessing

needs, and the promise of descendants was especially meaningful for him in light of Sarai's barrenness (11:30). In that ancient context, these two items ensured one's future, one's dreams for achievement and fulfillment in life. The Abram narrative thus teaches us how to discover true security in life. Here we learn the role of home and family, and discover that our walk of faith produces a future.

The promises are intriguingly similar to the three things Abram sacrificed in order to follow the call of God.

Genesis 12:1a	Genesis 12:1b–3
country / land (ʾereṣ)	land (ʾereṣ)
people / clan / family	descendants / great nation
father's house	blessing

The earthly things to which we cling in our desperate search for security and comfort are actually the very things that get in the way of true security. In the life of Abram and the other patriarchs, Genesis reveals to us that true security and fulfillment in life are achieved by living for God and depending on his promises. We are liberated through bondage to him. We are freed through our servitude. The key term of the promises is "blessing," a word that occurs five times in 12:2–3. Abram will be blessed by God, but he will also become God's instrument for blessing others. Part of fulfillment in life is living for others. We never experience God's best for us until we are used by him to touch the lives of someone else.

Were the promises of God fulfilled in Abram's lifetime? The promise that Abram and Sarai would have children was fulfilled in Genesis 21, when Isaac was born. But God did not promise just to give Abram a single child, but to turn him into a "great nation" (12:2). This promise was later broadened to emphasize the extent of that nation. God promised Abram that his offspring would be countless, like the stars of heaven and the grains of sand on the seashore (Gn 15:5; 22:17). But this is not the kind of promise that could have been fulfilled in Abram's lifetime: it simply had to be accepted on faith. Likewise the promise that he would inherit Canaan was for a far distant future (as Gn 15:13–16 makes clear). So Abram had to give up the known for the unknown. Genesis emphasizes this very facet of his personality and the magnitude of his great faith.[7] The nature of the promises meant they, for the most part, *could not* be fulfilled in Abram's lifetime. He personally would not have all the promises of God. But better—he had the God of all the promises.[8] As such, he becomes the paradigm for Christian faith.

Genesis 12:4 is one of the most amazing verses of the Bible. The account states simply, "So Abram left . . ." We are not told what must have gone on between 12:1–3 and 12:4. Did Abram argue with God or question his calling? Did he agonize during the night about how difficult the trip would be, and how unreasonable it seemed to forsake everything in his past? We are not told. Sometimes the Bible is as important for what it does not say as for what it does say. Genesis is not concerned to give us those details. They are not necessary to the point of the narrative. The central message is that Abram launched out in radical obedience to God's call on his life. Such obedience is what God desires from all of us.

Abram in Egypt (12:10–20)

Genesis 12:10–20 relates the sudden and unexpected departure of Abram from Canaan to Egypt. There was nothing wrong with his trip to Egypt necessarily, especially in a time of severe famine. One could even argue that God had providentially provided for Abram in this way, since Egypt was usually the last to suffer from drought in the region. But as you read about this event, you may have been surprised to hear Abram asking his wife to lie to Pharaoh about the nature of their relationship in order to save his own skin (12:13, not the only time this occurs in Genesis, as we shall see). And you may have questioned his rather shady means of acquiring wealth (12:16).

Suddenly, our hero's actions are not very heroic, as he moves from faith to fear. Abram fell victim to the old lie that telling a half-truth is permissible if you can get away with it. Sarai was in truth his half-sister (read 20:12), so he could justify his actions as not really all that serious an offense.[9] But Abram meant to deceive, and using one half of the truth to conceal the other is no less a lie! As her brother, he would be treated with respect and honor. As her husband, he feared he would be killed.

We learn from this episode that all is not perfect with our main character. He has lost faith in God's protection, and has taken matters into his own hands. Though he has set out on the path of faith, following God with radical abandon, Abram's action threatens to counteract the program God has set in motion. This is the first appearance of a theme that recurs as we travel through the patriarchal narratives of Genesis. The theme is a threat to God's promises of Genesis 12:1–3. The promises are threatened by the actions of one of the characters of the narrative.[10] In many episodes to follow, the promises of God are jeopardized by sin. Abram is motivated by fear for his life. But there are options open to God that Abram does not see. Here, as in other cases where the promises are threatened, God proves faithful to his Word. He rescues Abram from a threat that Abram himself created, and provides a means of preserving his promises.

Abram's descent and return from Egypt also prefigure the later experience of national Israel. Like Abram, the family of Jacob was forced to move to Egypt by famine. Just as Abram acquired wealth in Egypt, the Egyptians gave the children of Israel gold and precious stones when they left (Ex 12:35). God sent plagues on Egypt both times in order to liberate first Abram and later the Israelites. There are other parallels, but this is enough to demonstrate that Abram's time in Egypt foreshadows Israel's bondage there and their subsequent exodus.[11]

Trouble with Lot (13–14)

Abram had returned from Egypt a wealthy man. But there were more troubles ahead.

Study Questions

1. How may it be said that Abram is the beginning of the solution to the sin problem identified in Genesis 1–11?

2. Why is the fact that Abram's story begins with the genealogy of Terah so important?

3. Describe the three sources of security God called Abram to forsake, and comment on that which God called Abram to.

4. How are the three promises of God to Abram an example of the "re-creation" spoken of in chapter 4? (How are these promises related to issues broached at creation?)

5. In what way is Abram the paradigm for Christian faith?

6. How does Abram's journey to Egypt prefigure the later experience of the nation Israel?

7. What do the choices made by Abram and Lot reveal about the character of each?

Genesis 13 and 14 tell of another kind of threat, this time because of his nephew Lot. Since Abram and Sarai had no children, Lot was the presumed heir of Abram's estate. But these two chapters reveal serious flaws in Lot's character and explain how he came to drift out of the picture as a central figure.

Some people seem always to take the path of least resistance. It is not that Lot was evil; he simply seemed to be adrift without an anchor. He lived life on the edge, and like so many of us, he eventually lost his way. When faced with hard decisions, he acted selfishly and, in some cases, indecisively (as we shall see in Gn 19:10).

The threat to the promises of God begins, not with Lot, but with another inadequacy of this land God has promised. First there had been famine in the Promised Land, and Abram had been forced to flee to Egypt. Now the land was proving once again to be incapable of supporting both Abram and Lot. Lot had also acquired great possessions. As so often happens, human nature got in the way. Strife developed between Lot's herdsmen and Abram's. They decided it would be better to separate and live in different portions of the land.

Abram was the elder and would have been justified in choosing the best for himself, while sending Lot off to fend for himself. But Abram rose to the occasion and offered Lot a choice between life in the rugged hills of central Canaan or life in the rich plains of the valley. Abram's wisdom in this situation is the result of his faith.[12] He had relinquished his hold on all material things when he set out to follow God (Gn 12:1–3). This was merely an opportunity to renew that decision. And when Abram started his journey "even though he did not know where he was going" (Heb 11:8), he had learned not to base his decisions on visible appearances, unlike Lot, who "looked up and saw . . ." and "chose for himself" (13:10–11). Abram's obedience in following the call of God had prepared him well for this challenge.

Lot chose the best share of land without regard for his uncle's welfare, or the fact that his choice would put him in close proximity to Sodom, a city noted for its sinfulness. The reference to Lot's pitching his tents "near Sodom" implies that he was unconcerned about associating with the wrong crowd, a trait that would eventually get him into trouble (Gn 19). He also walked away from the blessings of God he had enjoyed because of his association with Abram (12:3).

Genesis 14 is the account of an ancient war in which Sodom and Gomorrah were captured. Lot unfortunately was taken captive and carried into exile. Abram mustered his personal forces and rescued Lot, delivering also the cities of Sodom and Gomorrah. How quickly we see the consequences of Lot's choices in the previous chapter. At the close of Genesis 13, Lot anticipates future prosperity in Sodom, while Abram was content to worship and live at Hebron (13:18). But Lot's selfish decision gains him a prize soon lost, and Abram's response places him in a position of honor among the kings of the plain (14:17–24).

In the midst of these problems, God reassured Abram of his promises. After Lot chose to live near Sodom, God told Abram to examine the land in which he lived, and with one brief statement confirmed both the promises of land and descendants: "Lift up your eyes from where you are and look north and south, east and west. All the land that you see I will give to you and your offspring forever" (13:14–15). Abram was learning that a life of faith was possible if he kept his eyes on the promises of God, even while the circumstances around him seemed abysmal. Though Abram did not realize it, this was just the beginning of his woes. But God rewarded his magnanimity toward Lot by reiterating the land-promise. God increases our understanding of his riches according to the needs we have at the time. As Abram's problems seemed to increase, he also began to grasp the extent of God's great land-promise: "Go, walk through the length and breadth of the land, for I am giving it to you" (13:17).

6 Tracking Abram and His Family

History and Geography of the Patriarchal Narratives

So Abraham left the land of the Chaldeans and lived in Haran until his father died. Then God brought him here to the land where you now live.

—Stephen, Acts 7:4 (NLT)

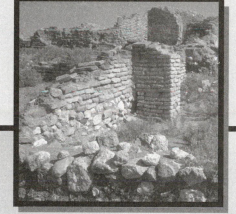

Objectives

After reading this chapter you should be able to

1. Locate and describe the significance of major cities and geographical regions associated with Abram.
2. List the major archaeological periods of ancient history, including the dates, major events, predominant cultures, and significant leaders of each era.
3. Describe the linkages that have been made between the archaeological periods of history and the biblical accounts of Abram and other biblical patriarchs.
4. Summarize the evidence supporting or refuting each of the linkages between the patriarchs and archaeological periods.
5. Identify possible comparisons and contrasts between the names the Bible uses for God and those the surrounding Canaanite religions use.
6. Compare the concept of covenant with predominant cultural and religious practices of the time.

Reading Genesis without a road map can be confusing. We have encountered many places in the Promised Land already, places where Abram lived: Hebron, Bethel and Ai, Beersheba, etc. Besides Canaan we also must remember the patriarchal homeland in Mesopotamia, specifically the city of Haran, which continued to play an important role in the narrative even after Abram settled in Canaan. This chapter will explore these places during the patriarchal period in order to give you the road map you need.

Where in the World Are These Places?

We have described the areas known generally as Mesopotamia and Canaan (or Syria–Palestine) in chapter I.3 above. Now we will look at a few specific places in which Abram and his family traveled.

Mesopotamia

The patriarchal homeland was apparently in an area called "Aram-Naharaim" in Genesis 24:10 (meaning "Aram of the two rivers"). This refers to a region in central Mesopotamia, or more specifically, to that district near the Habor and Euphrates rivers.

The two main cities mentioned in the narratives are Ur and Haran.

Ur of the Chaldeans (11:28, 31; 15:7)

Abram's roots are in a city known as "Ur of the Chaldeans." A later editor or scribe was aware of more than one city called "Ur" in the ancient Near East. Since the Chaldeans did not exist in the ancient world until nearly a thousand years after Abram's day,[1] the designation "of the Chaldeans" was without question added by a later scribe in order to distinguish *which* Ur was meant.

Unfortunately for modern scholars, this has not really resolved the problem. As many as three cities have been considered as candidates for Abram's hometown.[2] The most likely candidates are Urfa (now called Edessa) about twenty miles northwest of Haran and the more famous Ur in lower Mesopotamia. For the present, we will assume the Ur of lower Mesopotamia

is the one intended in the text.[3] If this is correct, Abram came from one of the most important cities of the ancient Near East. Ur was the administrative, economic, and legal capital during a Sumerian renaissance near the end of the third millennium B.C. After the Amorites took control of the region at the turn of the millennium, Ur continued to play a significant role as a cultural center.

Haran (11:31, 32; 12:4, 5; 27:43; 28:10; 29:4)

The city of Haran is located on the banks of the Balih River, a tributary of the Euphrates (see map on page 79). The city is often mentioned in Akkadian texts from the city of Mari as an important Amorite center during the first half of the second millennium B.C. This is precisely the period of the patriarchs, as we shall see.

You may have noticed that Abram had a brother by the same name (Gn 11:27). It may seem confusing, but the name is only similar in English and is completely coincidental. The Hebrew spelling of the city name is different and not related to Abram's brother (and Lot's father) named Haran.

The patriarchal narratives make frequent reference to the city of Haran. In addition, Haran is probably the unknown city of Nahor, Laban, and Rebekah in Genesis 24. All of these references seem to point to Haran as the patriarchal homeland, the area where Abram's extended family originated. How he and his smaller family came to live in Ur is a matter of speculation. But his sojourn from Ur to Haran to Canaan means he was going against the stream of Amorite migration at that time, which tended to flow from Syria–Palestine into Mesopotamia.

Canaan

In Genesis 12:4, we read about Abram's remarkable obedience. He set out following God, "even though he did not know where he was going" (Heb 11:8). This section will trace a few of the places Abram traveled in the Promised Land, and will prepare us for reading the rest of the patriarchal narratives.[4]

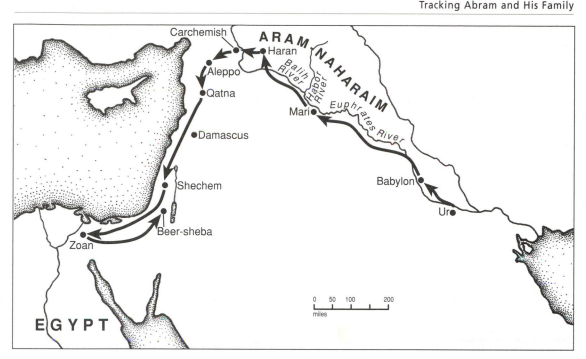

Map of Abram's Journeys

Remains from the ancient city of Haran.

Many artifacts have been discovered from Ur in lower Mesopotamia. The Standard of Ur depicts the leaders of Ur celebrating a victory.

Shechem (12:6)

When Abram left Haran, he probably followed the famous highway known as the Via Maris through Damascus, along the north shore of the Sea of Galilee to Megiddo. From there he may have continued south along the Via Maris for a short distance before detouring inland toward the central highlands, where he eventually came to Shechem (Gn 12:6).

Remains from the ancient city of Shechem.

Shechem has a long-standing tradition as an important city of the second millennium B.C. It has been identified as Tell Balata, near modern Nablus. Archaeologists have discovered inscriptions in Egypt referring to Shechem, revealing that it had become a major urban center during the time of Abram.[5] Here, in the heartland of Canaan, the Lord appeared to Abram to assure him of his future in the land (12:7).

Oak of Moreh (12:6)

Somewhere near Shechem was a famous oak tree noted probably as a place where one could seek divine oracles. The name "Moreh" means "teacher," and it may suggest this was a place where people regularly attempted to meet their deities.[6] It may anticipate God's appearance to Abram in 12:7.

Bethel and Ai (12:8)

These two cities were located approximately ten miles north of Jerusalem (see map II.6.2). They undoubtedly had different names during Abram's day. Bethel was known as Luz during the earlier Canaanite period (Gn 28:19), and archaeologists are not quite certain about Ai.[7]

Having come to Shechem, Bethel, and

Ai, Abram has arrived in the heartland of Canaan. All of these cities were to play important roles in Israel's future history, and their inclusion in the Abram narratives attests to the faithfulness of God in fulfilling his covenant promises to Abram.

The Negev (12:9)

Next Abram traveled into the Negev, a Hebrew term for the desert south of Judah (literally, "the dry land"). It also means simply "the South," and signifies broadly the desert between the hills of Judah and Kadesh-barnea. Kadesh and Bered are cities of the Negev that appear in the Abram narratives (16:14; and see 20:1). Since the Negev lacked enough rainfall for agriculture, we might expect any source of water to draw attention. So the wells at Beersheba (21:31–33) and Beer-Lahai-Roi (16:14; 24:62; 25:11) are featured as prominent Negev sites.

When Abram reached the Negev, he had arrived at the traditional southern border of Canaan. In Genesis 12, Abram began in Haran at the northwestern border of the Promised Land, and traversed all the way to the Negev in the south. "He not only sees what has been promised to him; he walks through it, and he lives and wor-

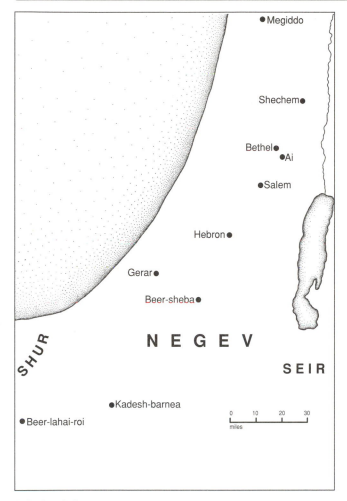

Palestine during the time of Abram

Oaks of Mamre (13:18; 14:13; 18:1; 23:17, 19; 25:9)

When Abram moved into a new area, he tended to settle not in the established city, but at an open-air sanctuary with trees. When he first entered the Promised Land, he settled at the Oak of Moreh near Shechem, where he built an altar to the Lord (12:6–7). At Hebron, he likewise settled at the Oaks of Mamre, where he also built an altar to the Lord (13:18). Archaeologists have speculated that this may be Ramat el-Khalil, approximately two miles north of Hebron.[9] The term "Mamre" is the name of an individual Amorite in Genesis 14:13 and 24. But elsewhere it refers to the woodlands near Hebron, presumably owned at one time by Mamre. It, like Shechem's Oak of Moreh, may have been noted as a place where one could commune with the gods. If so, it seems appropriate Abram would build an altar to Yahweh in both locations.

Gerar and Beersheba (20:1; 21:31–33; 26:1–6)

On more than one occasion, the patriarchs visited Gerar, near Gaza (20:1; 26:1–6; and see map II.6.2). At one point, Abram appears to have roamed between Kadesh and Shur in the extreme south, while either setting up camp or making periodic visits to Gerar (20:1).[10] This and other areas of the south became particularly important as sources of water during periods of drought and famine.

Wells in the Negev were especially important. The city of Beersheba ("well of seven") is the site of a treaty between Abram and Abimelech, king of Gerar (Gn 21). The Hebrew word for "swear," used in the treaty ceremony (v. 31), would create an interesting wordplay on the place-name. But more important, Abram now has access to the much needed water supply in the Negev.

Looking for Mr. Abram

It is important to use maps to follow where the patriarchs are in their journeys. Unfortunately, it is more difficult to locate Abram in time than it is to follow him geographically. You may have noticed as you read

ships in it. Symbolically he has taken possession of it."[8]

Hebron (13:18; 23:2)

One of the most important sites in the Abramic narrative is Hebron, which is situated approximately twenty miles south of Jerusalem in the heartland of Judah (see map II.6.2). "Hebron" is the Israelite name for the city, its former Canaanite name being Kiriath-Arba (Gn 23:2). Hebron and the nearby Oaks of Mamre (see below) are the locale for many of the most important events of the story of Abram. After he moved to Hebron in Genesis 13:18, Abram settled there until he "moved on" to dwell deeper in the Negev, eventually settling in Beer-sheba (20:1, and 21:31–33). Sarai and Abram were both buried in the cave of Machpelah near Mamre at Hebron, which Abram bought from Ephron the Hittite (23:17; 25:9).

Abram traveled through the Negev, which literally means the dry south land.

Early Bronze Age

Middle Bronze Age

Late Bronze Age

cuneiform

hieroglyphics

these first few chapters of the patriarchal narratives that the Bible gives no precise dates when Abram lived. Genesis contains no exact synchronisms with other events of world history that would make it possible to locate Abram in time. The rest of this chapter will attempt to place the patriarchs in historical perspective based on what we know about the world at that time.

Categories for Ancient History

Many events described in the Bible, especially in Israel's early history, cannot be dated precisely. In fact, history in general is without absolute chronology until the later Assyrian and Babylonian periods of the first millennium B.C. As a result, when archaeologists and historians deal with early periods of history, such as the period of the patriarchs of Genesis, they divide the millennia into periods according to the technology available at that time: stone, bronze, and iron.[14] After the various stone ages (Paleolithic, Mesolithic, Neolithic, and Chalcolithic), human beings relied first on bronze and then on iron for tools, weapons, and other utensils. Thus we refer in the broadest of terms to the Bronze Age and the Iron Age.

By these terms, archaeologists do not mean to imply that ancient peoples switched from stone to bronze suddenly, and later from bronze to iron. Nor do we mean that only bronze was used for tools and other utensils during the Bronze Age while only iron was used in the Iron Age. In a much more general way, we can say that around 3300 B.C., bronze technology spread throughout the ancient Near East, and that around 1200 B.C. people discovered the benefits of the use of iron.

The Bronze Age (3300–1200 B.C.) is customarily divided into three periods: the

Early Bronze Age (3300–2000 B.C.), the **Middle Bronze Age** (2000–1550 B.C.), and the **Late Bronze Age** (1550–1200 B.C.).

The Early Bronze Age (3300–2000 B.C.)

The Early Bronze Age (3300–2000 B.C.) witnessed the birth of human civilization. Prominent features were the invention of writing and the beginning of recorded history. In Mesopotamia, the Sumerians first used **cuneiform** extensively for writing, and in Egypt the use of **hieroglyphics** is well attested. In Mesopotamia a series of strong city-states began to grow, and by the end of the Early Bronze Age the first great Semitic empires gained control of all of southern Mesopotamia. In Egypt, the Early Bronze Age was the era of the great pyramids and the apex of Egyptian culture. So the period marked the rise and fall of humankind's first great empires: Old Kingdom Egypt and the Sumero-Akkadian empires in Mesopotamia. By the close of this period, all the main features of human civilization and culture had appeared that characterize human history in the ancient Near East for centuries to come.

In reference to Syria–Palestine, this period is also known as the Canaanite Age. The Early Bronze Age witnessed a sudden flourishing of population and urbanization in Syria–Palestine. There was rapid transition from life in unwalled villages to fortifications at a number of sites.

This period is often further subdivided by archaeologists into four smaller periods: Early Bronze I (3300–3000 B.C.), Early Bronze II (3000–2800 B.C.), Early Bronze III (2800–2400 B.C.), and Early Bronze IV (2400–2000 B.C.). EB IV is also known as MB I or Intermediate Bronze. It was a pastoralist culture in which there were no

The Historicity of Abraham

Some scholars doubt Abraham existed. Since the Bible lacks historical synchronisms for Abraham with extrabiblical events, literary critics near the end of the nineteenth century challenged the historicity of Abraham (see Part V, below). One leading scholar called Israel's great ancestor "a free creation of unconscious art."[11] Later scholars assumed either that Abraham was a distant ancestor from Israel's shadowy past, about whom we can know almost nothing, or that he was simply a literary creation of later Israelite authors. In either case, many scholars today consider whether he lived an irrelevant question.

However, the literary critical positions formulated at the turn of the twentieth century, and which continue to influence so many working on the Old Testament today, were done so in a scholarly context where the ancient Near East was hardly known. An enormous amount of valuable evidence has come to light in the twentieth century for scholars working on the ancient Near East: Hammurapi's famous law code, Hittite texts from Asia Minor, religious and literary texts from Ugarit, sociologically important texts from ancient Nuzi, letters from Mari, letters from Israelite Lachish, the Dead Sea Scrolls, and thousands of texts from Ebla and Emar in Syria, to name a few.

If Genesis were a newly discovered ancient manuscript, and if it were treated with the same investigative methods developed in the twentieth century for work on other ancient Near Eastern texts, it is doubtful that such skepticism would prevail.[12] When the literary approaches of the nineteenth century are properly balanced with other methods, including comparisons with ancient Near Eastern societies, cultures, and texts, the results are much different. The historicity of Abraham has not been proved by these methods. But the ancient Near Eastern context has illuminated the biblical account and made it possible to portray Abraham as a real historical person, whose life story has been reliably preserved in the Genesis narratives.

Genesis accurately portrays Abraham early in Hebrew history. Sociologically, his culture is seminomadic among Canaanite city-states rather than controlled by the later Israelite laws of Moses. Religiously, he is conscious of God's uniqueness, perhaps even his transcendence as the only God. Here also, Abraham is clearly prior to the cultic laws of Moses and later Yahwism. It is doubtful whether a later Israelite author could have conceived of and invented such an ancestor, without any of the features that would come to characterize Israelite life and faith.

The ancient Near Eastern comparative material confirms that the biblical portrait of Abraham is possible. Scholars have been able to verify that features of the Abraham narratives, such as his ancestral role, his career and life-style, his name and his faith, are all possible in an early-second-millennium context.[13] Though these observations cannot prove that he existed, the ancient Oriental parallels confirm the Bible's portrayal of Abraham as possible and perhaps even likely.

Nor is this an irrelevant question. The Bible links faith and history together inextricably. The concept of "blind faith" is in effect absent in Scripture, where faith is always informed by historical events. The Bible uses the exemplary faith and life of this great ancestor of Israel as one of the most important pillars of our Christian heritage (Rm 4).

major cities that followed the destruction of the mighty urban centers of Early Bronze.

The Middle Bronze Age (2000–1550 B.C.)

This period of ancient Near Eastern history is marked by the movement of ethnic groups and new empires replacing the older powers of the Early Bronze Age. In Mesopotamia, after a brief renaissance of Sumerian culture at the old city of Ur (Ur III dynasty, 2112–2004 B.C.), the country came under the control of a new Semitic element, the Amorites. Early in the Middle Bronze Age, the Amorites ruled Mesopotamia

Table 6.1
Archaeological Periods of Ancient Near Eastern History[1]

Approximate Dates (B.C.)	Archaeological Period	Israel	Ancient Near East
Before 14,000	Old Stone Age (Paleolithic)		Pre-cave culture
14,000–8000	Middle Stone Age (Mesolithic)		Cave culture
8000–4200	New Stone Age (Neolithic)		Neolithic Revolution: cultivation of crops and beginning of rain-based agriculture, domestication of animals, first permanent settlements
4200–3300	Copper-Stone Age (Chalcolithic)		Metal replaces stone in the production of tools and weapons
3300–2000	Early Bronze		Invention of writing Birth of human civilization Egyptian Old Kingdom Sumerian and Akkadian kingdoms in Mesopotamia Old Canaanite culture at Ebla
2000–1550	Middle Bronze	Israel's patriarchs	Arrival of Amorites and other ethnic groups in Mesopotamia Old Babylonian Empire Egyptian Middle Kingdom
1550–1200	Late Bronze	Egyptian bondage Birth of Moses The exodus Wilderness wanderings Israelite conquest of Canaan	International contacts and balance of power Powerful Egyptian New Kingdom exerts influence in Syria–Palestine Rise and fall of the New Hittite Empire Kassite control in Mesopotamia
1200–930	Iron Age I	Period of the judges United monarchy: Saul, David, Solomon	Invasion of Sea Peoples and disruption of major powers Rise of new ethnic groups, including Arameans and Israelites Rise of Assyria
930–539	Iron Age II	Divided Kingdom Fall of Israel in 722 Fall of Judah in 586	Weakened Egypt Assyria reaches greatest strength before fall in 612 Neo-Babylonian Empire: Nebuchadnezzar
539–332	Iron Age III	Return of Jewish exiles Ezra and Nehemiah Building of Second Temple and walls of Jerusalem	Cyrus captures Babylon in 539 Persian Empire

[1]Philip J. King, *American Archaeology in the Mideast: A History of the American Schools of Oriental Research* (Philadelphia: ASOR, 1983), 282, and Keith N. Schoville, *Biblical Archaeology in Focus* (Grand Rapids: Baker, 1978), 8–9.

from several strong city-states in an uncertain balance of power. Then one individual from the city of Babylon was able to consolidate his strength and establish a new empire throughout Mesopotamia: Hammurapi. He rose to power in 1792 and established the Amorite empire known as the Old Babylonian Empire, which endured until 1595 B.C. Hammurapi is most famous for his collection of laws, many of which bear striking resemblance to the laws of Moses in the Pentateuch.

In Egypt, after a period of darkness and confusion called the "First Intermediate Period" (2200–2000 B.C.), the country once again flourished during the Middle Kingdom Period (2000–1700 B.C.). The Middle Kingdom was a time of peace and stability, and one in which Egypt engaged in trade with Syria–Palestine, resulting in the acquisition of considerable wealth. But toward the end of Middle Bronze, Egypt also succumbed to the rise of Semites, which is characteristic of this period throughout the ancient Near East. Native Egyptian control of the country ended when the Hyksos, Semites probably from Syria–Palestine, took control of northern Egypt. The Hyksos ruled Egypt for approximately 150 years in what is called the "Second Intermediate Period" (1700–1540 B.C.). For the first time in Egypt's history, the country was conquered and dominated by foreigners.

In Syria–Palestine, too, there were Semitic peoples settling in. After an initial period of decline, the Amorite culture brought a resurgence of sedentary life and the development of urban centers. The Canaanites who had settled the coastal plains and valleys as early as the third millennium may have been of the same Amorite stock as those who were now leading a rebirth of urbanization. The towns and cities of the Abram narrative were likely flourishing as part of this development. And the covenant promises we read about in Genesis (numerous descendants and the land to support them) were uniquely suited for a transitory, migrant Amorite looking for land to settle.

The Middle Bronze is also further subdivided: Middle Bronze I (2000–1800 B.C.),

An example of Egyptian hieroglyphics.

Middle Bronze II (1800–1650 B.C.), and Middle Bronze III (1650–1550 B.C.).

The Late Bronze Age (1550–1200 B.C.)

Archaeologists and historians refer to the Late Bronze Age (1550–1200 B.C.) as a period of internationalism and communication in the ancient Near East. It was a time of international trade and balance of world powers, with Syria–Palestine caught in the middle.

The Late Bronze Age is marked by Egypt's powerful New Kingdom, which exerted considerable influence on the coastal areas of Syria–Palestine. The Egyptians successfully ended their subjugation to the Hyksos and entered the period of their greatest political strength (1550–1100 B.C.). The powerful rulers of New Kingdom Egypt sought to govern the coastal areas of Syria–Palestine in order to control commercial trade with the Aegean and the rest of western Asia. Their antagonists were the powerful Hittites, who ruled from central Asia Minor. Hittite kings fought the pharaohs of Egypt for control of Syria–Palestine, eventually coming to a draw in the mid-thirteenth century. Toward the end of the Late Bronze Age, the Hittites and Egyptians agreed to a peace treaty, ending the hostilities between the two nations. For most of the period, however, the Egyptians successfully dominated trade and acquired tremendous wealth and prosperity.

While Egypt was dominant throughout this period, Mesopotamia experienced a time of political weakness. After the fall of Hammurapi's Old Babylonian Empire, southern Mesopotamia was controlled by foreigners known as Kassites. The long rule of the Kassite dynasty (over three hundred years) brought peace and stability to Babylonia, though not military superiority. The Kassites preferred peace treaties and other nonmilitary means of diplomacy to defend their borders. They adopted many elements of traditional Babylonian culture and raised southern Mesopotamia to a new level of international prestige during this period. The Babylonian dialect of Akkadian became the *lingua franca* (or international language) of the day.

The Iron Age (1200–332 B.C.)

Around 1200 B.C., cataclysmic changes occurred in the ancient Near East. The major powers (notably Egypt and the Hittites) suddenly declined and the political map changed dramatically. Most scholars assume the changes started with the fall of Troy (around 1250 B.C.) and the subsequent fall of the Mycenaean cities on the mainland of Greece. Survivors must have fled by sea along the coasts of the Mediterranean, disrupting all the major powers of the ancient world. These newcomers are known collectively as "Sea Peoples." One group of these Sea Peoples, known from Egyptian sources as "Peleset," settled on the southwest coastal plains of Syria–Palestine. They are known in the Old Testament as "Philistines," a term that also gave rise to the term "Palestine."

One result of the arrival of the Sea Peoples was the spread of new metalworking technology, particularly the use of iron for making weapons. Gradually, iron technology replaced bronze altogether, and archaeologists and historians refer to the period after 1200 B.C. as the Iron Age (1200–332 B.C.). This period is marked by the rise of the first genuinely world empires, all from a Mesopotamian base: Assyria, Babylonia, and Persia. The Iron Age is commonly subdivided into three periods: Iron Age I (1200–930 B.C.), Iron Age II (930–539 B.C.), and Iron Age III (539–332 B.C.; see table II.6.1). This was the period of Israel's monarchy, exile, and restoration. Biblical history from the close of the Pentateuch to the end of the Old Testament fits within the Iron Age.

Possible Dates for the Patriarchs

After this brief overview of the archaeological periods of history, we are now ready to attempt a more specific dating for Israel's patriarchs. Precision will be impossible—the most we can do is review the common proposals for when Abram, Isaac, and Jacob lived. Most suggestions range from the Early Bronze Age to the Late Bronze Age.[15]

A Date in Early Bronze III (2800–2400 B.C.)

The exciting discovery of the ancient Syrian city of Ebla along with thousands of cuneiform tablets generated a lot of attention from Old Testament scholars. Among some of the more spectacular claims for these recovered texts was the alleged historical synchronisms with Genesis 14, the account of Abram's rescue of Lot. The Ebla texts, it was claimed initially, listed the five "cities of the plain" in the same order in which they occur in Genesis 14.[16] But it is now clear that the reading of these city names (and one of the kings mentioned in the biblical text, Birsha) was erroneous. Though such an early date for the patriarchs is possible, the evidence currently in favor of this option is questionable.

A Date in Middle Bronze I (2000–1800 B.C.)

One of the most popular theories a few decades ago was the idea that Abram was an itinerant merchant, a donkey-caravaneer, who traveled back and forth between Ur and Haran, and later between Damascus and Egypt. As a traveling merchant, Abram would have used the trade routes extending throughout Mesopotamia, Syria–Palestine, and the Negev into Egypt. William F. Albright and Nelson Glueck believed the rise of caravan trade under the Twelfth Dynasty pharaohs could be synchronized with certain settlements in Syria–Palestine.[17] The activities of Abram seemed to fit well into this context.

But it was subsequently determined that Albright's dates for the Palestine sites were incorrect and that these settlements were active before the Twelfth Dynasty. For a variety of reasons, the Albright–Glueck theory has now been abandoned.[18]

A Date in Middle Bronze II (1800–1650 B.C.)

The most likely date for Israel's patriarchs is Middle Bronze II, based on the so-called Amorite Hypothesis.[19] It is possible to associate the pastoralist life-style of the patriarchs with the resurgence of city life in MB I and the flowering of Amorite culture in MB II.

At the close of the Early Bronze Age, urban life was disrupted throughout Syria–Palestine. All the major cities were destroyed and the culture of EB IV (or the Intermediate Bronze Age) witnessed the gradual sedentarization of Amorite newcomers. But during MB I, a second wave of Amorites appears to have contributed to a renewal of city life, and MB II experienced a flowering of Amorite culture and a return to the great city-states of ancient Syria–Palestine. This portrait of Amorite migration and sedentarization at the end of MB I and during MB II presents an attractive context in which to view the patriarchal life-style described in Genesis. A leading proponent of this approach has also argued for ethnic continuity between the Amorites and the later Arameans, which would explain the early Israelite description of the patriarch as a "wandering Aramean" (Dt 26:5).[20]

A Date in the Late Bronze Age (1550–1200 B.C.)

A few scholars have argued that Abram and Jacob lived in the fourteenth century B.C.[21] Evidence for such a date comes from the social and legal customs described in fifteenth- and fourteenth-century texts from Ugarit, and especially Nuzi. These Late Bronze Age texts contain cultural parallels with patriarchal practices depicted in Genesis. However, such a late date cannot be reconciled with the biblical chronology, and many of the proposed parallels have now been called into question.[22]

A Late Bronze Age date for the patriarchs seems impossible to defend, though some of the parallels with ancient Near Eastern materials is still valid. Just because a social or legal parallel is attested in texts only from a later period does not mean that custom was not part of the culture from an earlier period. The Amorite population at Ugarit would obviously have a shared cultural heritage with Israel's ancestors. And the Hurrian population of Nuzi had contacts with Amorites early in Nuzi's history. Certain of the parallels with Genesis are valid, though they do not require a Late Bronze Age date for the patriarchs.

A Date in the Iron Age (1200–330 B.C.)

Finally, a number of authors today are arguing for an Iron Age date for the patriarchal narratives. This is not really a date for the *events* recorded in the patriarchal narratives, but for the *narratives* themselves. In other words, these scholars would maintain that the patriarchs were not historical figures, but rather the narratives about them merely reflect the Iron Age setting in which they were written. Later Israelites created these narratives in order to explain their origins. Abram and Joseph become "typological prefigurations" of the later Israelites, and may or may not have been actual historical individuals. Isaac and Jacob are eponyms, or fictitious persons from whom the names of the later groups were supposed to be derived.[23] Obviously, this position does an injustice to both the evidence of the biblical texts and the parallels from ancient Near Eastern texts.

Religion of the Patriarchs

It should be obvious by now that precise dates for Israel's patriarchs are impossible to determine. In this presentation of the various possibilities, I have assumed Abram fits most naturally in the Middle Bronze Age.[24]

One other issue that is related to the question of when Abram lived is the nature of Abram's religion. A look at the religious beliefs and practices in the patriarchal narratives of Genesis reveals several interesting features. First, you may have noticed that the Abram narrative uses a variety of names for God, almost all beginning with "El": El-Shaddai (17:1), El-Elyon (14:18), El-Roi (16:13), El-Olam (21:33), etc. In general, most of these El-type names are used in dialogues and speeches of the patriarchal accounts in Genesis, but not in the narrative framework.[25] This probably indicates that the narrator of Genesis equated the God of the patriarchs with the Mosaic Yahweh (read Ex 6:2–3). Yet the ancient sources used to compile the patriarchal narratives did not refer to Yahweh, only to El-Shaddai, or Elohim, or other El-type names. This seems to demonstrate that the narrator has accurately and faithfully preserved the information in the original sources. (We shall return to this point in Part V, below.)

Second, the idea of "covenant" with its attendant promises is at the heart of Abrahamic faith. Though there seems to be much about patriarchal religion that is found in other ancient Near Eastern cultures, the use of the covenant to explain God's relationship with Abram is unique.[26]

Study Questions

1. Describe the ancient cities of Ur and Haran, indicating their position in the ancient world and their importance in the patriarchal narratives.

2. How does our knowledge of world conditions in the Middle Bronze Age contribute to our understanding of the story of Abram?

3. Where do historians believe the "Sea Peoples" originated? Why is their influence so important? How do their descendants figure in the biblical narrative?

4. Describe the various positions held by scholars on possible dates for the life of Abraham, noting especially the factors that lead many scholars to place him in Middle Bronze II.

5. Compare and contrast the religion of the patriarchs with the religion of the Canaanites. How do these factors contribute to discussions on the dating of events in the patriarchal narratives?

6. Explain how ancient Near Eastern comparative material aids in evaluating the historicity of Abraham.

Third, the relationship between Abram's faith and the religion of the Canaanites is complex. On the one hand, there is no mention of Baal or the polytheistic fertility cult in the patriarchal narratives. This is striking confirmation that these narratives are genuine Middle Bronze accounts, since Baal rose to prominence in the second half of the second millennium. Sometime during the Late Bronze Age, Baal be-

Key Terms

Early Bronze Age

Middle Bronze Age

Late Bronze Age

cuneiform

hieroglyphics

came the chief deity in the pantheon of Syria–Palestine as illustrated in the texts from Ugarit. El, the benevolent creator god of the Canaanites, became less significant in their mythology. The rest of the Old Testament bears eloquent testimony to the struggles Israel had with Baalite cults. And the utter lack of reference to Baal in the patriarchal accounts betrays their Middle Bronze origins (at least).

On the other hand, there is much in the faith of Abram that appears to have been appropriated from Canaanite religion. The patriarchs were comfortable with the Canaanite El-type names for God and with sacrificing on temporary, makeshift altars without priest or prophet. And Abram could commune freely and openly with Canaanite worshipers who were committed to El as the loving father God, creator of the universe (Gn 14:18–20).

These features are quite different from the religion of the later Israelites, and they support an early second-millennium date for the patriarchal events and for the traditions used in compiling Genesis.

7 "Then God Gave Him the Covenant" (Acts 7:8)

Genesis 15:1–17:27

Abraham never wavered in believing God's promise. In fact, his faith grew stronger, and in this he brought glory to God.

—Paul, Rom 4:20 (NLT)

Supplemental Reading: Romans 4:1–25

Outline

- **Melchizedek and the King of Sodom (14:17–24)**
- **Defining Abram's Special Relationship with God (15)**
  "I Am Your Shield" (15:1–6)
  "I Am the Lord" (15:7–21)
- **Hagar and Ishmael (16)**
- **Signs of God's Covenant (17)**

Objectives

After reading this chapter you should be able to

1. Identify key events and related concepts of the developing relationship between God and Abram.
2. Contrast Melchizedek with the king of Sodom, including their respective interactions with Abram.
3. Define the concept of covenant in the ancient world, the specific promises God made in his covenant with Abram, and the theological significance of this covenant.
4. Summarize Abram's attempts to apprehend God's promises by adopting Eliezer of Damascus and later taking Hagar as a substitute wife, and contrast these with God's plan for fulfilling those promises.
5. Describe the ratification of God's covenant with Abram, and the additional promises God makes and requirements made of Abram.
6. Summarize the theological significance of the change of Abram's and Sarai's names.
7. State the theological import of the rite of circumcision.

All of us understand what it is like to feel insecure. Even if we have friends and family who love us and give us every reason to feel secure, occasionally we all get the feeling that life is about to cave in on top of us. We may know in our heads that we are safe and protected, but our feelings tell us otherwise. We all have to balance what we know to be true with what we feel, to balance faith and feelings.

Imagine the insecurity and uncertainty Abram must have felt. He abandoned everything in order to follow God to an unknown land, with only a set of intangible promises to sustain him. We might expect Abram to require more information from God; to bargain with him as a prerequisite to obedience. But instead, Genesis portrays a picture in which Abram's relationship with God intensifies. As they grow closer together, God gives Abram more and more assurances that his Word is true and that all will be well for the patriarch. Instead of bargaining with God, Abram learns gradually to trust him more and more.

Melchizedek and the King of Sodom (14:17–24)

After Abram's dramatic rescue of Lot and the cities near the Dead Sea (Gn 14), there were obviously many people who were grateful. Upon his return, two kings greeted him: Melchizedek, king and priest of Salem (probably Jerusalem), and the unnamed king of Sodom (presumably the Bela of 14:2). Their response to Abram is a study in contrast. One is gracious and appreciative; the other, suspicious and surly. Their meeting with Abram posed yet another threat to fulfillment of the promises, and presented Abram with a greater temptation than he had so far encountered.

Melchizedek's name means "my king is righteous,"[1] and he is one of the most mysterious figures of the Bible. In a book like Genesis, which is so concerned with genealogies, Melchizedek suddenly appears on the scene with no such reference. As the author of the New Testament Book of Hebrews states, "Without father or mother, without genealogy, without beginning of days or end of life, like the Son of God he remains a priest forever" (7:3). Like Jesus, Melchizedek combined the offices of priest and king in the city of Jerusalem (Ps 110:4). The author of Hebrews sets out to explain why the priesthood of Jesus rightly replaces the ancient levitical priesthood of the Old Testament, since Jesus was of the tribe of Judah and not the priestly tribe of Levi. The levitical priesthood had been preceded by that of Melchizedek, a type or forerunner of the priesthood of Jesus. Levitical priesthood had an intrinsic obsolescence, which was now replaced by the superior priesthood of Christ.[2] Melchizedek is not necessarily a critical part of the story of redemption, but he is a divine intimation of the Son of God.

Melchizedek greets Abram with a banquet fit for a king[3] and blesses him. His blessing is the first time the promises of Genesis 12:1–3 have found explicit fulfillment in the text, since here another human blesses Abram. According to God's design, this means Melchizedek will receive the blessings of God (12:3). In contrast, the king of Sodom seems rude. He offers Abram nothing and speaks to him curtly: "Give me the people and keep the goods for yourself" (14:21). As returning victor of the war, Abram was entitled to keep everything: people, animals, and captured property. Presumably, the king of Sodom feared he would do just that. So he proposed a compromise, without the usual common amenities that were associated with friendlier ancient Near Eastern conversations.

This was a greater threat to Abram than the enemy kings had been. To have accepted the riches of the king of Sodom would have been a compromise of his calling. "More hinged on this than on the most resounding victory or the fate of any kingdom."[4] After giving one-tenth of the spoils to Melchizedek, Abram offers all the rest to the king of Sodom, except for a share to those who assisted him in the battle. He refused to accept anything from the king of Sodom, and his motivation is telling: "I have raised my hand to the LORD, God Most High, Creator of heaven and earth, and have taken an oath that I will accept nothing belonging to you" (14:22–23).

Mount Sodom.

Melchizedek had blessed God, and we may presume was blessed by God. If the king of Sodom's abrupt treatment of Abram may be taken as a curse, then we can only expect he will be repaid in kind (12:3). This will not be the last we will hear of the city of Sodom.

It would have been easy for Abram to rationalize and justify accepting Sodom's wealth. But he had learned his lesson from his earlier mistake in Egypt. To accept wealth from pagan rulers can lead to compromises of faith (Gn 12:16). Abram was learning to depend totally on the provisions of the Creator of heaven and earth for his future.

Defining Abram's Special Relationship with God (15)

Without a doubt, you have now come to one of the most important chapters of the Bible. The rest of the Bible turns on the two

---

Table 7.1
Parallels of Genesis 15

	Verses 1–6	Verses 7–21
1) God reveals himself to Abram	"Do not be afraid, Abram. I am your shield your very great reward."—verse 1	"I am the Lord, who brought you out of Ur of the Chaldeans to give you this land to take possession of it."—verse 7
2) Abram asks clarifying question regarding a promise:	"O Sovereign Lord, what can you give me since I remain childless . . . ?"—verse 2	"O Sovereign Lord, how can I know that I will gain possession of it?"—verse 8
3) God gives further assurances	Children as numerous as the stars of heaven.—verses 4–5	A smoking firepot with a blazing torch—verses 9–21

God's **WORD**

God's **COVENANT**

main ideas of Genesis 15: faith and covenant. The apostle Paul saw Abram's justifying *faith* (Gn 15:6) as the centerpiece in his definition of Christianity (read Rm 4 and Gal 3:6). The *covenant* described here and in Genesis 17 became the foundation of the Sinai covenant between Moses and the nation of Israel (Ex 19–24). These two, *faith* and *covenant,* are the truths that bind together Old and New Testaments, describing how God loves and redeems first Israel and then the Christians of the early church.

Genesis 15 has two sections that are parallel to each other: verses 1–6 and verses 7–21. Both relate dialogue between God and Abram. These conversations reaffirm two of the promises of God to Abram in Genesis 12:1–3: descendants and land. In both, God initiates the dialogue with a statement meant to reassure and comfort Abram. Then, Abram asks a question of clarification. Finally, God responds with further details about the fulfillment of the promises.

Abram's questions are not questions of doubt or confusion. Rather, he seeks further confidence that God will bring his promises to fruition. Any wandering Semite of the ancient world would have sought at least as much. We should see here an honest attempt by God's servant to wrap his mind around the Word of God in a better effort to understand more completely and to follow more faithfully God's will.

"I Am Your Shield" (15:1–6)

Melchizedek's blessing in the previous chapter had stated succinctly "Blessed be God Most High, who delivered your enemies into your hand" (14:20). Now, God speaks to Abram to confirm that the military victory of Genesis 14 was due to his special relationship with God. The verb "delivered" in Genesis 14:20 is a Hebrew wordplay, since it sounds very similar to the word "shield" used in Genesis 15:1.[5] In other words, God used the historical circumstances of Genesis 14 as an opportunity to take Abram further in their relationship (note the "after this" of Gn 15:1). Just as God had protected and delivered Abram in the war with the enemy kings, so he will be his shield in the future. And because Abram had declined to accept the spoils of warfare, God will see that he will receive "great reward" (15:1).

The comforting assurances that God would protect and reward Abram were given as reasons for Abram not to be afraid. Apparently God was aware of Abram's needs. Abram was in fact afraid, and with good reason. He had just defeated enemy nations, and his closest city-state (Sodom) had not seemed unappreciative of Abram's rescue efforts. God was speaking to Abram's emotional needs with rational and timely assurances. We should remember to allow God's truth to penetrate our minds when our emotions threaten to carry us away.

Perhaps it would have sounded more pious to simply thank God for this recent revelation, with its assurances of safety and compensation. But Abram was a man on a mission. He could not forget, nor did he want to forget, the original promise that he would have a son. At his age, and with a barren wife, it seemed impossible.[6] His response in verses 2–3 honestly sought more from God. This was the first time Abram had actually addressed God in response, which reveals the depth of his need. God had delivered Abram's enemies into his hand, but now would he also deliver a son into Abram's household?[7]

Abram mentioned a certain Eliezer of Damascus in verse 2. There has been much debate among scholars about Abram's relationship with this individual and its possible parallel with ancient Hurrian practices.[8] Though scholars are not agreed, it appears that some sort of adoption was in view. A childless man could adopt an individual who would be expected to care for him in his old age. The adopted child would give him a proper burial, and in exchange could expect to inherit the estate upon the adopter's death. It was a means of social security for the elder individual and a potentially profitable business deal for the adopted son. We know nothing else about this Eliezer, but apparently Abram felt this was his only option. The fact that Eliezer's name is recorded drives the point home vividly. Abram is now advanced in years and the promises of God have not been fulfilled. God has delayed in fulfilling his promises. The lack of a son creates an acute need in Abram's life.

God's reassuring response was both astounding and graphic (Gn 15:4–5). He clarified his earlier promise by stating that it would not be necessary for Abram to adopt a son. He would have a biological son, "a son coming from your own body." But then God went far beyond Abram's concern for a single son. He invited Abram to step outside and gaze at the stars. Not only would Abram father a son, but his descendants would be as countless as the stars of heaven. This confirmed the promise of Genesis 12:2 to make Abram a "great nation." The apostle Paul explains that the promise was fulfilled in the multitude of believers in Christ (Rm 9:7–8; Gal 3:6–9). If you are a believer, you are a child of Abraham!

At his age, to accept such a word from God certainly required an enormous faith. But Abram was up to the challenge. The classic statement of Abram's faith in Genesis 15:6 reveals how Abram embraced God's Word as true. The verse has two parts.

15:6a—Abram believed the LORD,

15:6b—and he credited it to him as righteousness

Hebrew has no abstract noun for "faith," but the verb in 6a means "believe in," "rely on," or "give credence to." The particular form used here can mean repeated or continuous action, implying that faith was Abram's usual response to God's words. The object of Abram's faith is the Lord, Yahweh, which is Israel's sacred covenant name for God.

This was more than a mere intellectual acknowledgment that God's Word was true. It *was* that, but it was much more. Abram was also accepting the plan of God, the design and pattern of God for his life. This was an abandonment into God's will for Abram's life and a forsaking of his own ambitions and plans.

The second half of the verse is God's response to Abram's faith. The verb "credited" (now with God as subject) can also be understood as "counted" or "reckoned" (NRSV), and can have a legal accrediting sense: "He accounted it to him for righteousness" (NKJV). Some translate it with a declarative sense: "The Lord declared him righteous because of his faith" (NLT). The word "righteousness" is not some abstract

ideal that is unattainable for human beings. Rather, as illustrated in the life of Abram, righteousness is a right relationship with God. God alone defines what is right and what is wrong. And he alone knows what is right for us. To live for him in faith, accepting his will for us, is to live a life of righteousness. Such a life may be characterized as God-pleasing, or Godlike. Righteousness is not an absolute standard, but a right personal relationship with him who alone is righteous.[9]

In Genesis 15:6, Abram is designated as one well pleasing in God's sight. Israel's patriarch has discovered what it means to be fully human, to be acceptable and righteous before God. In a sense, this is a return to the Garden of Eden. Not that humans can ever go back to the pre-Adamic perfection of the Garden, but God can be pleased with us and accept us as his own. This faith is to trust God's future for us, even while we live in the deathly present. The faith that results in righteousness means "the end of every '-ism' (not only moralism, dogmatism, pietism, but also existentialism, positivism, Marxism, capitalism, humanism), for every -ism is a way of keeping control of the present. This new righteousness means to relinquish control of the present for the sake of a Genesis."[10] Abram has become a "new creation; the old has gone, the new has come" (2 Cor 5:17).

The influence of Genesis 15:6 on the New Testament cannot be overestimated. As we have said, the verse's definition of faith was especially important to Paul's arguments in Romans 4 and Galatians 2–4. Also, James uses the verse to demonstrate that true saving faith always expresses itself in actions (Jas 2:20–24).[11]

"I Am the Lord" (15:7–21)

As we have said, Genesis 15 has two parallel sections. The first half (vv. 1–6) instructs us about saving faith. The second half (vv. 7–21) introduces the concept of "covenant," a key theological idea in the rest of the Bible. As the first unit confirms the seed-promise, verses 7–21 confirm the land-promise.

This unit opens in much the same way as the first. God reveals himself to Abram with comforting words: "I am the LORD,

Animal Sacrifice in Ancient Near Eastern Treaty Ceremonies

The ancient Near East has provided several examples of treaty ceremonies from the early second millennium B.C. using slaughtered animals. These examples are not perfect parallels to the use of animals in Genesis 15, but they add graphic background to this odd ceremony and support the early origins of the patriarchal account.[12]

1. Excerpt from a text from the city of Alalakh in northern Syria, dated to the eighteenth century B.C.

Abba-AN swore an oath of the gods to Yarimlim and he cut the neck of one lamb (saying): (May I be cursed) if I take what I have given to you.

—*RANE* #22, pages 96-97

2. Another eighteenth-century text, this time from the city of Mari on the Euphrates, describes a treaty ceremony involving slain animals.

I went to Ashlakka and they brought to me a young dog and a she-goat in order to conclude a covenant (lit. "kill a donkey foal") between the Haneans and the land of Idamaras. But, in deference to my lord, I did not permit the use of the young dog and the she-goat, but instead had a donkey foal, the young of a female donkey, killed, and thus established a reconciliation between the Haneans and the land of Idamaras.

—Moshe Held, "Philological Notes on the Mari Covenant Rituals," *BASOR* 200 (1970): 33; and see *ANET* 482

who brought you out of Ur of the Chaldeans to give you this land to take possession of it" (v. 7). This is deliberately stated in language that later Israelites would recognize instantly. The terminology is a familiar expression, used often to introduce or summarize the significance of the Sinai covenant between Yahweh and the Israelites: "I am the LORD your God, who brought you out of Egypt to give you the land of Canaan . . ." (Lv 25:38; and see also Ex 20:2 = Dt 5:6). "Ur of the Chaldeans" is simply substituted for "Egypt." Thus, the covenant between Abram and God foreshadows Yahweh's great salvation for Israel in the exodus from Egypt and the subsequent covenant at Sinai.

God refers to "Ur of the Chaldeans" as a means of grounding his present covenant with Abram in the past act of salvation from Mesopotamia (Gn 11:28, 31). And this foreshadows the Sinai covenant, which is grounded in the past act of divine salvation from Egypt (Ex 20:2).[13] The formula shows the relationship between the two covenants, the Abrahamic and the Mosaic. What God did through Moses at Sinai was part of a larger design, a continuation of his work through the patriarchs. And all of this is God's solution to the sin problem that had plagued creation since the loss of the Garden of Eden.

As in the first unit of Genesis 15, God's words of comfort prompted a question from Abram. In 15:2–3 Abram asked about the promise of seed, and in 15:8 he asked how he can have assurance that he will possess the land (review table II.7.1). His questions are no sign of doubt or unbelief, especially since the first part of the chapter stressed the exemplary nature of Abram's faith. Rather, he acknowledges his feelings of insecurity, and simply seeks confirmation. Such emotions are only natural, especially in a genuinely vulnerable situation like Abram's. We should take Abram's lead and not hesitate to express ourselves to God.

God's response would hardly seem comforting to us: "Bring me a heifer, a goat and a ram, each three years old, along with a dove and a young pigeon" (v. 9). Abram apparently understood the divine instructions to be initiating some sort of sacrificial ritual. He slaughtered and cut the animals down the middle, laying the halves side by side. However, the birds he did not divide in half. That night, Abram fell into a deep sleep. God then revealed to him pertinent details of the future in order to assure Abram that his Word was true. God related to Abram a brief synopsis of the history of Israel. The descendants of Abram would be enslaved by a foreign nation for four hundred years. But God would miraculously deliver the children of Abram, and after four generations would bring them back to Canaan to possess the land as their inheritance (vv. 13–16).

The text then describes an unusual ceremony in which a smoking firepot with a flaming torch passes between the pieces of the animals (v. 17). What is the meaning of this odd event? Sometimes the Bible describes customs and practices that are unique to that ancient culture. Such practices seem strange, and we may not always understand why biblical characters do some of the things described. Occasionally these customs are illuminated by archaeological discoveries from other cultures closely related to ancient Israel's. But at other times, we simply cannot be assured of the precise significance of certain cultural practices. Fortunately, we can almost always tell from the biblical context what the custom signifies even if we cannot know all the details. Abram clearly understood what he was to do with the animals God requested.

This event is described as a "covenant" (Hebrew *běrît*) in the next verse. This term in the Bible describes binding relationships between human partners, or between God and humans. The concept has a legal background and describes an agreement between two parties where no such agreement existed by nature. Such agreements had binding obligations on both parties. This is a rich theological concept in the Bible, since God commits himself to covenant relationships with humans in which he accepts obligations. To under-

stand fully just how important this concept is in the Bible, you should realize that this is the same notion behind the English word "testament" in our labels "Old Testament" and "New Testament." The message of the New Testament is really the story of Jesus' new covenant, which has its historical and theological roots firmly planted in Israel's old covenant with God.

Though some would deny that Genesis 15 describes a genuine covenant,[14] this binding agreement between Abram and God is the first in a series of such covenants in the Bible. This is the foundation on which the covenant between God and the Israelites is based (Ex 2:24–25). This is also the foundation of the Davidic covenant, in which God promised David an eternal dynasty to rule from Jerusalem (2 Sam 7), and the new covenant, in which God sent a Son of David to establish his eternal kingdom (read Lk 1:31–33).

Though we can be confident of this general understanding of the covenant between God and Abram, the precise significance of the details escapes us. An intriguing parallel in Jeremiah 34:18 may indicate that both parties of the agreement

Polygamy in the Bible

Polygamy, or the practice of having more than one spouse at the same time, was not God's ideal plan for marriage ("polygyny" refers more specifically to multiple wives). The Bible clearly sanctions marriage as the union of one man and one woman (Gn 2:18, 24). In the New Testament, Jesus confirmed monogamy as the legitimate form of marriage (Mt 19:4–6).

Yet the Bible nowhere specifically condemns polygamy. Rather, it often narrates the unfortunate effects of the practice. The first polygamist, Lamech, was a ruthless man (Gn 4:19–24). Jacob had

two wives and two concubines. It was through this multiple marriage that God blessed the patriarchal family and began to fulfill his promises to multiply the descendants of Abraham. But the family was also rife with favoritism, deception, jealousy, and betrayal (Gn 25:28; 27:1–45; 35:22; 38:18–28; etc.). Some of the future kings of Israel would also have more than one wife, but always with dreadful consequences: David (2 Sm 3:2–5; 13:1–29; 15:1–18:33) and especially Solomon (1 Kgs 11:1–4).

Polygamy was not the norm among Israel's neighbors in

the ancient Near East, but did exist as it does in many cultures where women are not valued highly.[15] It was not widespread among the ancient Israelites, where it was the exception rather than the rule. Wherever it was practiced among Israelites, it may be seen as an accommodation to the surrounding cultures.

Abram and Hagar are unique because of the cultural parallels, and their relationship may not strictly be considered polygamy. Yet it, too, had negative consequences (Gn 16:4–16).

normally passed between the pieces of animals and thereby imposed a curse on themselves: "And those who transgressed my covenant and did not keep the terms of the covenant that they made before me, I will make like the calf when they cut it in two and passed between its parts." As each party of the agreement went between the pieces of slain animals, they were symbolically decreeing a self-imprecation or curse on themselves. By implication, they were swearing, "May I become like these slain animals if I break my part of the agreement." In Genesis 15, it was the holy, creator God who bound himself to his Word, who swore to perform his promises to Abram under penalty of death. God's role in the covenant-making is heightened by the fact that it was completely unilateral; Abram was entirely passive, having fallen into a trance (15:12).

Though this traditional way of understanding the covenant ceremony is possible, it is increasingly being recognized that the covenant of Genesis 15 may not involve self-imprecation. The slaying of the animals may simply ratify the sacred covenant without constituting a symbolic curse.[16] The text appears to omit any such curse deliberately so as to adapt the covenant idea without necessarily requiring the concept of divine self-imprecation. God has taken the most somber and serious type of oath to commit himself to Abram. Regardless of the details of this ceremony, God has given himself without reservation to Abram's future. Abram can rest assured in the promises of God. He will bring them to pass.

So Genesis 15 asks the question: Can Abram, in fact, *trust* God? But it also asks if God, in fact, can *be trusted*. "It is faith which permits [Abram] to trust and God to be trusted. It is unsure faith that wonders about the delay. The issues are set here. The remainder of the Abrahamic narrative explores the answers."[17]

herit Abram's estate. But he would never do so now that he had withdrawn from the family and moved to Sodom. Then Abram made arrangements to adopt Eliezer of Damascus. But God had insisted that Abram's own seed, a son from his own body, would carry forward the divine promises. Then the first verse of Genesis 16 reminds us of the stark reality: "Sarai . . . had borne him no children."

As you read this chapter, you may be astonished at the solution Sarai recommended. She took her Egyptian maid, Hagar, and gave her to Abram as a substitute wife. According to long-established custom in the ancient Near East, a child born to Hagar would then count as Sarai's.[18] This was perfectly acceptable in that culture. And after ten long years of barrenness (Abram is now eighty-five, and Sarai seventy-five), this surely seemed like God's purpose.

But the narrative of Genesis 16 is clear that this was a matter of God's people making other arrangements without his direction, trying to "help God out" of a predicament. The chapter contains deliberate echoes of Genesis 3 and the sin of Adam and Eve—Abram "obeying his wife," and Sarai "taking and giving to her husband."[19] This is an instant replay of the original sin and a definite delay in God's redemptive plan. Yet God is able to use even the failures of his people. God often calls on us to wait for his timing. We only complicate things when we take over for God and launch out where he never intended for us to go.

At the end of Genesis 16, Abram has had a son, Ishmael, through Hagar. The question now becomes: "Is Ishmael the son of the promise?" God certainly has specific plans for this descendant of Abram (16:10–12). Perhaps Abram and Sarai were right to take matters into their own hands. The question is answered quickly in Genesis 17, where God brings his promises to Abram into sharper focus.

Hagar and Ishmael (16)

Abram and Sarai decided to take matters into their own hands. First, Abram's nephew, Lot, seemed the logical one to in-

Signs of God's Covenant (17)

In Genesis 15, God ratified his covenant with Abram; in Genesis 17, he confirmed

and established it. This chapter opens with a similar pattern as the two sections of Genesis 15. God reveals himself to Abram in another important "I am" statement meant to comfort Abram and draw him into more intimate dependence on God.

Genesis 15:1—"I am your shield, your very great reward."

Genesis 15:7—"I am the LORD, who brought you out of Ur of the Chaldeans to give you this land to take possession of it."

Genesis 17:1–2—"I am God Almighty. . . . I will confirm my covenant between me and you and will greatly increase your numbers."

Genesis portrays a loving God who seeks at every turn to reveal his true nature to humans in order to invite them into deeper relationship with him. In each case, his self-revelation presents Abram with an opportunity to draw closer to God.

This time, God also reveals his deepest desire for Abram: "walk before me and be blameless" (17:1). This expression is a call for Abram to live a life of unequivocal surrender to God's will. Perhaps you wonder what else Abram could surrender, having left everything to follow God's calling (Gn 12). But the previous episode with Hagar is a subtle warning that Abram still has more to learn about dependence on God.

The chapter opens with the statement that Abram is now ninety-nine years old. Thirteen years had passed since the birth of Ishmael. During those years, we must assume Abram had accepted the fact that Sarai was not going to have children and that Ishmael would be the heir of the divine promises. God begins by bringing his covenant promises into sharper focus (17:4–8). Abram will not only have children; he will become the "father of many nations," and kings will come from him. The "whole land of Canaan" will be an "everlasting possession" for his descendants.

So far, these are wonderful reaffirmations of the covenant promises stated earlier. But God also announces that Abram's eighty-nine-year-old wife, Sarai, will have a son within a year (v. 21). She will become the mother of nations, and kings of peoples will come from her (v. 16). The as-tounding declaration is too much for Abram. He falls on his face and laughs (v. 17). What about Ishmael? God agrees that Ishmael will be blessed and will become a great nation (v. 20), but not the promised nation. Sarai and Abram are going to have a baby! Because Abram laughed, he is instructed to name the son "Isaac," which means "he laughs." Both parents laughed incredulously when told they were going to have a son (18:12).

Genesis 17 also occasions the change of names—Abram to Abraham and Sarai to Sarah. The name "Abram" probably means "father is exalted." But now his name will mean "father of a multitude" (17:5).[20] From this point forward, the Bible knows him as Abraham. Sarai's name is also changed to Sarah, though both mean "princess." Her new name is merely an alternative pronunciation of the old.

Here we see an important principle that is repeated often in the Bible. Personal names in our modern context are often little more than identification labels. But in the Bible, they signify an individual's personal character. At times, they can reveal a person's destiny, at least as perceived by his or her parents at birth. Any midlife change of name is a momentous event that symbolizes a change of that person's character, and in this case, a transformation of destiny. What's more, the name is changed by God himself! This is more than a hopeful expression of a proud new parent. The name changes represent God's own seal on the future destiny of Abraham and Sarah in his divine plan. The essence of their personalities is changing, and so is their role in history. Christians familiar with the New Testament will immediately think of the changes from Simon to Peter and Saul to Paul (Mt 16:17–18 and Acts 13:9). Those who encounter God will never be the same, and name changes are appropriate means of symbolizing the transformation.

In addition to the name changes, God also marks this turning point in Abraham's life by giving him a new sign of the covenant—circumcision. The act of circumcision was well known in ancient times and widely practiced by many of Israel's neighbors.[21] Elsewhere in the Old Testament, Israel's traditional enemies, the Philistines, are mockingly called "the

Study Questions

1. Describe the way Abram was treated by Melchizedek and by the king of Sodom. What may we surmise about each in them in light of Genesis 12:3?

2. How do the historical events of chapter 14 prepare Abram for his encounter with God in chapter 15?

3. Explain both the meaning and significance of Genesis 15:6.

4. In what ways does God's covenant with Abram foreshadow the covenant at Sinai?

5. Define "covenant," and explain the remarkable nature of the covenant in Genesis 15.

6. How does the account of Abram's dealings with Hagar represent "Adam and Eve all over again"?

7. What can we as modern believers learn about faith and covenant from the story of Abraham?

uncircumcised," which probably indicates the Philistines were unique in their failure to practice circumcision. We may assume that most ancient peoples practiced circumcision for hygienic reasons and because it came to be viewed as socially acceptable.

But like nearly ever other facet of ancient Israel, God transformed this social custom into a religiously significant act. Rather than instituting a totally new ritual to signify the covenant, he adapted and transformed an ancient and familiar custom, investing it with new meaning. It will forever be associated with God's eternal covenant and his irrevocable claim on Abraham's life. No longer can Abraham be passive in his covenant with God (as in 15:12). This is a painful, self-inflicted action carried out in response to God's unique covenant. The performance of circumcision symbolized for Israel God's eternal promises. It also established constitutive identification of each male member of the covenant community.[22] And the decision was permanent! The sign could not be reversed, so there could be no turning back on God's covenant. Elsewhere the Bible develops the idea of "circumcision of the heart" (Dt 10:16; 30:6; Jer 4:4; Rom 2:28–29).[23] Covenant faithfulness is more than mere physical conformity, involving the deepest attitudes and intentions.

Genesis 17 is clearly a central chapter in the Abrahamic narratives. Several literary features of the entire narrative seem to converge in this chapter.[24] The Lord appears to Abram as "God Almighty" (Hebrew *El Shaddai*), a name that emphasized God's invincible power and faithfulness to fulfill his promises. This name would come to be viewed as distinctively significant for the patriarchs (Ex 6:3). The new names for Abraham and Sarah form a pivotal point in the story. All the important aspects of Abraham's life intersect in this ninety-ninth year of his life, when Sarah conceives Isaac. After the Hagar and Ishmael episode (Gn 16) and the passage of thirteen long years, one might have questioned whether God's promises had changed. Perhaps after all this time, the covenant was no longer intact. But God assured Abraham that he was still at work and that the covenant promises were sure.

8 Standing on the Promises of God

Genesis 18:1–25:18

Faith certainly tells us what the senses do not, but not the contrary of what they see; it is above, not against them.

—Blaise Pascal, French scientist and philosopher (1623–62)[1]

Supplemental Readings: Acts 7:2–8, Hebrews 11:11–19

Outline

- **Promised Son and Problem Nephew (18–19)**
  Abraham and Sarah Entertain Guests (18)
  Sodom and Gomorrah (19)
- **Abraham and Abimelech (20)**
- **The Promised Son—At Long Last! (21:1–21)**
- **Agreement with Abimelech (21:22–34)**
- **Abraham's Great Test (22)**
- **Family Matters (23:1–25:18)**
  The Death of Sarah (23)
  A Suitable Wife for Isaac (24)
  The Death of Abraham (25:1–18)

Objectives

After reading this chapter you should be able to

1. Describe the interactions among Abraham, Sarah, and their three guests in Genesis 18, highlighting God's promise of descendants, the plan to destroy Sodom, and the bargaining for the deliverance of Sodom.
2. Summarize the character traits and activities of Lot in Genesis 19, contrasting his compromises with the surrounding environment to the faithfulness of Abraham.
3. Discuss the significance of Abraham's half truth to Abimelech, the curse that resulted, and the result of Abraham's prayer.
4. Describe the events surrounding the birth of Isaac and the agreement between Abraham and Abimelech in Genesis 21.
5. Examine the literary, cultural, and theological components of God's command to sacrifice Isaac, Abraham's response, and God's last-minute substitution.
6. List the events involved in the purchase of the field and cave for Sarah's burial, and the relationship the transaction had to God's promises.
7. Identify the reasons Abraham sent a servant to find a wife for Isaac, the events surrounding the quest, and the significance of those events.

The opening quote from a great Christian philosopher reminds us that there are times when we must live our lives based on faith in God, and faith need never be contradictory to life's circumstances. Rather, our relationship with God gives us a different perspective on life and the world. We make decisions and take actions based on our conviction of faith, and at times this means we act without the assurance of tangible certainty (Heb 11:1).

As we have seen, Abraham becomes the prime example of such faith for the authors of the New Testament. The previous unit of Genesis went to great lengths to demonstrate how this faith was the central component in Abraham's covenant relationship with God. Now we shall see how Abraham's faith plays out in several routine affairs of his life, and some that are not so routine.

In this final collection of episodes from Abraham's life, we begin to see a gradual growth in his personal piety. As he grows in his understanding of God and God's nature, he also matures in his personal walk with God; he learns what it means to stand on God's promises. The New Testament also teaches that there is a commensurate growth between head knowledge and heart purity (Jas 1:2–5). Just as Abraham illustrated the nature of saving faith, so he also illustrates for us the process of Christian maturity.

Promised Son and Problem Nephew (18–19)

In these two important chapters, we read of the prediction of Isaac's birth and the final dismissal of Lot as a possible heir.

Abraham and Sarah Entertain Guests (18)

With their new covenant names and renewed promises of their relationship with God (Gn 17), Abraham and Sarah must have felt they were ready for anything in life. But they could not have anticipated what was about to happen. The event described in Genesis 18 is one of the most remarkable in the Bible.

Abraham and Sarah had established their home near Hebron, in a tent-dwelling among the Oaks of Mamre (v. 1). One day three visitors came their way, and Abraham treated them royally as was ancient Near Eastern custom. He did not wait at his door, but ran to meet them. Bowing to the ground, he offered to wash their feet and provide rest. He also offered a snack, which turned out to be a feast (vv. 2–8). In the ancient world, a person's reputation was often determined by the ability to provide such extravagant hospitality. Such kindness is also suitable for modern Christians, who might unwittingly entertain angels (Heb 13:2).

The identity of these visitors is clear from the opening verse: "The LORD appeared to Abraham near the great trees of Mamre. . . ." The next verse describes how the visitors appeared to Abraham, as "three men." But as the narrative progresses, it is clear that these are no ordinary mortals. In the conversation that occurs after the meal, one of these visitors appears to be omniscient; he seems to know things that no human could know. This first happens when he asks Abraham, "Where is your wife Sarah?" (v. 9). But then he announces that, in about a year, Sarah will give birth to a son (v. 10). When Sarah, standing out of sight behind the tent door, overheard the prognostication, she laughed to herself (v. 12). But the visitor knew that Sarah laughed, and even what she thought to herself (v. 13).

The identity of one of these visitors as "the LORD" in verse 1 is gradually confirmed as the narrative progresses. At first all three appear to be speaking with Abraham (v. 9). Then one of them makes the startling prediction that Sarah will have a son (v. 10).[2] Then the text clearly states that it is the "LORD," or Yahweh, who speaks with Abraham (v. 13), which the patriarch gradually begins to realize, as is clear from his petitions in verses 16–33 (especially v. 25b). In 19:1, two of the visitors are called "messengers" or "angels." This means Abraham and Sarah were honored to host Yahweh himself with two of his messengers in their home! This is one of the most human-like manifestations of God in the Bible. And the meal he shared with Abraham illustrates the most intimate and personal type of fellowship in the ancient world. Truly, Abra-

Lessons in Prayer

The well-known dialogue between God and Abraham in Genesis 18 illustrates a general principle of Christian life: maturity means caring for others. As one matures in his or her relationship with God, one naturally learns to intercede for the needs of others. This is truly the flowering of Abraham's faith. Abraham's intercession has four distinct elements.

1. *Divine Intentions* (vv. 16–19). Yahweh ponders whether he should conceal his plans from Abraham his servant. He concludes that certainly he will reveal to Abraham what he intends to do because he has known him (NIV's "chosen him"), and wants him to learn to do what is right (v. 19). Having thus decided, Yahweh reveals his plans to Abraham (vv. 20–21).

2. *Divine Hesitation* (v. 22). This verse contains a rare and obscure feature of the Hebrew text. Eighteen times in the entire Old Testament, ancient Jewish scribes chose to alter a text that seemed irreverent, idolatrous, or otherwise inappropriate (known as the *tiqqûnê sōfĕrîm,* see note 5, below). It is possible that verse 18 originally had "Yahweh remained standing before Abraham." If so, this reading heightens the idea that God hesitated in order to give Abraham time to intercede for Sodom.

3. *Servant's Intercession* (vv. 23–33). In Abraham's tentative, yet bold prayer, he bases his plea on God's character (v. 25). Abraham is also persistent with his concerns, which is the point of his descending conditions for mercy: fifty righteous people, forty-five, forty, and so on.

4. *Divine Response* (19:29). Lot and his two daughters were the only ones really saved, and they were reluctant participants. Yahweh answered the intent and spirit of Abraham's prayer, however much that prayer was inadequately prayed.

Though Abraham is the one who prayed, it was God who initiated the prayer, even goaded and coached his timid servant in prayer. It seems perfectly obvious that intercessory prayer was God's plan and desire. This was the next logical step in Abraham's spiritual development, and something God very much wanted him to do.

Furthermore, this same pattern of divine revelation and hesitation, followed by prayer and response, is repeated elsewhere in Scripture. These steps of successful intercessory prayer are demonstrated by Moses (Ex 32:7–14 and again in Nm 14:11–20), Amos (Am 7:1–9), and Daniel (Dn 9:2–21), among others. All of these examples of intercessory prayer seem to have certain shared features. They are the result of mature servants of God taking the next step in his plan for them. When believers mature in their faith, they find themselves naturally turning to the needs of others rather than always petitioning God for their own "needs" (which are often just desires). Such prayer is also people-driven. Abraham's concern for Lot drove him to prayer. He was bold with God because of his compassion and love for his nephew.

ham has become "the friend of God" (Jas 2:23; and see Is 41:8, NLT).

The purpose of the divine visit was to draw Sarah into full ownership of the covenant promises. In the previous chapter, God had been just as precise; it was Sarah who would give birth to the promised son (17:16, 19, 21). Abraham's response, like Sarah's here, had been laughter (17:17). As a reminder of their laughter, the proud new parents would name the child Isaac, "he laughs."

We are not told if Abraham had informed Sarah that God intended to give her a son after all these years. If he had not, her reaction to this news was certainly understandable. But even if Abraham had prepared her, she could hardly bring herself to believe that after years of barrenness, and long past the age of childbearing, God would now—at the age of ninety—grant her conception and motherhood (18:11–15). Her laughter and doubts were not the result of stubborn resistance to God's will, but of hopelessness and years of disappointment.[3] In the context of the patriarchal period, ninety is not hopelessly old. But this comes after years of longing for children, and now the text makes it clear, Sarah had been through menopause (18:11). In human terms, the visitor's pronouncement was impossible.

But Sarah's reaction also solicited from the Lord one of the great statements of Scripture: "Is anything too hard for the LORD?" (18:14).[4] Rather than rebuke Sarah for her unbelief, Yahweh gently reminds her that the one who knew her name and heard her innermost thoughts is able to bring it to pass. Her long years of disappointment and sorrow were about to end, because nothing is too hard for God. It was time for her to claim her role in the covenant promises, and to prepare herself to become the "mother of nations" (17:16).

The famous account of Abraham's prayer for the righteous of Sodom (18:16–33) reveals that the patriarch's relationship with God had taken on a new dimension—concern for someone other than himself. The previous dialogues between Abraham and God (Gn 12, 15, 17) had all concerned the covenant promises, and Abraham's need for assurances that the promises were true and irrevocable.

As the three were leaving Abraham, they "looked down toward Sodom," in an ominous tone that hints at what is to come. Yahweh considers, apparently aloud with the others, whether he should take Abraham into his confidence and relate to him his plans. Abraham will certainly become a great and mighty nation. But God decides to relate his intentions to Abraham primarily because he has "chosen him" (or simply, "known him," 18:19). Yahweh succinctly informs his servant that he intends to determine whether Sodom should be destroyed due to its surpassing wickedness.

The two messengers start their descent from the hills near Hebron to the city of Sodom. Abraham and Yahweh remain on the road overlooking the Dead Sea plain with the city of Sodom below. There is good reason to think that 18:22b contains a rare intentional change in the text. The text currently states "Abraham remained standing before the LORD." But there is evidence that early Jewish scribes made an intentional change, and that the text originally read, "The LORD remained standing before Abraham."[5] It seemed inappropriate to have the Sovereign Lord stand patiently waiting before his servant. Either way, the

phrase paints a striking picture. Whether Yahweh waits for Abraham to speak, or whether he waits while Abraham speaks, the passage portrays God patiently, even longingly, waiting for his servant to come to the rescue of potential victims of the crisis. The account teaches as much about God's view of intercessory prayer as it does about the nature of prayer itself.

Once Abraham gained assurance that God would not destroy Sodom if there were fifty righteous inhabitants, he reasoned that a just God would also have mercy on forty-five, forty, thirty, twenty, and finally ten righteous people. Of course, Abraham was not simply acting on behalf of ten anonymous individuals, but for his own family. Lot and his immediate family were in jeopardy, and Abraham was the only one who could help. The point of Abraham's hesitant bargaining is not that God needs us to cajole and bicker with him. Rather, this is a bold exploration of God's mind and heart. This was new territory for Abraham. He knew of God's intentions to destroy the city, but he was not sure of the limits to God's mercy. For Lot's sake, he was willing to find out.

In the end, Yahweh answered his prayer, though not exactly as Abraham had prayed it. God did destroy the city, even though there were not ten righteous to be found. Nevertheless, God remembered Abraham and delivered Lot (19:29). A perfect and righteous God had granted the spirit of his servant's imperfect and inadequate prayer. Abraham had not yet become a blessing to "all peoples on earth" (Gn 12:3), but this episode anticipates and foreshadows that reality.

Sodom and Gomorrah (19)

The nighttime events of chapter 19 present an unmistakable contrast with the those of the previous chapter, which occurred in the bright noonday sun.[6] The details of this encounter are as seedy and disreputable as the others were intimate and full of promise. The previous chapter culminated in Abraham's exemplary concern for others. This chapter ends in the ignoble Lot committing incest with his daughters while in a drunken stupor (19:30–38).

As you read Genesis 19, you should review the conflict between Abraham and

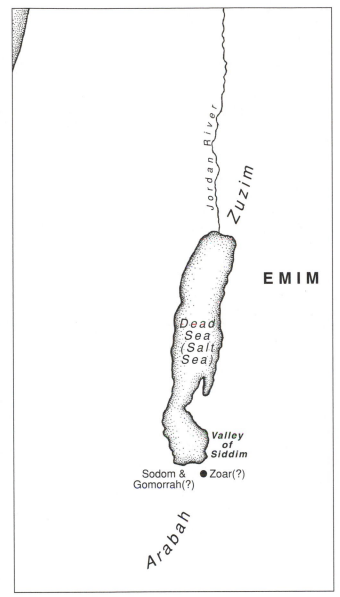

Location of Sodom and Gomorrah. Many believe that Sodom and Gomorrah were located beneath what is now the southern end of the Dead Sea.

known they would need protection from the depraved men of Sodom. There was enough decency in his character to try to intervene on their behalf. Ironically, he would learn that the visitors would have to intervene on his behalf.

However, as you read the narrative of chapter 19, you probably realized how reluctant and almost befuddled Lot seemed to be. When the men of Sodom threaten to rape the two visitors, Lot offers them his virgin daughters instead (vv. 4–8). It is possible that Lot was hoping his daughters' fiancées would come to their rescue, or that the homosexual attackers would not be interested in his daughters. We might argue that Lot was fulfilling his responsibility in trying to protect his important visitors at any cost. But his offer of the daughters probably also reflects how much the evil practices of his iniquitous surroundings had influenced Lot.

In the intervening years, Lot and his family had become enamored with the sensuality and apparently the wealth and prestige he had acquired in Sodom. Rather than influencing his culture, Lot had himself been shaped by his surroundings. He was a righteous man with a holy heritage, but one who lived day after day among the "filthy lives" of lawlessness, and who "was tormented in his righteous soul by the lawless deeds he saw and heard" (2 Pt 2:7–8). The years of compromise made Lot waver. When told to run for his life, he hesitated (19:16). It had become too difficult to leave the tantalizing life near Sodom. So modern Christians must guard against the subtle and beguiling influences of an irreligious environment.

Lot was delivered from the conflagration, but only because of Abraham's faithfulness (19:29). When Lot's wife disobediently looked back, she was trapped and overpowered by the explosion's molten debris and became a "pillar of salt" (19:17, 26). Her actions revealed a desire to keep her life, and therefore she lost it (read Lk 17:32–33).

This narrative illustrates both the surpassing mercy of God (in rescuing an undeserving and reluctant Lot) and his anger toward sin (in destroying the cities). It also teaches us to analyze our relationships. Lot was the nephew of a man of singular righteousness and faith. His uncle would become the means by which God would

Lot in Genesis 13. When they decided to separate, Lot chose to live near the wicked city: "Lot lived among the cities of the plain and pitched his tents near Sodom" (v. 12). He had been motivated by greed and pleasure, and it was a decision he would come to regret.

When the Lord's messengers came to destroy the city, Lot suddenly found himself in an unbearable situation. He welcomed and entertained the visitors as was the demands of his culture and as Abraham had done in chapter 18. He could not allow these visitors to spend the night in the public square (19:2–3). Lot must have

What Was the Sin of Sodom?

It has long been assumed that the sin of the Sodomites was homosexuality. Genesis 19:5 says simply that the men of Sodom demanded, "Bring them out to us and we will know them." Most translations assume the sexual nature of this statement: "Bring them out so we can have sex with them" (NLT, and see also NIV and NKJV). Our English word "sodomy" illustrates the long-standing assumption that this sin was homosexuality.

Under pressure from pro-homosexual groups, some modern scholars have argued the sin of Sodom described in Genesis 18–19 was not homosexuality. Instead, it is argued, the sin of the Sodomites was a more general disorder of a society organized against God, or one of abuse of justice.[7] But how legitimate is this claim?

Genesis had earlier noted the unusual sinfulness of Sodom: "the men of Sodom were wicked and were sinning greatly against the Lord" (NIV, Gn 13:13). But specifically what was the nature of their sin that God himself said was "extremely evil" and which Lot, with all his shortcomings, recognized as "a wicked thing" (NLT, 18:20 and 19:7, respectively)?

The Hebrew word "know" (*yāda‹*) in the expression, "we will know them" (19:5), has a wide range of meaning, and it is true that the word is used for sexual intercourse in only a minority of occurrences. However, context is the most important feature in determining the meaning of a given word in any particular context. The term "know" clearly has sexual connotations elsewhere in Genesis (4:1, 17, 25; 24:16) and seems the most likely meaning here in light of Lot's response. The offer of his virgin daughters, "who have never slept with a man" (19:8, literally, "who have not *known* a man") makes no sense otherwise. The use of the term "know" with a clear sexual meaning only three verses later seems to settle the issue.

We even have a parallel episode in the Book of Judges. In Judges 19, a Levite had entered Gibeah of Benjamin as a visitor to spend the night. A resident of the city invited him to lodge in his home, washed his feet, fed his donkeys, and then they shared a meal together. That night, the wicked men of the city surrounded the house, pounded on the door, and demanded the guest be brought outside so they could "know" him (v. 22). Likewise, the vile request was met with an offer to substitute a virgin daughter in place of the male guest.

It seems perfectly obvious in both these contexts that homosexuality is the nature of the request. Any doubt about this interpretation should be dispelled by Jude 7: "Sodom and Gomorrah and the surrounding towns gave themselves up to sexual immorality and perversion. They serve as an example of those who suffer the punishment of eternal fire."

Homosexuality is resolutely condemned in the Bible (Lv 18:22; 20:13; Rom 1:26–27). Israel's neighboring nations appeared to view it as little more than an oddity, which makes the Old Testament's condemnation even more striking. But more specifically, what is proposed in Genesis 19 and Judges 19 is homosexual gang rape, which is emphatically denounced as deplorable even by Israel's neighbors.[8] Modern scholars who deny this interpretation are more influenced by contemporary cultural pressure than by the facts of the immediate context of Genesis 19.

offer salvation to the entire world. Yet, because of his association with a sinful culture and his inclination to be shaped by that culture rather than by his relationship with God, Lot had a much less glorious part to play in God's plan.

In fact, the account ends with a rather contemptible event. Lot had pleaded to live in a smaller city of the plain, Zoar, rather than be banished to the hills (19:18–22). But after the terrible devastation, Lot was frightened. He settled in the mountains after all, living in a cave with his two daughters (vv. 30–38). The daughters, motivated by desperation and fear, set out to preserve male descendants for their father themselves. After intoxicating Lot, they conceived children by their own father on successive nights. This pitiful sequel to the narrative of chapter 19 serves an etiological purpose by explaining the origins of Israel's future enemies, the Moabites and Ammonites (on etiology, see chapter 2, note 16, above). But it also illustrates the end result of Lot's tendency to compromise with the culture around him. Sadly, he and his family had been influenced by their sensual and impetuous surroundings. Lot learned what many worldly Christians today need to remember: too close an association with unbelieving friends can have devastating results.

Abraham and Abimelech (20)

After the devastation at Sodom, Abraham traveled south again. Perhaps the cataclysmic changes in the area of Hebron necessitated his search for water (as the dispute over wells might indicate, 21:22–34). His family seems to have dwelt at Gerar, while he was in the south between Kadesh and Shur (see Gerar on map II.6.2, above).[9] Motivated by fear, Abraham once again announced that Sarah was his sister, and Abimelech, king of Gerar, takes her for his wife (20:2).

The promises of God are placed in jeopardy again, this time traded away for personal safety. This is all the more disheartening, coming as it does on the heels of the double assurances that Sarah is about to conceive the longed-for and promised baby (17:16; 18:10). Abraham had been such a stalwart saint in his intercession for Sodom, the wicked city. But now before the god-fearing king of a "righteous nation" (20:4, NIV's "innocent nation"), Abraham seems incapable of confidence in God. Out of fear, he passes Sarah off as his sister in order to ensure safety in a foreign land.

Try as we might, it is difficult to understand how Abraham could make the same mistake twice. Sarah was indeed his half-sister (20:12), and on an earlier trip to Egypt, he had concealed the whole truth in order to deceive Pharaoh (12:10–20). On that occasion disaster was narrowly averted by God's intervention. God rescued Abraham from a threat that Abraham himself had created (see pages 73–74, above).

How could Abraham have fallen into the same trap again? The circumstances of his stay near Gerar were similar to those of Egypt. He was living in close proximity to a powerful ruler. Abraham was afraid on both occasions that the ruler would kill him in order to have his wife. He lied in order to protect himself rather than trust God. In this way, the life of Abraham teaches us that faith in God does not usually remove every temptation we may have immediately. There may be certain temptations that present particular difficulty for the new believer. In this case, a sinful act had become a sinful pattern, and Abraham, our hero of faith, appears to have a problem with the truth.

Genesis 20 also, however, emphasizes that even though he is guilty, the prayer of Abraham is effective. Abimelech's family and slaves were all barren because of Sarah (v. 18). In a dream, God revealed to Abimelech that our hero is "a prophet" and that his prayer will result in life for the king (v. 7). As undeserving as he is, Abraham is still the means by which God grants life and blessing to the nations (12:3). He prays for the foreign king, his wife, and all the women of his household, and God grants fertility to them all (20:17). Ironically, God had not yet granted fertility to Abraham's own wife.

The Promised Son— At Long Last! (21:1–21)

The suspense has been building from Genesis 12, when God first promised descendants for Abraham. If you can imagine you had never read this story or heard the outcome, you can also imagine the impact of this literary crescendo, with its unanswered questions. So God would make a nation of Abraham. But through whom: Lot, Eliezer, Ishmael? And what will become of this covenant promise if Abraham is killed by an Egyptian pharaoh or a Canaanite king, or if Sarah becomes the wife of another man? Even though Abraham has reached new spiritual heights in his covenant relationship with God and has learned to intercede for others, will he ever stop deceiving his neighbors and learn to trust fully in the promises of God?

The suspense is finally resolved in Genesis 21, when Isaac is born to Sarah. But the resolution is not due to Abraham or Sarah. Rather, *Yahweh* was "gracious" to Sarah, just "as he had said," and he did for her "what he had promised" (21:1). Sarah gave birth to Isaac "at the very time *God* had promised him" (v. 3). Likewise, the proud parents gave the baby the name "Isaac" ("he laughs"), again confirming the fulfillment of God's intentions (17:19). This birth extols God's faithfulness, not Abraham's accomplishments. This might be obvious when the text reminds us that Abraham was a hundred years old at Isaac's birth (21:5).

Isaac's name is a reminder of his parents' incredulous reaction when Yahweh predicted his birth (18:12). Yet now, as wonderful as it is mysterious, his name no longer conjures up stunned disbelief, but joy and wonderment. Sarah's words ring out: "everyone who hears about this will laugh with me," and "Who would have said to Abraham that Sarah would nurse children? Yet I have born him a son in his old age" (21:6–7).

It is unfortunate that one person's cause for rejoicing is another's cause for resentment. At a feast to celebrate Isaac's weaning (approximately three years later), his mother saw him being mocked by Ishmael, now in his mid-teens.[10] In Genesis 21:8–21 we read the difficult story of Sarah's demand to expel Hagar and Ishmael from the family. As difficult as this was for Abraham, God assured him that he would bless Ishmael also and make him the father of a great nation (cf. 17:20, and page 97, above). Nevertheless, Isaac was the chosen son of promise: "it is through Isaac that your offspring will be reckoned" (21:12; read also Gal 4:21–31).

Agreement with Abimelech (21:22–34)

Abraham has continued to live in the south near Gerar, and the Philistine king, Abimelech, requested a long-term treaty with him.[11] This powerful king's respect for Abraham proves that God's promises are gradually taking hold. Abraham has become a formidable presence in the area. Though he does not possess the land (he continued to live in the land of the Philistines "for a long time," 21:34), the king is confident of God's blessings on Abraham and that the patriarch has a secure future. Abimelech desired to protect his own future by forming an alliance with the Israelite patriarch (21:23).

Abraham took the opportunity to clarify a dispute about an important well, which Abimelech's servants had seized. In a treaty typical of equals in the ancient Near Eastern, the well becomes Abraham's permanent possession in exchange for seven lambs. After the many recurrences of "oath" and "seven" (words from the same Hebrew root *šbʿ*), we are not surprised to learn that the place was called Beer-sheba, "Well of the oath" or "Well of seven." At long last, Abraham "now has at least a well he can call his own in the land of Canaan."[12]

Abraham's Great Test (22)

With Genesis 22, you have now reached the summit of the Abrahamic narratives, in terms of both literature and theology. Its literary quality is recognized by all, having been called "the most perfectly formed and polished of all the patriarchal stories."[13] Its profound theological insights have stirred Jewish and Christian readers for thousands of years. Were it not for the narrator's opening intimation ("Some time later God tested Abraham," v. 1), the reader would be left without a clue about the outcome.

The promise of a baby has been the all-consuming need and drive of the Abrahamic narratives. The hope for a son is obviously the central promise of the threefold patriarchal promises: land, descendants, and blessing (12:1b–3, and see pages 71–73, above). Without Isaac, Abraham could never hope to have a multitude of descendants, inherit the land, and become a blessing to the nations.

The narrative now takes a shocking twist. With the removal of Ishmael (21:8–21), the way was clear for the one and only heir of the patriarchal promises.

Tel Beersheba. It was here that Abraham and Abimelech sealed their treaty.

Isaac's future seemed certain. Then comes the unsettling command to sacrifice Isaac as a burnt offering (22:2). Abraham had been growing and learning many new things about God and about living in relationship with him. Could this possibly be true? Could God be like the other deities of the ancient world after all? As difficult as it might be for Abraham to understand, perhaps Yahweh now desired child sacrifice like other gods of Canaan.

Or, Abraham must have thought, was there any possibility he misunderstood the command? The astonishing clarity of verse 2 dispels all such possibilities. The command itself entails three verbs in the imperative: Take! Go! Offer up as a sacrifice! The lead imperative ("take") has a polite and formal spelling, which is rare when God addresses humans (something like "take, please"). It indicates that God is about to ask Abraham to do something staggering.[14] Furthermore, in a grammatically surprising way, this verb has three direct objects, each marked specifically as such in the Hebrew. These three objects move from the general to the more particular in a way that is obscured by most English translations:

TAKE
your son
your only son, whom you love
Isaac

Thus far, it would be impossible to misunderstand.

Early Jewish interpreters illustrated graphically just how specific the command was using an imaginary dialogue between God and Abraham.

> "Abraham, take your son!"
> "Which one, God? I have two sons."
> "Take your only son!" came God's reply.
> "But Lord," argued Abraham, "Ishmael is the only son of Hagar, and Isaac is the only son of Sarah."
> "Whom you love," answered God.
> "Lord, I love them both."
> "Isaac!" was God's solemn reply.[15]

So far the command was clear, but not necessarily alarming. That was about to change. The second imperative "Go!" had a familiar and foreboding ring in Abraham's ears. The specific Hebrew spelling of this verb only occurs one other place in the entire Old Testament—Genesis 12:1. There God had used the same particular form in a similar literary device. God's initial command to "Go!" also had an intensifying list of threes: from your country, your people, and your father's household. Whatever remaining hopes Abraham may have had about the command were dispelled by the final imperative, "Sacrifice him . . . as a burnt offering." This was the most widely used sacrifice in the Old Testament period, and involved cutting up

A famous portrayal of Abraham sacrificing Isaac from the Church of the Holy Sepulcher.

and burning the entire animal on an altar. As much as Abraham may have studied and analyzed these words in the hopes of altering their meaning, the command of God was undeniable.

The climactic role of this episode is clear from the way our author has paralleled Genesis 22 with Genesis 12. The initial call of Abraham and this supreme test of his faith have been deliberately cast in the same literary mold.

Not only is the verb "Go!" unique to these two passage in this particular spelling, but so is the use of three specifying qualifiers, and the patriarch's radical obedience is prevalent in both passages. All of these parallels serve to highlight one significant difference between these chapters: Genesis 22 contains no promises. At precisely the place where the call of Abraham contained promises and assurances of God's protection and blessing (12:2–3), the test of Abraham has only silence. There are no assurances here; no certainty of the future.

Clearly the author intends us to see the binding of Isaac as the concluding and climactic episode in Abraham's journey of faith, just as Genesis 12 was the beginning of that journey. These two episodes, therefore, create a sort of literary frame for the Abraham narratives. The correspondence of Genesis 12 and 22 also has profound theological significance. The call of Abraham forced him to let go of everything familiar and dear to him, everything that could provide security. But the call to sacrifice Isaac was a challenge to release the promises of God. After twenty-five years of hoping and praying, the long-awaited son of promise had arrived. Everything Abraham hoped for was focused on Isaac. Genesis 12 called

Parallels of Genesis 12 & 22

	Genesis 12	Genesis 22
Command:	Go!	Take, Go, Sacrifice!
	To a land	To a mountain
	unknown	unknown
	("I will show you")	("I will tell you")
Response:	12:4—obedience	22:3—obedience[16]

Abraham to leave his past; Genesis 22 called him to leave his future!

God, of course, did not permit Abraham to sacrifice Isaac, but he provided a ram to die in Isaac's place (22:13). But the episode illustrates the patriarch's radical abandonment into God's will. The nature of Abraham's action is clear in the words, "Early the next morning Abraham got up and saddled his donkey" (v. 3). Our instincts may lead us to speculate about what went on during the night. Surely Abraham must have tossed and turned, and even argued with God during a sleep-less night. But the Bible is only interested in Abraham's actions of faith; his exemplary surrender to God's Word, regardless of how difficult to understand or how painful to perform.

It may be difficult for us to comprehend how Abraham could have even considered obeying God's appalling command. But this is due to our lack of understanding the request as a test of Abraham's faith, as the narrator stated from the outset (22:1). Many scholars have argued that Genesis 22 is based on a more ancient story about a child sacrifice, which was resolved

The Sacrifice of Isaac and the New Testament

Christians have always recognized profound parallels between the offering up of Isaac in Genesis 22 and Jesus' death on the cross. For several New Testament authors, Abraham and Isaac were types of God the Father and his Son, Jesus. The examples are so pervasive it seems likely the comparisons go all the way back to Jesus' own self-interpretation of his identity and mission. Others have suggested the relation between Isaac and Jesus goes back to Jewish rabbinic tradition, which sometimes had Isaac actually being sacrificed as expiation for the sins of Israel.[21]

Paul's words in Romans 8:32 appear to be an intentional echo of the offering of Isaac: "He who did not spare his own Son, but gave him up for us all—how will he not also, along with him, graciously give us all things?" (compare Gn 22:12, 16). With this subtle comparison to Abraham and Isaac, the apostle Paul emphasized the Father–Son relationship in the atoning work of Christ. The suffering and death of Christ is thereby also placed in the context of the suffering of God the Father, since he had to yield up his Son for the salvation of humankind. The well-known "For God so loved the world that he gave his one and only Son" (Jn 3:16) probably also makes the same point.

This attention to Isaac as a type of Christ is only hinted at in the New Testament, but it is made possible because of a connection already drawn in the Old Testament. Later tradition associated Mount Moriah (Gn 22:2) with Jerusalem, or more specifically, with the mount on which Solomon built the temple (2 Chr 3:1). Thus this was the very site on which the Israelite sacrifices were routinely offered. In the fullness of time, their atoning significance was replaced by the atoning sacrifice of Christ. "This type already pointed to the antitype to appear in the future, when the eternal love of the heavenly Father would perform what it had demanded of Abraham; that is to say, when God would not spare His only Son, but give Him up to the real death, which Isaac suffered only in spirit."[22] The New Testament authors would no doubt have elaborated on this comparison were it not for one major difference between Isaac and Jesus: the New Testament has no ram caught by its horns in the thicket! Indeed, Jesus *was* sacrificed, and became the Father's atoning gift to us all.

The New Testament makes several other allusions to the sacrifice of Isaac, but there are at least two passages that use this text explicitly. The author of Hebrews states that when Abraham offered his only Son, he believed that God could raise him up from the dead (11:17–19). James uses Abraham's actions as an example of how faith and works always work together in the life of the believer (Jas 2:21–23). Thus James and Hebrews chose to emphasize Abraham's act of offering instead of Isaac's atoning sacrifice. Abraham becomes the paradigm for faithful obedience.

Many have noted that this artifact from ancient Ur resembles a ram caught in a thicket.

came after Abraham, he would certainly have been aware of such practices.[18]

Rather than a simple repudiation of child sacrifice, the author has emphasized this account as a test of Abraham's faith (22:1).[19] God was not trying to make Abraham fail spiritually. Rather, this account illustrates the spiritual truth taught in the New Testament: trials successfully endured strengthen the believer's ability to trust and obey God (read Jas 1:2–4). God wanted Abraham not to sacrifice Isaac on an altar, but to sacrifice him in his heart. In other words, this was the supreme test of Abraham's faith because he was asked to forsake that which he loved supremely—his only son, whom he loved, Isaac.[20] Our love for God should never be forced to compete with our love for someone (or something) else (Mt 10:37).

Abraham passed his test! Because he did not withhold anything from God, but even surrendered his own son, God blessed him (Gn 22:15–18). God took the opportunity to reaffirm all three covenant promises to Abraham. His descendants would be as numerous as the stars above and the grains of sand on the seashore. They would capture the land of their enemies, and become a blessing to all nations on earth, "because you have obeyed me" (vv. 17–18).

Family Matters (23:1–25:18)

The time-honored account of Abraham's life and faith is now over. There remain only a few final issues related to the patriarchal family: a suitable wife for Isaac, and the deaths of Sarah and Abraham.[23]

The Death of Sarah (23)

Abraham was still landless; he remained "an alien and a stranger" in Canaan (23:4), though his wealth and reputation meant everyone recognized him as a "mighty prince" (v. 6). When Sarah died at the age of 127, Abraham found it necessary to seek a proper place for burial. He purchased a field with its cave near Hebron from Hittite settlers from the north for four hundred shekels of silver.

The scene with Ephron and the Hittites

when a ram was substituted for the child. This story was then appropriated by a later Israelite author as an example of the patriarch's faith, and as a polemic, or formal argument against the practice of child sacrifice. As such it marks the rejection of the detestable practice and establishes the norm of substituting an animal in place of the child (so the ram for Isaac).[17]

Though such practices were performed in ancient Canaan and were not unknown even in Israel, it is clear that the norm in the ancient Near East was animal sacrifice rather than child sacrifice. The idea of substituting an animal for a child would have occurred long before Abraham's day. Yet the idea was still known and we must assume it was one with which Abraham was familiar. Biblical law makes provisions for animals to be substituted for the firstborn son, who was expected to be dedicated to God (Ex 22:29; 34:20). It is this background that makes God's command to Abraham a suitable test. Though the Israelite law

This fifth- or sixth-century basilica-type church stands on the traditional site of the Cave of Machpelah. Beneath it are chambers, in which explorers in A.D. 1119 reportedly found the bones of the patriarchs.

ship, and he was willing to pay top shekel for it.

At long last, Abraham was in possession of at least a portion of Canaan. The narrator is careful to say that the cave and field of Machpelah were near Mamre (that is, Hebron) "in the land of Canaan" (23:19, and see v. 2). At the end of his journey he holds a well (Beersheba, 21:22–34) and a cemetery as downpayments on God's promise.[24] It was faith in the ultimate fulfillment of that land-promise that led Abraham himself (25:9–10), and later, Isaac, Rebekah, Leah (49:29–32), and Jacob (50:13) to join Sarah in this family tomb. In death, the patriarchs were victorious in a way that escaped them in life. Though their voices grew silent, their family sepulcher bore eloquent witness that death could not prevent them from entering further into the promises of God, and in this way they are examples for us all. The New Testament author concludes: "All these faithful ones died without receiving what God had promised them, but they saw it all from a distance and welcomed the promises of God" (NLT, Heb 11:13).

A Suitable Wife for Isaac (24)

The account of the binding of Isaac had ended with a genealogy of his cousins back in Haran (22:20–24). Nahor, the brother of Abraham, had twelve sons. But the genealogy also mentions one granddaughter, Rebekah. It is unusual to include daughters in the list, and the author did not inform us why Rebekah would become important. But after the angel stopped Abraham from killing Isaac, he assured Abraham that his descendants would be too numerous to count. This meant presumably Isaac would need a wife. The brief genealogy in Genesis 22 had anticipated this search for a suitable companion for Isaac.

Abraham had a problem. He refused to allow Isaac to return to Mesopotamia, the land of his origins, yet he was just as adamant about Isaac marrying a Canaanite woman. Twice he warned his chief servant who was responsible for finding a suitable daughter-in-law, "do not take my son back there" (24:6, 8). Having come so far, Abraham was not about to allow Isaac to look back now (Heb 11:15–16). But

may seem odd to us because we are not accustomed to such negotiations. Their polite bargaining before the witnesses at the city gate (v. 10) was actually a formal business transaction, and quite typical in ancient Near Eastern times. Before the witnesses, Ephron offered to give both the field and cave of Machpelah to Abraham, who had requested the cave only. Abraham insisted that he would pay full price. Ephron politely mentioned the value of the property, but seemed almost ashamed to appear so mercenary: "What is that between me and you?" (v. 15). Everyone knew what was happening here; they all knew the procedure. Abraham paid the full asking price for the property, which may be the only surprise in the transaction.

Though we do not have enough information about property values in the patriarchal period, it seems that four hundred shekels of silver was an enormous amount. It could be that the field associated with the cave was substantial. It is more likely that Ephron actually expected half as much as a fair price, and Abraham granted the full four hundred shekels as a sign of good will. It was important for Abraham to have uncontested owner-

Table 8.1
The Family of Terah
(Genesis 11:27–29; 22:20–24; 29:16)

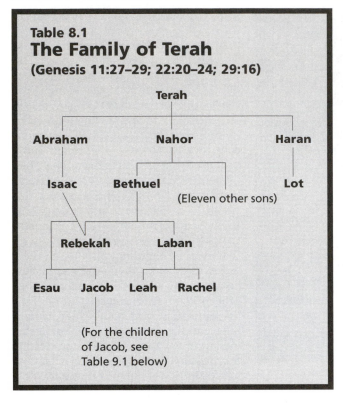

Terah
Abraham — Nahor — Haran
Isaac — Bethuel — Lot
(Eleven other sons)
Rebekah — Laban
Esau   Jacob   Leah   Rachel

(For the children
of Jacob, see
Table 9.1 below)

1:8). Abraham understood the critical role of the mother. If Isaac had an unbelieving wife, there would be little chance of having godly children.

The solution was to send his trusted servant back to the patriarchal homeland in search of a suitable wife for Isaac. The chief servant of a "mighty prince" (23:6) like Abraham would have been an important and powerful man in his own right.[25] Having taken an oath (the meaning of placing one's hand under the thigh), the servant went back to Haran with the formidable task of locating the right kind of young woman. In a fashion that only God could ordain, the servant meets Rebekah and her family, relates the nature of his mission, and persuades them all that the young and beautiful Rebekah should return to Canaan with him to become Isaac's bride.

As you read this narrative, you were probably impressed by the devotion and faithfulness of Abraham's unnamed servant, and with Rebekah, the industrious young girl. Indeed, all the characters of this amazing drama display surpassing trustworthiness and exemplary character. But ultimately, the episode is about God's faithfulness. *He* protected and guided the servant on his journey, and *he*

equally dangerous was the prospect of marrying a Canaanite woman. In the Old Testament period, the family was the most important educational unit (Dt 6:6–7; Prv

Study Questions

1. What purpose does the divine visit of Genesis 18 serve?

2. Contrast the events of Genesis 18 and 19. How does the author portray Abraham, and how is this different from his depiction of Lot?

3. What are the similarities between Genesis 12 and Genesis 22? What are the differences? How may the events of Genesis 22 be construed as the climactic episode in Abraham's journey of faith?

4. Discuss the significance of the patriar-chal tomb with respect to God's promise.

5. Why was Abraham insistent that Isaac not take a Canaanite wife?

6. What appears to be the sin of Sodom, and why does this appear to be the case?

7. What New Testament authors explicitly reference the story of Abraham's sacrifice of Isaac? Which character do these authors emphasize, and why?

8. In what ways can the reading of Genesis 12 and 22 enhance our faith as Christians?

salvation
history

brought Rebekah along with just the right servant-spirit at just the right time. From our historical perspective centuries later, we can see how he used the remarkable obedience of a few family members dealing with an intimate issue as the framework for accomplishing his purposes in our **salvation history**. For it was through this union of Isaac and Rebekah that the covenant and its wonderful promises were to be perpetuated.

The Death of Abraham (25:1–18)

Abraham's marriage to Keturah probably occurred earlier in his life.[26] The narrator of Genesis prefers to describe the events involving the main characters without distractions. Thus we can follow the fulfillment of the promises in a straight line before doubling back to read the other details of Abraham's life.

Key Term

salvation history

Abraham lived to the ripe age of 175 (v. 7). His sons, Isaac and Ishmael, buried him in the cave of Machpelah, which as we have seen, became the patriarchal cemetery (v. 9). His burial in the land of promise anticipates the fulfillment of God's Word.

With Genesis 25:11, we have finished the *tôlĕdôt* of Terah, which began in 11:27 and details the life of Abraham. But before the narrator continues with the promised line of Isaac, he rounds out the episode with the *tôlĕdôt* of Ishmael (25:12–18).

This, too, highlights the faithfulness of God in fulfilling his promises concerning Abraham. God had pronounced that Ishmael's descendants would "live in hostility toward all his brothers" (16:12), which finds its fulfillment pattern in 25:18b.[27] Furthermore, God had assured Abraham that Ishmael would father twelve princes and become a great nation (17:20), which is fulfilled according to 25:16.[28] Thus even in the peripheral characters of this great salvation history, God is faithful to his Word. This drives the reader to continue with the narrative, since God would certainly bring his promise to fruition for Isaac, just as he did for Ishmael.

Part
3

Encountering Jacob:
God's Troubled Servant

Genesis 25–36

"You have striven with God and with humans."

—Gn 32:28

9 Jacob Struggles with His Family

Genesis 25:19–31:55

O, what a tangled web we weave,
  when first we practice to deceive!

—Sir Walter Scott
(1771–1832)[1]

Supplemental Readings: Hosea 12:2–5, Romans 9:10–13

Outline

- **Of Twins and Birthrights (25:19–34)**
  Birth of the Twins (25:19–28)
  Stolen Birthright (25:29–34)
- **Isaac and Abimelech (26)**
- **Jacob Steals the Blessing (27)**
- **The Ladder (28)**
  Jacob's Escape from Esau (28:1–9)
  Jacob's Dream (28:10–22)
- **Jacob and Laban (29–31)**
  Jacob Marries the Daughters of Laban (29:1–30)
  Jacob's Children (29:31–30:24)
  Jacob's Prosperity (30:25–43)
  Trouble with Laban (31)

Objectives

After reading this chapter you should be able to

1. Contrast the character traits of Jacob and Abraham, and the character traits of Jacob and Esau.
2. List the events preceding and surrounding the birth of Jacob and Esau.
3. Summarize the privileges and responsibilities of being the firstborn, and the events that shifted the birthright from Esau to Jacob.
4. Discover parallels between the lives of Isaac and Abraham.
5. Describe how all four participants contributed to the wrong that occurred in the stealing of the blessing incident.
6. Imagine what Jacob felt and experienced as he left home for Mesopotamia.
7. Explain the personal and theological significance of Jacob's dream and the responses he made to the dream.
8. Describe the events leading to the marriage of Jacob to Leah and Rachel.
9. Compare the relationships Jacob had with Leah and with Rachel, the competition that was fostered, and the long-term bitterness and strife between the two families of Jacob that resulted.
10. List the events leading to the departure of Jacob and his families, the pursuit and accusation by Laban, and the resulting covenant established with Jacob.

The next major unit of Genesis is sometimes called the Jacob cycle (25:19–37:1). The great Scottish novelist and poet, Sir Walter Scott, captured the spirit of the Jacob cycle with the famous stanza cited in the opening paragraph. The web Jacob wove through deception was indeed tangled. But as we shall see, God was able to use and bless even Jacob.

After reading the Primeval History (1:1–11:26), and the Abrahamic narratives (11:27–25:18), you are now ready for the third section of Genesis, which gives an account of Abraham's family: Isaac, Esau, and particularly Jacob. You will soon realize that this is a very different narrative. Instead of following the encounters of a righteous man and his relationship with God, you will be left wondering how God could bless (and use) a man like Jacob.

In Genesis 1–11, you learned about the beauty of God's perfect creation, the entrance of human sin into the world, and the devastating consequences of sin. The problem of sin detailed in the Primeval History is a problem for all of us. But then in Genesis 12–25, you learned that Abraham is the answer to the world's sin problem, or at least the beginning of the answer. God considered him righteous because of his surpassing faith, and God established a personal relationship with him through the covenant and its promises for the future. From our modern, post–New Testament perspective, we are able to look back across the ages and realize that God raised up the nation Israel as the fulfillment of those covenant promises to Abraham. Eventually God's Messiah (or "Christ") came from that nation, and lives today as the permanent solution to our sin problems (read Heb 9:28; 1 Pt 2:24; 3:18).

But suppose for a moment you were *not* reading Genesis from your modern perspective. Suppose you did not already know the end of the story recorded in the New Testament. Jacob, son of Isaac and child of the promises of Abraham, is a questionable character, with a unique and entirely predictable personality. He was willing to use (or abuse?) anyone at any time for personal gain. At times he was manipulative and deceitful; at other times, clueless about God and his calling. This is not supposed to be the way of Abraham's children. The account creates a tension between the present reality (Jacob's questionable character) and the future hope of the covenant promises. It leaves us asking "Why?" of the way things were, and "Why not?" of the way they were supposed to be.

If you did not know better, you might think the covenant promises were in serious jeopardy in the hands of this scoundrel. And in fact, if the outcome depended on Jacob alone, we would have cause for alarm. But Genesis wants us to get this point: the promises are *of* God and *from* God. He will not let his Word fail (Is 40:8).

Of Twins and Birthrights (25:19–34)

In Genesis 25:19, a new *tôlĕdôt* section begins: "This is the *account* of Abraham's son Isaac." As we have said, the editor of Genesis has arranged the eleven *tôlĕdôt* sections into four larger units (review pages 17–18, above). So far, you have covered the Primeval History and the Abrahamic narratives. This third major unit has the *tôlĕdôt* of Isaac (which is actually the story of Jacob) and Esau (36:1–37:1).[2]

Genesis 25 has described the children of Abraham and Ishmael (vv. 2–4 and 13–15, respectively). Both had an impressive number of children, including Ishmael's twelve "princes" or tribal rulers (v. 16). But as elsewhere, the author of Genesis hastens on to the promised line, having dutifully marked what became of Ishmael's descendants.

The total number of Isaac's sons was two! This rather modest offspring may at first appear to us less impressive than Ishmael's twelve tribal chiefs. But the author of Genesis devotes nearly twelve chapters (25:19–37:1) to Isaac's two sons, while Ishmael's are covered in a few short verses.[3] In God's plan of salvation, appearances can be deceiving, and it is the seed of God's covenant promises that the author wishes to relate.

Genesis 25:19–34 narrates the birth of twins and the question of birthright. The author moves on promptly to describe the all important birth of Abraham's grandsons before Isaac's own brief story (which comes in Gn 26). This illustrates the importance of tracing the patriarchal promises through the birth of the promised progeny. Isaac quickly becomes a peripheral character once the twins are born.

Birth of the Twins (25:19–28)

The "account" *(tôlĕdôt)* of Isaac begins with the birth of twins to Isaac and Rebekah. The comment that Rebekah was unable to conceive (25:21) presents the dreaded problem of the barren wife again. Just as Sarah before her (and Rachel after her, Gn 29:31; 30:1–2), Rebekah had been unable to provide the all-important male offspring promised by God. And, just as Sarah and Abraham had waited twenty-five years before Isaac was born, Rebekah and Isaac waited twenty (compare vv. 20 and 26).

In the Abrahamic narratives, the birth of the promised one was delayed in the narrative. We followed Abraham and Sarah in their journeys and agonized with them over their childlessness. Isaac was finally born in Genesis 21, and by then we had watched as Abraham and Sarah grew in their relationship with God. But the issue of barrenness is treated much differently here. This time the matriarch's barrenness and the news that she has conceived is recorded in one startling verse near the beginning of the unit (25:21). Though there is a twenty-year delay, the author's concern is not to narrate the actions and struggles of Isaac and Rebekah during the delay, as it had been with Abraham and Sarah. This time the concern is with the actions and behavior of the promised son, Jacob, once he has arrived.

During Rebekah's difficult pregnancy, the Lord revealed to her the nature of her twins' relationship, which becomes an important theme for the rest of the Jacob narrative.

Two nations are in your womb,
and two peoples from within
you will be separated;
one people will be stronger than
the other,
and the older will serve the
younger (25:23).

Jacob and Esau will eventually become the important nations of Israel and Edom, thereby fulfilling the promises to Abraham in Genesis 12:1–3 and elsewhere. In addition, this illustrates the common biblical theme of the younger brother displacing the older, as we have already seen with Cain and Abel, and Isaac and Ishmael.[4] It is this struggle between Jacob and Esau that dominates the "family history" of Isaac. And this divine revelation detailing the main theme of the Jacob cycle occurs at the beginning of the unit, playing a similar role as the promises of God at the beginning of the Abraham cycle (Gn 12:1–3).[5]

The newborn twins were already different as babies (25:25–27). The red and hairy Esau grew into a daring and hardy outdoors man. Jacob, the younger of the two, was a quiet homebody. Even at the time of their birth, their future battles were anticipated. Jacob emerged grasping his older brother's heel, and is therefore named "Jacob," a name that means something like "May God Protect," but also sounds like the word "heel." Through Jacob's own actions, he devalued the name into a synonym for "Supplanter," "Deceiver," or "Cheater" (see Gn 27:36).[6] Remembering that Old Testament names often reflect one's character, Jacob's name does not portend an optimistic future for his relationship with Esau. As we shall see, Jacob is aptly named. He is the deceiving trickster, who seeks to supplant his older brother.

The prophet Hosea suitably summarized the life of Jacob.

In the womb he grasped his
brother's heel;
as a man he struggled with God
(12:3).

It is his struggles with his family and with God that consumes most of the rest of Genesis.

The birth account ends on a distressing and foreboding note: "Isaac ... loved Esau, but Rebekah loved Jacob" (25:28). Parental favoritism would plague this family for years to come and cause monumental grief (read Gn 37:3).

Stolen Birthright (25:29–34)

The right of the firstborn son brought several benefits in Old Testament culture.[7] At the death of the father, the firstborn son inherited a double portion of the estate (Dt 21:17). The eldest son also enjoyed special status throughout his lifetime, ranking second only to the father as the head of the family (Gn 43:33). These responsibilities and privileges would ordinarily be formerly conferred on the firstborn son in the father's deathbed blessing.

Esau, as the firstborn of Isaac, had particular responsibility and privilege because he would also be called on to continue the faithful line of Abraham and was heir to the patriarchal promises of God's covenant. In this sense, the red soup incident continues the presumed heir theme of the Abraham narrative. First Lot was the presumed heir of Abraham, then Eliezer, then Ishmael. Would Esau now become the heir of Isaac, and the one to carry on the patriarchal covenant?

Jacob's offer to purchase Esau's birthright may not have any of these particular rights (or responsibilities) in view, but rather deals with family priority in general. Jacob is positioning himself for the prior claim of the elder brother.[8] By doing so, he has prepared the way to acquire the greater privilege of the blessing in Genesis 27.

Our narrator does not condemn Jacob's actions, but rather judges Esau's indifference toward his family responsibilities and privileges: "So Esau despised his birthright" (25:34). In this assessment, the New Testament author agrees, using Esau as the example of someone who missed the grace of God and caused trouble and defilement because of a "bitter root" in his life (Heb 12:15–17). Esau chose immediate gratification of his physical desires over continued position in the patriarchal family, thereby also forfeiting his role in the covenant line of Abraham. Such foolish decision making is characteristic of all of us when we relinquish the long-term benefits of faithfulness for the sake of instant gratification of ordinary human appetites.

Although the narrator condemns Esau, it is also clear that Jacob was no innocent and unwilling participant. He was eager to seize the opportunity for his own advantage, without concern for his brother's well-being. In this he was like Cain, who killed his brother Abel. Jacob was unwilling to be his "brother's keeper" (Gn 4:9), choosing instead to manipulate Esau in his constant struggle to gain the upper hand. Clearly, this unscrupulous fellow, this "Deceiver," Jacob is not cut from the same cloth as Abraham. As we learn more about Jacob and his unprincipled character, the question of the narrative is, "What will become of Abraham's covenant and the promises of God now?"

Isaac and Abimelech (26)

Once the twins, Jacob and Esau, are born, Isaac quickly fades into the background. This is the only chapter of Genesis devoted to Isaac, and after chapter 27, he is scarcely mentioned again until his death (35:28–29). The placement of the chapter is not as disruptive as it appears, since it plays a literary role in the symmetrical design of the Jacob cycle.[9]

This chapter relates how Isaac is forced to flee his home because of famine, claims his wife is his sister in a pathetic effort to save his own skin, endures controversies over water rights with the surrounding Philistines, and, most important, accepts in faith the promises of God to Abraham. If the details sound familiar, it is with good reason. The point of this account seems clear: Isaac is a worthy successor to his father Abraham, even including the same flaws.[10]

Just as famine forced Abraham to flee the promised land (12:10–20), so now Isaac journeys to Gerar, another of Abraham's former base camps (20:1). Just as Abraham had dealings with the Philistine king Abimelech, so now does Isaac, though this was probably a subsequent king with the same throne name.[11] Isaac, like Abraham, claims his wife is his sister, falsifying the relationship for fear of his life, again like Abraham (compare 26:7 with 12:13; and 20:11). Isaac made the same mistake as Abraham, and yet was delivered by the mercy of God in the same way.

As unthinkable as it seems that Isaac could make the same mistakes as his father, the point of the narrative is that he

The Philistines of the Patriarchal Period

It is commonly assumed that the Philistines of Genesis 21 and 26 represent a historical anachronism. The Philistines do not play a dominant role in Old Testament history until the time of the judges and the rise of the monarchy (see the books of Judges and 1 and 2 Samuel). Extrabiblical sources refer to the arrival of the Philistines in southern Syria–Palestine around 1200 B.C. Egyptian texts include as a subgroup of the Sea Peoples, the "Peleset," who settled on the southwest coastal plains of Palestine, and in fact, gave rise to the word "Palestine."[12] Their presence in the patriarchal narratives, therefore, is believed to be a historical incongruity or chronological misdating by several centuries. Many people today assume the author of Genesis mistakenly projected the political circumstances of his own day (the much later monarchy, when the Philistines were so powerful) on the distant patriarchal period.[13]

But this assumption raises more questions than it answers. The later Philistines, who were the bitter enemies of Iron Age Israelites, were different from these in Genesis in both demeanor and government.[14] The later Philistines were warlike and lived in the five cities of the coastal plain (the "pentapolis," consisting of Gath, Gaza, Ashkelon, Ashdod, and Ekron). These later Iron Age Philistines were administered by "lords" (*sĕrānîm*). By contrast, the Philistines of Genesis lived around Gerar and Beersheba, and were ruled by the kings of Gerar, known by the throne name "Abimelech." These fundamental differences between the Bronze Age Philistines portrayed in the patriarchal accounts and the later Iron Age Philistines make it difficult to view the Genesis references as anachronistic. An Iron Age author reflecting his own historical period would have invented Philistines who were much different from the ones we read about in the patriarchal narratives. The Genesis descriptions seem to be authentic accounts of a true Bronze Age historic situation, rather than retrojections of later history.

It is more reasonable to compare the Philistines of Genesis with such people as the Caphtorim from Crete (Dt 2:23). Thus the term "Philistine" could be used for an earlier Aegean group that was a precursor to the later Philistines. In a sense, these Caphtorim would represent the first wave of Sea Peoples from the Aegean.

also believed the Word of God in the same way, and acted on the promises of God as Abraham had. The great promises of the covenant are restated and confirmed to Isaac (26:2–5, 24). Not only are Abraham's great promises repeated, but they are expanded and enhanced for Isaac. God emphasizes that he will grant Isaac his own presence in the land ("I will be with you" 26:3; and see v. 24), and urged him not to go down to Egypt but to live in the confines of the Promised Land. It took an act of faith for Isaac to stay in Canaan during the famine, but God granted mercy with the Philistines. Not only that, but remarkably Isaac reaped "a hundredfold" harvest within the year (26:12). God had truly been faithful in blessing Isaac.

The controversies with Abimelech over water rights illustrate Isaac's faithful character. If we were disappointed by his failure at Gerar, we have to be impressed by Isaac's victory at Rehoboth (26:16–22). The previous arrangement between Abraham and the Philistines had been forgotten or ignored. Isaac had prospered so much, the jealous Philistines drove him from Gerar. Twice his father's wells were captured and he was expelled from the region. Finally at the third location, they were left in peace, so that Isaac named the place Rehoboth, or "Open Spaces" (26:22). Isaac has wisely sought to avoid confrontation, and graciously accepted whatever ground the Philistines conferred. When Abimelech and his corps arrived and requested a treaty, Isaac affably agreed. But immediately upon their departure, a fresh well was discovered with abundant water (26:32). Despite his failures, Isaac has not

The Philistines of the patriarchal age differed in several respects from the Iron Age Philistines depicted here.

lost faith in the promises, or in God's ability to grant success.

Jacob Steals the Blessing (27)

Genesis 27 presupposes a precise understanding of the deathbed blessing. In Old Testament thought, the final fatherly blessing was much more than a prayer for the future of his children. Rather, the blessing actually played an important role in determining the destiny of his descendants, as Jacob's blessings of his children near the close of Genesis so aptly illustrate (chaps. 48–49). Thus, the blessing was a right entrusted to the father in which he was guided by God's grace to bestow spiritual and material possessions, all of which were irrevocable.[15] Rather than a prayer, the final blessing was more like a prophecy, the fulfillment of which was ensured by God himself.

All four participants in this episode are almost equally at fault.[16] Esau had married two Hittite wives from Canaan, who had made the lives of his parents miser-able (26:34–35). The importance of avoiding such marriages is clear from Abraham's insistence that Isaac marry within the patriarchal family of Yahweh worshipers from Haran (24:3–4). Yet Isaac is also at fault for not making the same insistent demand of Esau. Abraham had carefully arranged for Isaac to marry Rebekah; why did not Isaac make the same arrangements for Esau? Isaac's patience (almost passivity) in his dealings with Abimelech was a noble characteristic (Gn 26), but it surfaces here as indifference or neglect. Rather than call both his sons to receive a blessing as was customary, he foolishly summons only his favorite son, Esau, whose "tasty food" is the kind he likes (27:4). Though we may be tempted to blame only Rebekah and Jacob for their part in the ruse, the narrator has enough blame to share with Isaac and Esau.

But Rebekah and Jacob have their own guilt to bear. Rebekah had received the assurances of God himself while the twins were still in her womb: "the older will serve the younger" (25:23). This divine pronouncement standing at the head of the Jacob narrative made clear God's will, just as the promises of Genesis 12:1–3 did for the Abrahamic narratives. Yet even with the promises of God in her hands, Rebekah refused to act in love and charity and to wait for God's timing. Rather, she took manipulative action to guarantee the future of her favorite son. Jacob, for his part, willingly went along with her scheme. His only objection unveils a fear of detection rather than moral disapproval: "What if my father touches me? I would appear to be tricking him and would bring down a curse on myself rather than a blessing" (27:12).

The consequences of all these actions are telling. At first glance you may have thought Jacob and Rebekah got away with it. But Rebekah was forced to send her beloved Jacob away to Mesopotamia for what she hoped would be "a few days" (27:44, NKJV), but in reality was twenty years. She would never see Jacob again. Jacob, for his part, had to flee for his life. While in Mesopotamia, he was tricked into marrying the unattractive Leah, in order to marry Rachel also. His favoritism for Rachel and her children would result in conflict for the rest of his life. Like Abraham before them, these characters were unwilling to wait on the Lord to accomplish his will in their lives. Though ultimately God was faithful to his Word and accomplished his purposes through them, they made their lives difficult by pursuing their own designs.

While other biblical narratives illustrate the exemplary behavior of our great heroes of faith, this chapter depicts the fallibility of each member of the chosen family. All four characters are guilty: Esau in reckless marriages, Isaac in stupefied favoritism, Rebekah in calculated brazenness, and Jacob in deceitful exploitation. Yet despite all of this, God's grace endures and his purposes for the chosen seed of Abraham advance.

The Ladder (28)

Esau's unfortunate marriages became Rebekah's excuse for sending Jacob away (27:46). In reality, she was privy to the news that Esau was planning to murder Jacob. The urgency of the situation led her to approach Isaac and insist that Jacob be sent back to the patriarchal homeland to ac-quire a suitable wife, as Abraham's servant had done for Isaac (Gn 24). The only hope for finding a godly wife for Jacob was Bethuel's household back in Mesopotamia (see table II.8.1). Perhaps without knowing the circumstances, Isaac would also be saving Jacob from Esau's wrath.

Jacob's Escape from Esau (28:1–9)

Isaac's farewell blessing became an occasion to review and restate the all-important covenant promises for Jacob. As Isaac sent the son of the promise back to Paddan Aram, the homeland of Abraham's family,[17] he reiterated the threefold blessing that now must become Jacob's life charter (28:3–4). The "blessing of Abraham" (NRSV) contained the now familiar assurances of land and descendants, pronounced in the name of "God Almighty," the patriarchal name for God (El Shaddai, Gn 17:1).

Jacob set out presumably to find for himself a suitable wife, but really to escape Esau's anger. He was vulnerable for the first time in his life. He was the home-lover being forced to leave home. He has estranged his own brother, and now must leave his parents to journey to a land that must have seemed foreign and totally unfamiliar to him. He has the promises of God in his hands, but he has not the experience with God nor relationship with God necessary to find much comfort in the "blessing of Abraham." This was a time for Jacob to find out his convictions, about God and about himself.

Try to imagine reading this narrative as though you did not know the outcome. Will Esau pursue Jacob and attempt to murder him? Will Jacob ever return to Canaan? What will happen once he reaches Mesopotamia? Will he marry someone in Abraham's family and continue the promised line? The suspense is heightened by this picture: the *promised* son, Jacob, running for his life *away* from the *Promised* Land. How can this be, and how will it ever be resolved? Even if he does marry a suitable wife and returns to Canaan, how can the promises of Abraham be fulfilled in the life of someone so far removed from the *faith* of Abraham?

As Jacob goes off into the horizon (28:5), all of these questions beg for resolution.

Jacob's Dream (28:10–22)

We will not have to wait long for the answers. At "a certain place" on his way from Beersheba to Haran, Jacob has to stop for the night (28:10–11). Lonely and afraid, and on his own far from home, it must have been a harrowing experience. Customarily in the Old Testament, travelers forced to spend the night in a strange location were taken in by local residents (review Gn 19:1–3, and compare Jgs 19:11–21). It was ancient custom not to allow a visitor to brave the elements out of doors overnight (see especially Jgs 19:15, 17–20). Whether Jacob was unable to locate a friendly host, or unwilling to accept aid, the result was the same. He was alone, and forced to bed down under the stars.

Taking a stone and preparing a place to sleep, Jacob settles down for the night (28:11). He could not have anticipated what happened next. In a dream, he saw a ladder (more likely a stairway, with steps rather than rungs) connecting heaven and earth.[18] The stairway was a two-way street: angels were "ascending and descending on it" (v. 12). The significance of the angels is not explicit in the passage, but they were probably God's patrolling forces who had access to both heaven and earth—all of earth. Wherever Jacob roamed on his journeys, God's forces would be guarding and protecting him (see also God's statement in v. 15).[19] Until now, these were forces that Jacob had not considered. He had relied all his life on his own ability to manipulate and deceive. Now in this vulnerable moment in a dream from God, he is made aware that a larger design is at work in his life.

The central core of the passage is God's appearance in the dream and his pronouncement of the covenant promises of Abraham for Jacob (vv. 13–15). Here God affirms the threefold covenant promises of Abraham—land, descendants, and blessing: "I will give you and your descendants the land on which you are lying. . . . All peoples on earth will be blessed through you and your offspring." Similar words were still ringing in Jacob's ears, for his father had sent him on his journey with a reminder that he was the heir of "the blessing given to Abraham" (vv. 3–4). But this was different. It was one thing for Jacob's father to charge him with the significance of his relationship to God. This dream was an entirely different matter. Jacob's loneliness and dangerous vulnerability in the open spaces made him particularly receptive to God's message. Now it was time for him to decide what he really believed. No longer could he live on the strength of his parents' faith. It was time for the God of Abraham and Isaac to become the God of *Jacob* as well.

The covenant promises have a similar function in this narrative as in the previous Abrahamic narratives. As God's assurances of covenant promises to Abraham in Genesis 15 anticipated later events in Abraham's life (and the rest of the Bible), these assurances to Jacob point to the subsequent events in the Jacob narratives.[20] The circumstances of Jacob's life, narrated in the next several chapters of Genesis, fulfill the promises made here and illustrate once again that God is faithful to his Word.

Jacob had much to think about on his journey: the threat of Esau, the necessity of leaving home, the danger of traveling so far alone, uncertainty about what he would encounter in Mesopotamia, and whether he would ever be able to return to Canaan. God's concluding promise seemed tailored particularly for Jacob's needs: "I am with you and will watch over you wherever you go, and I will bring you back to this land. I will not leave you until I have done what I have promised you" (28:15). As you read the next several chapters of Genesis, remember that God's Word will prove true in your life also.

When Jacob woke up, he had several worshipful responses to the dream, all of which were appropriate. He acknowledged the Lord's presence in the place, which had been given no name in the narrative to this point. He erected a monument with the stone he had used as a pillow, anointed it with oil, and named the place Bethel, or "house of God" (vv. 16–19). The fear that Jacob experienced was a reverential fear from having been in God's presence, and was a new experience for Jacob (v. 17).

We might be tempted to read Jacob's vow with skepticism (vv. 20–22). Jacob vows that *if* God indeed protects him on his journeys, provides for his needs, and allows him to return to Canaan, *then* Yahweh will be Jacob's God. In addition, Jacob pledges to give a tithe, a full one-tenth of all his income, back to the Lord. If we suspect Jacob of collusion or trickery, we would hardly be far from the truth about his personality traits to this point. This looks like Jacob's pathetic attempt to manipulate God as he has so far been able to do to everyone else.

However, the nature of vows in the Old Testament makes it more likely that Jacob's vow was also an appropriate response to God's revelatory dream, if not a mature expression of faith.[21] Most vows are conditional statements uttered in a situation of distress. It is most likely that such a vow as this was a natural response of faith, in which Jacob pledged himself to worship Yahweh again once the divine promises were fulfilled. The remainder of the Jacob narrative shows how God fulfilled his promises, and Jacob's vow later in the narrative makes this interpretation preferable (see Gn 35:1–3, 14–15).

This was Jacob's first encounter with God. The faith of his parents had become his faith as well. His was not a mature faith like Abraham's, but nonetheless it was a new step for Jacob. The recent turn of events in his family life made it impossible for him to rely solely on his own ability to trick, lie, and steal. When God confronted him at Bethel, he grew up spiritually, choosing to take responsibility for his own relationship with God. The promises of God came in a dream, but Jacob's response came in his wakefulness. He found the world of the dream more convincing and attractive than his old world of fear, deception, and guilt. He resolved to embrace the reality of the dream.[22] This is an important lesson for all of us to learn. At some point in time, all of us must claim the great promises of God for ourselves, and step out in faith, making our own commitments to him. God has no grandchildren!

In the dream, God committed himself to the conniving runaway, just as he had once committed himself to Abraham (Gn 15). The stairway dream is a graphic audiovisual lesson for Jacob that God has come down to him and is with him on his journey. Heaven has come to earth. Indeed, the Bible repeats the refrain. God comes to other runaways as well. This in fact is God's defining feature—he comes to rebellious people to be with them and to save them. When finally he chose to become a person to seek and to save the lost, he was given the name "God with us" (Immanuel, Mt 1:23). Just as Jacob was forced to respond to God's coming, so must we.

Jacob and Laban (29–31)

Jacob was a new man. But his newfound faith could not remove the necessity of facing up to decisions he had made earlier in his life. It was still necessary to escape Esau and Canaan, and there was no choice but to continue on to Mesopotamia.

Jacob Marries the Daughters of Laban (29:1–30)

In a pattern we have witnessed before, the opening scene of this unit has the patriarch arriving safely in a foreign land, and meeting his future wife at a well (compare Gn 24). God's protection and guidance is as apparent with Jacob as it was with Abraham's servant who went to Mesopotamia to find a wife for Isaac. When Jacob met the beautiful Rachel, his cousin, he was overwhelmed with emotion (vv. 10–11). So far, the promises of the stairway dream were working.

Jacob seemed more than willing to attach himself to Laban's household (v. 14). But in meeting his uncle Laban, Jacob met a man who also knew a thing or two about trickery and manipulation himself. In fact, Jacob had met his match. Through Laban, he would drink deeply "of his own medicine of duplicity."[23]

Jacob fell hopelessly in love with Rachel. Since he had arrived in Mesopotamia empty-handed and could not afford the normal marriage present (a bride price given to the bride's family), he offered a very considerable part of his work capacity—seven years.[24] His love was so profound that even this heavy cost "seemed like only a few days to him because of his love for her" (v. 20).

But Laban outtricked the great trickster.

As Jacob deceived his father and cheated his brother, now he gets a dose of his own medicine from his uncle. At the wedding feast, Laban substituted the unlovely Leah, his first daughter, for Rachel. The next morning Jacob found himself married to Leah instead of his beloved Rachel. When he complained to his uncle about the deception, Laban explained it was customary that the elder daughter should marry first, and that he could still marry Rachel in a week's time, provided Jacob was willing to work an additional seven years. Jacob was trapped. He agrees to the terms, and finds himself now with two wives. His resentment of Laban and his favoritism for Rachel will lead to family discord that will plague him the rest of his life. In his old age, he favored Rachel's son, Joseph, so much that Leah's sons wanted to kill him, as we shall see (Gn 37:3–4, 18).

One might reasonably ask how Laban could possibly have pulled off such an astonishing deception. How could Jacob have been so wrong? Certainly the lateness of the hour in the wedding chamber and Leah's heavy bride's veil contributed to the ploy. But surely there was more to it than this! It seems likely that the wedding feast hosted by Laban was an intentional ploy to dull Jacob's senses with wine (29:22). The text also includes lexical hints that inebriation was part of the story.[25]

Jacob's Children (29:31–30:24)

This unit shows that God was faithful to accomplish his purposes, even through the deceitful actions of Laban and Jacob, and the jealous hatred of Jacob's wives. He had promised a great multitude of descendants to Abraham's grandson, Jacob. It would be through the unfortunate Leah and her maidservant that eight of the tribes of Israel would trace their descent.

Jacob's marriages were stormy from the start: "Leah was not loved . . . but Rachel was barren" (29:31). Both women wanted what the other had. Leah felt that having sons for Jacob would somehow earn his love, while Rachel was as desperate for children as Sarah had been before her. Giving birth degenerated into competition. Each wife gave Jacob her maidservant (Zilpah and Bilhah) in an effort to have more children than the other. Even though this practice was acceptable socially in the ancient Near East, it had caused problems in the patriarchal family before (Gn 16). Rachel's desperate deal for the mandrakes (a primitive drug thought to produce fertility) had an ironic result, since it failed to help her but resulted in more children for Leah (30:14–21). Ultimately, Rachel would also have a son, but not because of the man-

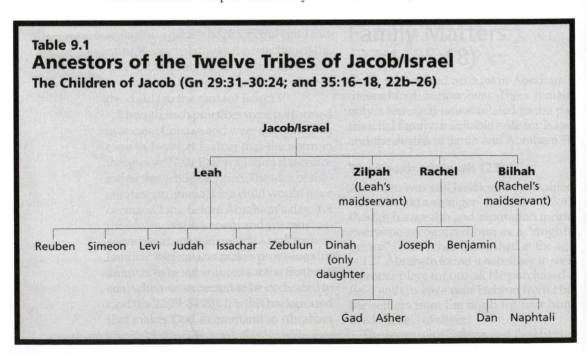

Table 9.1

Ancestors of the Twelve Tribes of Jacob/Israel

The Children of Jacob (Gn 29:31–30:24; and 35:16–18, 22b–26)

Jacob/Israel

Leah — Zilpah (Leah's maidservant) — Rachel — Bilhah (Rachel's maidservant)

Leah: Reuben, Simeon, Levi, Judah, Issachar, Zebulun, Dinah (only daughter)

Zilpah: Gad, Asher

Rachel: Joseph, Benjamin

Bilhah: Dan, Naphtali

Rachel's figurines may have included baked clay statuettes like these.

drakes: "Then God remembered Rachel; he listened to her and opened her womb" (30:22).

Through all the maneuvering and competition, God steadily fulfilled his promise of descendants for Abraham, Isaac, and Jacob. The birth and naming of Jacob's first eleven sons form the literary central point of an elaborate symmetrical structure in the Jacob narrative.[26] This is the turning point of the story, especially the birth of Joseph to Rachel (30:22–24). This was Jacob's purpose for living in Mesopotamia so long, though he may not have been fully aware of it. The children given to him by Leah, Rachel, and their maidservants will eventually become the twelve tribes of the nation Israel. In time, God will provide a Messiah for the world through Israel. From a human perspective we marvel at the rancor and bitterness that divide this family. Yet it is through this dysfunctional family that God's promises move forward in one giant step. From a divine perspective, God's grace is working in the lives of some very improbable subjects. We should be grateful that our salvation rests on the grace of God rather than on any human merit.

Jacob's Prosperity (30:25–43)

God blessed Jacob with children while he was in Mesopotamia. But he also blessed him by miraculously multiplying his share of Laban's flocks. His uncle, true to form, attempted to limit Jacob's success with the flock by removing all the spotted and speckled animals to a safe distance, making it unlikely that Jacob could increase his share. Jacob combined selective breeding with the superstitious beliefs of the time regarding animal husbandry. Miraculously, his share of the flock thrived and he became quite wealthy (v. 43). He no doubt owed his success more to God's grace than he realized.

Trouble with Laban (31)

Not only was Jacob surrounded by the bitter conflict between his wives, but he himself became embroiled in controversy with Laban. His success had led to jealousy and resentment (vv. 1–2), which suggested the time was ripe to return to Canaan. But Jacob was also a man on a divinely given mission, ever since the stairway dream of Bethel. Yahweh summoned Jacob in terms reminiscent of Abraham's initial call (v. 3; compare 12:1–2), and the time had clearly arrived to take leave of Laban's company.

What Were Laban's Household Gods (Gn 31:19)?

On the occasion of her quick departure from Mesopotamia to begin the journey to Canaan, Rachel stole her father's "household gods" *(těrā-pîm)*. Despite an enormous amount of scholarly attention given to these items, we still have unanswered questions about them. What exactly were the *(těrāpîm),* and why did Rachel steal them?[27]

Studies of the etymology of the word have not been conclusive. They are referred to simply as "gods" later in the chapter (vv. 30, 32). Comparison with other ancient Near Eastern cultures reveals that images of deities (usually figurines in human form) were sometimes thought to protect the family, and these may have been images of deceased ancestors. They were at times used for divining the will of the gods and for predicting the future.

But can any of these be behind Rachel's actions? Many have found a parallel in an Akkadian legal text from Nuzi, which is thought to reflect the social culture of northwestern Mesopotamia at that time.[28] In this case, possession of the family gods constituted a claim to the best inheritance portion, in which Rachel was guaranteeing her husband's financial future. But this interpretation has considerable problems, and has been generally discredited. More recently discovered texts from Emar (in Syria) have raised again the question of a link between possession of the family gods and the rights of inheritance. But these are also inconclusive.

We have some evidence that these figurines were viewed as amulets, or sources of protection and blessing—a sort of protective charm or good luck piece. In this case, they may have had little religious significance, nor were they legal and financial guarantees for Jacob's future. Rachel simply felt insecure about leaving home and following her husband and Leah, her rival sister, to a foreign land.

Was Rachel motivated by fear, piety, greed, or revenge? We may never know with certainty what the nature of these household gods were. But they were very important to Laban (31:30), and it seems probable that they continued to be a problem for Jacob until he purged them from his family before continuing on to Bethel (35:2).

It was time for Jacob's twenty-year sojourn to end. He had a vow to keep with God (at Bethel) and a brother to face at home.

Jacob Leaves Mesopotamia (31:1–21)

Jacob found it necessary to steal away surreptitiously, no doubt because twenty years had familiarized him with Laban's tactics. He knew his uncle would not willingly allow him to leave. Jacob's business was too important to Laban.

Rachel's theft of Laban's household gods *(těrāpîm)* has generated much scholarly speculation (v. 19). Whatever these items were, Rachel was probably trying to ensure good fortune for her trip to Canaan.

Laban Pursues Jacob (31:22–42)

Laban had been distracted while shearing the sheep, the busiest time of the year (v. 19). By the time he realized that Jacob had absconded, it was too late. But he gathered a sizable force and pursued Jacob and his family, overtaking them in Gilead, east of the Jordan River near the Promised Land. In the ensuing confrontation, Laban accused Jacob of stealing the household gods, about which Jacob knew nothing. He allowed Laban to search all his possessions, to no avail. Rachel coyly concealed the household gods from her father, and Jacob began a long diatribe in which he berated Laban for mistreating him all these years.

Jacob and Laban Make a Parting Covenant (31:43–55)

Laban's proposal to make a covenant or treaty must have surprised Jacob. He had departed in fear, but now Laban himself proposed peace. In a passage that illustrates ancient Near Eastern treaty making between equals, Laban and Jacob set up a stone monument, offered a sacrifice and

Study Questions

1. How does the birth narrative in Genesis 25 foreshadow the future relationship between Jacob and Esau?

2. Why does the biblical author say that Esau "despised his birthright"?

3. In what ways does Isaac prove a worthy successor to his father Abraham, both in his flaws and in his more admirable qualities?

4. How does the narrator reveal the guilt of all four characters in Genesis 27?

5. Why might it be appropriate to view Jacob's response to his dream as one of faith?

6. Describe two conflicts involving Jacob while he sojourned in Mesopotamia.

7. Explain the possible significance of the "household gods" of Genesis 31.

ate a celebratory meal together, gave appropriate names to the monument in their respective dialects (Laban's Aramaic name and Jacob's Hebrew), and declared the monument a witness of each man's commitment to peaceful nonaggression.

Jacob must have been more than willing to be free of the grasping and avaricious Laban. Now, nearly within view of the Promised Land, he certainly would have to deal with brother Esau. A pact of peaceful coexistence with Laban was infinitely better than leaving unfinished business back in Mesopotamia while he attempted to finish the business he had left behind twenty years before in Canaan. His very presence at the boundaries of the Promised Land must have reminded him of God's promises in the stairway dream of Bethel: "I am with you and will watch over you wherever you go, and I will bring you back to this land. I will not leave you until I have done what I have promised you" (28:15).

Would he really arrive safely in the land of promise with his new family of promise? And if so, what kind of reception would he receive from his estranged brother?

10 Jacob Struggles with God

Genesis 32:1–37:1

> Out of timber so crooked as that from which man is made nothing entirely straight can be carved.
>
> —Immanuel Kant, German philosopher (1724–1804)[1]

Supplemental Readings: Malachi 1:2–3, Hebrews 11:9, 20–21

Outline

- **Jacob Meets God, Jacob Meets Esau (32–33)**
  Jacob Prepares to Meet Esau (32:3–21)
  Jacob Meets God (32:22–32)
  Jacob Meets Esau (33)
- **The Violation of Dinah (34)**
- **Back to Bethel (35)**
- **Esau Epilogue (36)**

Objectives

After reading this chapter you should be able to

1. Given the fear Jacob had of his estranged brother, identify the means God used to reassure Jacob of divine protection.
2. Summarize the ways Jacob prepared for a confrontation with Esau, and the efforts he made to avoid conflict.
3. Specify the events involved in Jacob's encounter with God at Peniel and the change of character implied by the change of Jacob's name to Israel.
4. Compare the meeting of Jacob and Esau to Jacob's encounter with God.
5. Describe the events surrounding the violation of Dinah, emphasizing the command to avoid intermarriage with unbelievers, the less than noble actions by everyone involved, and the implied condemnation of Jacob for his role in the incident and his delay in the journey to Bethel.
6. Examine the response of Jacob to God's call to return to Bethel, including the purging of objects that might hinder them spiritually.
7. Describe God's appearance to Jacob upon his arrival at Bethel, the promises God made to him there, and the final events in the biblical account of Jacob.
8. Summarize the theological and literary significance of the five *tôlĕdôt* panels that form the basic structure of the patriarchal narratives.

So far we have little evidence that God has been able to carve anything entirely straight from this crooked timber, Jacob.

God has done many things for Jacob. He has granted Jacob his family's birthright and his father's blessing. God has miraculously protected Jacob and blessed him with abundant material wealth. He has given him a large family with many children, so important in that culture, and God has even restored peace to Jacob's relationship with Laban. Moreover, God has bestowed on Jacob the most important element of this entire Genesis narrative: the covenant promises.

But Jacob is still no Abraham. His response of faith to the stairway dream at Bethel (Gn 28) was a step in the right direction. But Jacob still has a long way to travel before he fulfills the vow he made there (vv. 20–22).

The next section of Genesis contains the rest of the Isaac tôlĕdôt (32:1–35:29, which is actually the Jacob narrative) and the Esau tôlĕdôt (36:1–37:1). The narrative recounts the experiences of Jacob and his family upon their return to the Promised Land.

Jacob Meets God, Jacob Meets Esau (32–33)

Jacob must have been greatly relieved to have settled the crisis with Laban at Gilead on the border of the Promised Land (ch. 31). Genesis 32–33 relates Jacob's return to Canaan. Given the fact that he had swindled his brother Esau twenty years before when he left Canaan, he could ill-afford to worry about two relatives holding grudges for separate reasons in different locations. With Laban appeased, he could now focus on the unresolved conflict at home in Canaan.

The last time Jacob had seen him, Esau was planning to kill him (27:41). Now that Jacob was returning to the Promised Land, the inevitable meeting with Esau loomed ahead. The anger of his estranged brother was a roadblock to Jacob's further growth. Geographically, he could have avoided meeting Esau on his way back to Bethel.

But spiritually, he had to be reconciled to his brother in order to reach Bethel, where he would fulfill his vows to God.[2]

In the brief paragraph between Genesis 31 and 32, the narrator tells us that Laban went his way, and Jacob went his (31:55–32:2).[3] But Jacob was not alone. After Laban's departure, Jacob was met by the "angels of God" at Mahanaim. Like the angels of the stairway dream of Genesis 28, the angels of this new vision were presumably intended to reassure Jacob of God's protective presence.[4] As the Bethel dream comforted Jacob when he departed Canaan, now the Mahanaim vision does so as he returns.

Jacob Prepares to Meet Esau (32:3–21)

In the hopes that Esau would receive him with open arms, Jacob sent messengers to Seir in southern Transjordan with the news of his return. Jacob's words were carefully chosen: "This is what you are to say to *my master* Esau . . . *your servant* Jacob says, . . . I am sending this message to *my lord*" (32:4–5). Though this sort of courtesy was common in the ancient Orient, such humility extended to one's twin brother is remarkable. The elaborate message is a tacit admission of guilt and an implied renunciation of the privileges Jacob filched from his brother.[5] His news that he has acquired cattle, donkeys, sheep, goats, and servants implies they are Esau's for the taking. Jacob's servile tone disavows God's prenatal pronouncement to Rebekah about which twin would rule the other (25:23), and Isaac's blessing to Esau, which was irrevocable in that culture (27:40). Jacob was placing himself at Esau's disposal, because he feared the worst.

The news brought back by the messengers was *not* reassuring. Esau was on his way to meet Jacob with a small personal army in tow, four hundred men. It was now clear that empty apologies would not suffice, and Esau's approaching troops presented Jacob with the greatest crisis of his life. He resorted to desperate means to win his brother over. First he prepared for the worst by dividing his family and property into two groups in a desperate attempt to save at least one group. Then he did what most of us do in extreme crises:

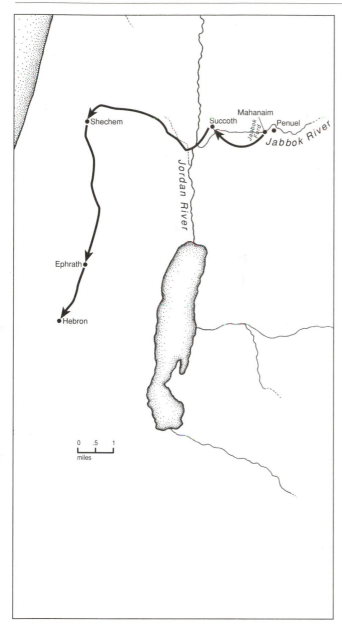

Jacob's travels in Palestine.

With each group of animals, he instructed his messengers to tell Esau "your servant Jacob" is coming behind us. Rather than a bribe, we should accept Jacob's own words as explanation of the gift: "I will pacify him with these gifts . . . perhaps he will receive me" (v. 20). Perhaps the repetition of Jacob's name would soften Esau's response. It would be easy to criticize Jacob for a lack of faith after so pious a prayer. But it seems more likely the narrator invites us to see Jacob as afraid and confused, with perhaps a measure of doubt mixed in with his faith."[7]

Jacob Meets God (32:22–32)

Jacob was paralyzed at the thought of meeting Esau. He had expended his energy in elaborate preparations for the impending encounter with his brother. But instead, he had this encounter with God, for which he was completely unprepared.[8]

Jacob's bizarre encounter with God at Peniel is the central episode in the description of Jacob's return to Canaan. It is framed literarily by his preparation to meet Esau (32:3–21) and the meeting with Esau itself (33:1–20). The central feature of this central episode is Jacob's name change to Israel. As elsewhere in the Bible, midlife name changes represent a change of character (Abram to Abraham, Simon to Peter). This was God's answer to the problem of Jacob's duplicitous and grasping tendencies. God was in the circumstances and affairs of Jacob's life, working to transform his character. The transformation was accompanied by the important blessing of God.

Jacob was apparently unable to sleep (he had intended to lodge that night in the camp, 32:21). He rose during the night, took his family, and embarked on a dangerous night-crossing of the river Jabbok, an east-to-west tributary of the Jordan approximately twenty-five miles north of the Dead Sea (see map III.10.1). Though we cannot be certain, it appears Jacob returned to the northern bank of the Jabbok after his family was safely across.[9] In any event, now he is inexorably alone (32:24). The solitude was God's timing for confrontation. "When everything is at stake a night of prayer is no burden, but rather a life-line."[10]

The text says simply, "a man wrestled with him till daybreak" (32:24b). The iden-

he prayed. In what is one of the great prayers of Genesis (32:9–12), Jacob seems clearly focused on his only hope of survival: "Save me, I pray, from the hand of my brother Esau." God's promises at Bethel to bless Jacob and be with him (ch. 28) are the sure foundation for Jacob's petition, as is evident in his words "But you have said . . ." (32:12).[6]

Not satisfied with prayer alone, Jacob prepares a substantial gift for Esau, consisting of a farmer's delight, which he sent to him in waves: goats, lambs, rams, camels, cows, and donkeys (vv. 13–21).

tity of the "man" is not clear at first. We as readers are left in the darkness of the night encounter, like Jacob who wrestles with his visitor until daybreak. But at dawn, Jacob prevailed over the man, who nevertheless maimed Jacob permanently. Jacob, perhaps suspecting that his was no mere human assailant, refuses to let go of the man without a blessing. The man responded with a question, "What is your name?" Jacob's answer is a confession, since he is admitting, as Esau observed years before, that he is rightly named (27:36). He has been a deceiving trickster from birth, and his current predicament with Esau is the result. The mysterious night visitor changed Jacob's name to Israel, "God fights / rules," because, he says, "you have striven with God and with humans, and have prevailed" (32:28).

Now convinced that he wrestles with no mere human, Jacob also asks for his name. Certain ancient religions considered possession of a person's name important as a means of gaining a power advantage, so the visitor refused. Instead, "he blessed him there" (32:29b). Without realizing it completely, this was what Jacob wanted and needed. He had acquired his father's blessing by deceit and treachery. Now wracked with fear at Esau's revenge, his wrestling turned to desperate determination, and he came away crippled, blessed, and renamed Israel. This time the blessing was rightfully acquired. In commemoration of this momentous event, he named the place Peniel, or "face of God," for he had seen the face of God and survived (32:30).

The struggle brought to a climactic conclusion the "battling and groping of a lifetime."[11] Jacob learned that it was with God he had been struggling all his life, not Esau in Canaan or Laban in Mesopotamia. He also learned that the true and best blessing results from submission to God's will, rather than from craftily wrenching it away from one's brother. Finally he learned that in God's economy strength comes through weakness, which prepared him to meet Esau.

Jacob Meets Esau (33)

The Peniel episode disrupts the flow of the narrative. It comes between Jacob's preparation to meet Esau and the meeting itself. But at the same time, Jacob's wrestling with God has prepared the way for his reunion with Esau, and therefore heightened the effect of one of the most touching reunions of the Bible.

Several features of the narrative suggest that Jacob is a new man after the Peniel experience.[12] When he saw his brother approaching, Jacob divided his family up again, as he had done before (32:7–8; 33:1–2). But this time there appears to be no military strategy involved, only a reverse order of his affection for his wives: concubines, Leah, and Rachel. The pre-Peniel Jacob was careful to remain behind his divided goods (32:17–21), whereas the post-Peniel Jacob "went on ahead" of his family to meet Esau (33:3). The degree of humility apparent in his formal greeting (33:3) and his insistence on repaying the "blessing" he had stolen from Esau (33:11) show to what degree Jacob is a different man.[13] Jacob has truly become Israel, leading one scholar to call this episode "Jacob at the Jabbok, Israel at Peniel."[14]

The great surprise (and relief!) of the narrative is that Esau too is a different man than he was twenty years before. Whereas he had wanted nothing but revenge against Jacob (27:41), now he runs anxiously to welcome his brother home (33:4). Apparently the four hundred men were not a military squadron sent to attack Jacob, but corps offered to protect Jacob the rest of the way home. The change in Esau is most apparent in the contrast between the way the brothers approached each other: Jacob "bowed down to the ground seven times," while Esau "ran to meet Jacob and embraced him; he threw his arms around his neck and kissed him" (33:3–4).[15] God had obviously been working in Esau's heart as well, and he was eager to be reconciled to his brother.

Jacob is so relieved to be forgiven and reconciled to his brother that he associates this meeting with Esau to his meeting with God in Genesis 32. He tells Esau, "to see your face is like seeing the face of God, now that you have received me favorably," in an obvious reference to Peniel (33:10). Just as Jacob saw the face of God in chapter 32 and yet lived, so now he has seen the face of his brother and survived.

After this cheerful reunion, the brothers part ways, Esau going back to Seir and Jacob traveling to the interior of the Promised Land (33:16–20). At Shechem, Jacob settled near the city, bought a plot of ground, and built an altar for worship (see map III.10.1). It was appropriate that Jacob worshiped God at Shechem, for this is where God first appeared to Abraham when he entered Canaan, and Abraham had built his own altar there (12:6–7). And, like Abraham, Jacob purchased a plot of ground in the land promised ultimately to belong to his descendants. The name of the altar, *El-Elohe-Israel*, "God is the God of Israel," acknowledges that Jacob has now come to appreciate fully the significance of that dark night at the Jabbok ford when his name was changed to Israel. The God of Abraham, the God of Isaac, has now, at long last, become the God of Israel.

What a wonderful ending this would have been for the Jacob narrative! Unfortunately the reference to Shechem is also a prelude to the next chapter.

The Violation of Dinah (34)

Sometimes it is difficult to understand why certain episodes were recorded in the Bible. The ravishing of Dinah is one of those horrible events that seems to have no redeeming value, and it is unclear what the narrator wants us to get from the account. Yet, as we shall see, it plays a fascinating role in the context of Genesis.

Dinah was the daughter of Leah, and therefore a member of the less appreciated portion of Jacob's family. Jacob had never loved Leah as much as he did Rachel (29:30), and he eventually favored Rachel's children, Joseph and Benjamin, more than those of Leah (review the family of Jacob in p. 126 above). Such favoritism had plagued the family since the days when Isaac and Rebekah showed unfair preferences for Jacob and Esau (25:28), and preferential treatment continued to be the source of considerable trouble throughout the rest of Genesis.

The hazards of intermarriage with the pagan Canaanites are never far from the surface of the narratives of Genesis. Abra-

ham had been concerned that Isaac might marry outside the patriarchal family, like Ishmael had done (21:21; 24:3–4), and Esau had disappointed his parents with marriages to unbelieving Hittites (26:34–35; 27:46; 28:8). The danger of Jacob's prolonged stay at Shechem, so near to his ultimate destination, Bethel, was at the very least unwise.

Dinah's new friends in Canaan got her in trouble. Too close an association with the inhabitants of the city made her vulnerable to the local prince, whose name was Shechem. Whether this was rape or seduction is not clear in the text, but the result is the same: "he took her and violated her" (34:2).

Jacob's response reveals indifference toward Dinah and indecisiveness: "he kept quiet about it" until Dinah's brothers came home from the fields (v. 5). If Jacob seemed reticent, the other children of Leah were openly enraged by Shechem's actions. Instead of Jacob taking charge in what was clearly a dangerous situation, he allowed Dinah's brothers to negotiate with the royal family of Shechem.

The proposed marriage was clearly not acceptable to Dinah's brothers. Yet they used the possibility of an imminent wedding as a ruse to deceive the inhabitants of Shechem (v. 13). They feigned acceptance of Shechem's request for marriage, with one condition: all the males of the city must agree to become circumcised like the sons of Israel. While the men of the city were incapacitated by the surgery, Simeon and Levi took advantage of them and slaughtered them. It is a pitiable illustration of the entire episode that God's great sign of his covenant with Abraham, circumcision (17:9–14), became a ploy on the part of the sons of Jacob to take revenge against the Shechemites.

Shechem is the only character the narrator thoroughly condemns, though even he is not completely rotten and without redeeming features (34:3, 19). The sad fact is no one in the narrative acts nobly. Dinah was at best naive and careless; her brothers, brutal and blood-thirsty. Simeon and Levi may have been motivated by justice, but they lied and acted imprudently in administering it.

The entire account is also a subtle condemnation of Jacob. He has delayed in his

The Bible and Mixed Marriages

The actions of Simeon and Levi in avenging their sister also highlight the Old Testament's stance on another issue: intermarriage with the unbelieving Canaanites. This is partly behind their statement, "We can't do such a thing; we can't give our sister to a man who is not circumcised" (34:14). The patriarchs understood that they were set apart from the surrounding nations, and that intermarriage would be unacceptable. The sons of promise (Isaac and Jacob) returned to the patriarchal homeland to find wives there, while sons of the non-elect line (Ishmael and Esau) married local women.

The Old Testament prohibits intermarriage with non-Israelites (Dt 7:3). The author of the Book of Kings goes to great lengths to show that Solomon's foreign wives led to his ultimate ruin (1 Kgs 11:1–6). Much later, Ezra and Nehemiah even used divorce as a means of reversing the vitiating national consequences of mixed marriages (Ezr 9–10 and Neh 13:23–27).

Yet in all of this, the overarching issue is religious faithfulness. When Israel was about to cross the Jordan and take possession of Canaan, the prohibition against mixed marriages focused on the problem of apostasy. The Lord warned that Canaanite wives "will turn your sons away from following me to serve other gods, and the LORD's anger will burn against you and will quickly destroy you" (Dt 7:4). Solomon became the tragic proof that this warning was necessary.

And yet there could be exceptions. Ruth the Moabitess, for example, became the wife of a prominent Bethlehemite, and she ultimately played an important role in salvation history. She became the great-ancestress of both David and Jesus (Ru 4:16–22; Mt 1:5). But Ruth had radically attached herself to the Israelite people, and more important, to the Israelite God, as her classic statement to Naomi shows: "Your people will be my people and your God my God" (Ru 1:16). Intermarriage was clearly not a racial issue in the Old Testament. Rather, the concern was the reality that marriage to someone with radically different commitments and convictions makes it intensely difficult to be faithful to God over the long haul. In fact, Israelite experience was that it was nearly impossible to be true to God while being married to a pagan.

This should never become a racial issue. It appeared to be racial in the Old Testament only because each racial group normally consisted of its own nation and religion. But in our multicultural, pluralistic environment, interracial marriages are not the issue. Rather, the New Testament is clear that marriage to unbelievers is the issue. The apostle Paul's words to the Corinthians stand as a warning that binding relationships with unbelievers result in compromise of one's relationship with God (2 Cor 6:14–16). Modern Christians should not condemn interracial marriages, but should consistently avoid interfaith marriages.

journey to Bethel, presumably because of the tempting benefits of trade with the Shechemites (34:10). His favoritism for the children of Leah leads to equivocation and evasion when Leah's daughter is abused. Rather than react strongly and decisively, he hesitated and allowed his overzealous sons to take charge. Jacob's indifference to Dinah's molestation is in stark contrast to his affection for Rachel's sons, Joseph and Benjamin, later in the Genesis story.[16] Likewise after the awful deed was done, Jacob despised Simeon and Levi, not because of their harsh judgment, their de-ception, or their abuse of the sacred rite of circumcision, but because the warlike act had potentially negative repercussions for him. Notice the pronouns in his rebuke of them: "You have brought trouble on *me* by making *me* a stench to the . . . people living in this land. We are few in number, and if they join forces against *me* and attack *me, I* and *my* household will be destroyed" (34:30). Simeon and Levi may have been zealous to a fault, but at least their concern was for Dinah as a sister, implying that Jacob had not cared for her as a daughter.[17]

theophany

The failure on the part of Jacob is evident when read in contrast with Genesis 32–33.[18] There Jacob had agonized and wrestled with God, coming away a new man. He had been quickly and humbly reconciled to his brother, and triumphantly reentered the Promised Land. But here once again he is wracked with fear and apprehension. And now ill-will had entered his family again, this time with his own children instead of his brother. He may have limped away from Peniel as "Israel," but this episode illustrates there remained features of the old "Jacob."

Back to Bethel (35)

The story of Jacob has been one of struggles, struggles between Jacob and Esau, between Jacob and Laban, and between Jacob and God. At long last, Jacob returns to Bethel to find peace with God, though peace with his family remained elusive.

Genesis 34 had ended on a note of fear; Jacob was terrified that the neighboring Canaanites would seek revenge for the Shechem massacre (v. 30). But God's command to go back to Bethel was a subtle reminder that he would protect Jacob. His first encounter with God was at Bethel (review Gn 28) when he was fleeing Esau's sword. God had assured him that he would go with Jacob and protect him on his journeys. Jacob had in effect vowed to return to Bethel and worship God there again, provided God faithfully kept his Word.

The sound of God's command to return to Bethel has a familiar ring. The imperatives "Arise, go up to Bethel!" are similar to those Rebekah and Isaac used to begin the story when they told him to run from Canaan and go to Laban in Mesopotamia: "Arise, flee . . . ," and "Arise, go . . ." (27:43; 28:2, NKJV). Furthermore, God's command to Jacob has parallels with the initial call of Abraham to begin his great walk of faith (12:1), and with the charge to go to Moriah to offer up Isaac as a sacrifice (22:2). With such an introduction, this final chapter on Jacob rounds off and finishes the Jacob cycle and places him alongside his grandfather Abraham as the rightful heir of the patriarchal promises.

In this instance, Jacob was as quick to obey as Abraham had been (12:4; 22:3). He purged his family of "foreign gods" and instructed them to cleanse themselves because of their defilement by war with Shechem (35:2–5). The exact nature of the "foreign gods" is unclear. They may long have been family possessions or recently acquired booty from the Shechem massacre (34:27–29). Whatever their origin, they were probably similar to good-luck charms, suggested also by the reference to earrings used sometimes as religious trinkets to ward off evil. Jacob's family took decisive action to remove anything that might stand in their way of a deeper relationship with God. Their burial beneath the oak at Shechem ridicules these cultic objects as worthless and pathetic items that are really no gods at all.[19] Indeed, anything that hinders us on our journey to spiritual maturity is useless, no matter how valuable it appears to the world (Heb 12:1).

So Jacob and his family returned to Bethel, where he fulfilled his vow made more than two decades earlier (28:20–22). The altar he built there (El Bethel, "God of Bethel," 35:6–8) links the end of Jacob's journey with its beginning, the stairway dream in which God first revealed himself to Jacob.[20] This is confirmation of that encounter. Jacob understands that God has been with him on his journeys and that whatever success he has seen is due to the gracious hand of God.

Like his first night in Bethel those many years ago, God appears to Jacob again (35:9–15). This **theophany** represents the strongest statement of the patriarchal promises Jacob ever received. God began by reminding Jacob of his Peniel experience. He is no longer the cheating trickster Jacob; he is now Israel. Such reaffirmation was necessary after the terrible episode at Shechem. God revealed himself as El Shaddai, God Almighty, to Jacob, as he had to Abraham (17:1). This patriarchal name emphasized God's invincible power and faithfulness to fulfill his promises. And indeed, God had been faithful! Jacob was now safely back in Canaan, and he had acquired enormous blessings.

But the promises of protection and return are short-sighted. God's vision for Jacob was much broader and deeper than Jacob's immediate concern to be safe and

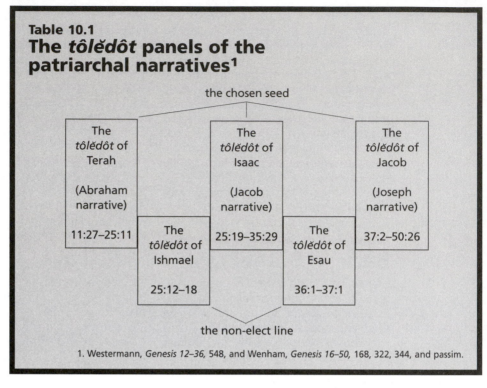

Table 10.1
The *tôlĕdôt* panels of the patriarchal narratives[1]

the chosen seed

| The *tôlĕdôt* of Terah (Abraham narrative) 11:27–25:11 | The *tôlĕdôt* of Ishmael 25:12–18 | The *tôlĕdôt* of Isaac (Jacob narrative) 25:19–35:29 | The *tôlĕdôt* of Esau 36:1–37:1 | The *tôlĕdôt* of Jacob (Joseph narrative) 37:2–50:26 |

the non-elect line

1. Westermann, *Genesis 12–36*, 548, and Wenham, *Genesis 16–50*, 168, 322, 344, and passim.

well-established in Canaan. The long-range promises given at the stairway dream are repeated here for Jacob: numerous descendants and land (compare 28:13–14 with 35:11–12). They would be hundreds of years in the making, and far beyond Jacob's expectations. In fact, this version of the patriarchal promises contains an element unheard since the days of Abraham: kings will come from Jacob's line (17:6, 16). This promise foreshadows the coming Messiah, the centerpiece in God's ultimate plan of salvation.[21]

The remaining sections of Genesis 35 contain various details intended to round off the story of Jacob (vv. 16–29). Here we read of the birth of Benjamin, the tragic death of Rachel, the death of Isaac, and Reuben's incest with Bilhah. There is also a list of the twelve sons of Jacob, complete now that Benjamin has been born. This collection of miscellaneous items with its account of two deaths (Rachel and Isaac) points backward into the patriarchal history. But the birth of Benjamin also points forward to the Joseph narrative (Gn 37–50), and ultimately to the fuller story of the nation Israel. As such, Genesis 35 serves as a transition from the patriarchal period to the beginnings of the people Israel.[22]

Esau Epilogue (36)

The *tôlĕdôt*-genealogy of Esau is recorded in Genesis 36 (more precisely, 36:1–37:1). This chapter explains how the descendants of Esau came to live in Mount Seir rather than Canaan proper (see map on page 81). Like his brother, Jacob, Esau grew into a great nation, the Edomites, inhabiting the area south and east of the Dead Sea. Thus this passage is the fulfillment of the divine oracle and the patriarchal blessing in Genesis 25:23 and 27:39–40. It also explains the future relationship between the nations Israel and Edom. This relationship was often hostile, though the sense of kinship was always just below the surface (Dt 23:7; Ob 10–12).

It is now clear that the five *tôlĕdôt* panels of the patriarchal narratives have a carefully crafted structure. After the death of Abraham was recorded (25:7–11), the genealogy of his elder son, Ishmael was given (25:12–18). The report of Isaac's death (35:27–29) has the same pattern, being followed by the genealogy of Esau (chap. 36). In both cases the genealogies serve as connecting links, holding together narratives in which one generation gives

Study Questions

1. Chronicle the events leading up to the meeting between Jacob and Esau. How did Jacob plan to appease his brother? How did his plans change following his encounter with God?

2. Explain the significance of the changing of Jacob's name.

3. How does Jacob's encounter with God prepare him to meet Esau?

4. Why was intermarriage unacceptable for the patriarchs? What sorts of intermarriages are Christians warned against, and why?

5. How is subtle condemnation of all of the main characters sprinkled throughout the account of Dinah's rape and the ensuing slaughter of the Shechemites?

6. Explain the carefully crafted structure of the five *tôlĕdôt* panels of the patriarchal narratives.

7. What can we as modern believers learn about the promises of God from the biblical account of Jacob?

Key Term

theophany

way to the next.[23] Thus the non-elect lines of Ishmael and Esau alternate neatly with the more complete family histories of the chosen seed: Terah's *tôlĕdôt*, which is the narrative of Abraham; Isaac's, which is the Jacob narrative; and Jacob's, which is the Joseph narrative.

The author has intentionally associated the careers of Abraham, Jacob, and Joseph in this way to highlight their role in salvation history. And, as we have come to expect in Genesis, the *tôlĕdôt* phrase introduces a new important step in the story by, in this case, covering briefly the ancillary branch of the family and then placing it aside before continuing with the main storyline.[24]

The role of Esau's foreign wives has been accented (36:2–5) in order to emphasize that Esau stepped outside the divine patriarchal promises. His genealogy also includes the detail that his descendants, like those of Ishmael before him, settled outside the land of promise (36:6–8; and compare 25:18). Having thus tied off the non-elect line of Esau, the narrator is now prepared to follow the promises of God through the descendants of Jacob, which he will do in the last major unit of Genesis, the Joseph narrative.

Part

4

Encountering Joseph: God's Model Servant

Genesis 37–50

The Lord was with Joseph, and showed him steadfast love.

—Gn 39:21

11 Joseph in Egypt

Genesis 37:2–41:57

Seek first his kingdom and
his righteousness, and all
these things will be given
to you as well.

—Jesus, Mt 6:33

Outline

- **The Context of the Joseph Narrative**
  Contrast between Esau and Jacob
  What Is Different about the Joseph Narrative?
  What Is the Same about the Joseph Narrative?
- **Joseph and His Brothers (37)**
  A Tale of Two Dreams (37:2–11)
  Joseph in the Pit (37:12–24)
  Joseph in Potiphar's House (37:25–36)
- **The Judah Interlude (38)**
  Judah and Tamar (38:1–30)
  The Place of Genesis 38
- **Joseph's Rise over Egypt (39–41)**
  Joseph in Charge of Potiphar's House (39)
  Pharaoh's Cupbearer and Baker (40)
  Pharaoh's Dreams (41)

Objectives

After reading this chapter you should be able to

1. Describe how God provides help during times of injustice and need, and uses moments of difficulty to produce growth, as exemplified by Joseph's slavery and imprisonment.
2. Recognize that the Joseph story is the second of a two-part Jacob narrative and it is about Jacob's family in general.
3. Identify the characteristics of Genesis 37–50 that make these chapters distinctive from the rest of Genesis, as well as characteristics that connect them with the first thirty-six chapters.
4. Summarize the source and results of favoritism shown by Jacob toward Joseph, and the intensification of these consequences due to Joseph's dreams and coat.
5. Recount the events leading to Joseph being sold into slavery and taken to Egypt.
6. Explain the significance of the Judah interlude in Genesis 38, including the idea that one sin tends to lead to others, that God accomplishes his purposes and changes individuals's character, and that the interlude contributes to literary suspense and contrast.
7. Trace the rise in Joseph's political power, recognizing the symmetry and other literary components in these chapters.
8. Contrast the Egyptian worldview with the perspective presented in the dream interpretation offered by Joseph.

Have you ever been tempted to care only about your own selfish interests at someone else's expense? You may be especially vulnerable whenever things seem impossibly set against you. If so, you will benefit greatly from reading the next section of Genesis.

In this chapter, you will read about Joseph and how he was shamefully treated by his own brothers and unfairly sold into slavery. Then he was slandered against and unjustly thrown into prison, where we was forgotten and left to waste away the best years of his life.

Through it all, the faithful young Joseph sought to do and be only what was right. This great section of the Scripture teaches us that God blesses those who seek first his lordship in their lives above everything else, including personal comfort, promotion, or safety. The great statement of Jesus about seeking God's kingdom and righteousness above all is no guarantee that we will be successful, the way Joseph eventually was. But Matthew 6 is referring to our *needs* (what we eat, what we wear, what will become of us). Joseph illustrates how those who are faithful to God have no cause for worry, even when all appears lost.

It is not as though these terrible events happened to Joseph within a relatively brief number of years, after which he was relieved of all these injustices. Rather, this took place over a great passage of time, and it appeared as though there would be no retribution or reversal of circumstances. Yet God provided for Joseph in the midst of the most difficult circumstances imaginable. Not only did he provide personally for Joseph, but, more important, God worked through and in the horrible circumstances of his life to preserve the nation Israel. This account explains how the children of Jacob came to be dwelling in Egypt instead of in the Promised Land. As such, this is the prelude to the story of redemption outlined in the Book of Exodus. The plagues and deliverance of the Israelites from bondage, the crossing of the Red Sea, and the Sinai covenant combine to form the central theme of Old Testament theology. It is the Joseph narrative that sets the stage for that drama.

The Context of the Joseph Narrative

In some ways the Joseph narrative is a continuation of the Jacob cycle. It can even be argued that the entire second half of Genesis (specifically, 25:19–50:26) is really about Jacob and his family.[1] His birth narrative is recorded at the beginning of this large unit and his burial at its conclusion (50:14). In this sense, Genesis 37–50 is actually part 2 of a two-part Jacob narrative. The author's concern in this last *tôlĕdôt* section of the book ("This is the account of Jacob," 37:2) is to narrate the history of the whole family of Jacob, not just Joseph. The leading figures are the sons, Judah and Joseph, who will eventually become the leading tribes of the future nation of Israel (as we will see in ch. 49).

Contrast between Esau and Jacob

The *tôlĕdôt* of Esau was included in Genesis 36, and explained how the descendants of Esau came to live in Mount Seir (see map on page 81). He grew into a great nation, the Edomites, who inhabited the area south and east of the Dead Sea. By contrast, the *tôlĕdôt* of Jacob, beginning here in Genesis 37:2, relates how Jacob's descendants had to go down to Egypt and eventually become enslaved by the Egyptians. From this point on, the biblical storyline will be devoted to the children of Jacob, the Israelites. The contrasting portrait of Jacob and Esau is part of the narrator's way of dispensing with the nonelect line briefly before continuing with the details of the chosen seed (see table 10.1, above).

What Is Different about the Joseph Narrative?

As you turn now to the last major section of Genesis, you encounter some of the best prose ever written. Scholars often comment not only on the author's masterful use of characterization and suspenseful drama, but on the larger overarching structure of the Joseph narrative.[2] The account is a carefully constructed unity more so than any other you have encountered in Genesis. This is not a negative reflection on the Book of Genesis as a whole, which is obviously edited carefully and well written. But the Joseph narrative in particular is noted for its literary artistry.

Genesis 37–50 is unique in other ways as well. Unlike the rest of Genesis, it can be said that the account of Joseph and his brothers is cast in a "secular" mold.[3] In other words, the miraculous or supernatural elements do not play as conspicuous a role as in the other patriarchal narratives. It was not unusual for God to appear to Abraham or Jacob, and to communicate directly through divine speech, or for God to appear in the form of a human being, and in Jacob's case, even wrestle with him physically. In earlier chapters of Genesis, God would occasionally intervene directly on behalf of the patriarchs, granting conception to their wives and fertility to their flocks or miraculously delivering them from peril. Here there are few such direct interventions, and God does not appear before Joseph to communicate with him through speech as he did frequently with Abraham.

This is certainly not to imply that the narrative is a secular novel in which the author gave little thought to God's role in the events. On the contrary, the subtle irony of the narrative is powerful testimony to the sovereignty and guidance of God, as we shall see. But this unit is clearly unique in its more subtle theological message. Even the use of dreams as a means of divine revelation, which is obviously central in the Genesis 37–45, is much more subtle and opaque than in Genesis 28, for example. So the Joseph narrative is unique in the Book of Genesis in its literary style and theological themes.

What Is the Same about the Joseph Narrative?

Despite the obvious uniqueness of the Joseph narrative, it also contains unmistakable links to the preceding patriarchal narratives. In fact, to miss these important connections with Genesis 12–36 would be to completely misread the story of Joseph.

On the surface, there are many ways in which the Joseph narrative is a continuation of the patriarchal stories. The characters involved have all been introduced in the earlier patriarchal stories, the narrator now picking up on the lives of the twelve

sons of Jacob. The nature of their lives as small-cattle nomads, constantly threatened by famine, is the same as their ancestors in Genesis 12–36. Details of the narrative also center on conflicts between members of the family, especially between brothers.[4] It seems obvious that the Joseph narrative is conscious of its roots in the earlier patriarchal accounts.

But beyond the surface-level connections, the Joseph narrative continues and develops the main themes of the patriarchal narratives (and indeed of the Pentateuch in general) by showing the gradual fulfillment of the promises made to Abraham in Genesis 12:1–3.[5] At the close of the narrative, the promises are clearly in process of fulfillment, and Abraham's descendants are growing in number and influence, even if still living in a foreign land. Furthermore, God is using them to bless the nations as he promised in Genesis 12:2–3 and elsewhere. Joseph's intervention in the affairs of Egypt to plan for the seven years of famine saved the lives of many peoples far beyond the borders of Egypt itself (41:57). This was all part of God's plan for the covenant people, who were descended from the patriarchs (50:20). So we must read the Joseph narrative in the light of the total patriarchal storyline.

Joseph and His Brothers (37)

The Joseph narrative is a masterfully told story of betrayal, suspense, and intrigue. But more than that, it illustrates how God is at work in the lives of those who trust him, and that even those experiences that are painful are not without redemptive value when they are entrusted to God's sovereign guidance. Read Genesis 37 as though you did not know the outcome. Put yourself in Joseph's position. This chapter relates how he was captured by his brothers and sold into slavery in Egypt.

A Tale of Two Dreams (37:2–11)

The opening paragraphs of the narrative set the stage by describing the internal strife of the patriarchal family. The narrator begins with the unfortunate relationship between Joseph and his half-brothers, and the even more unfortunate favoritism Jacob showed Joseph, the first-born son of his beloved Rachel (Gn 30:24). Without elaborating on the details, the narrator simply explains that Joseph had delivered a negative report on the activities of his half-brothers to their father (37:2).

We know from the terrible events at Shechem (review Gn 34) that Jacob's favoritism for Rachel over Leah, Bilhah, and Zilpah had continued with their children (review the family of Jacob in table III.9.1, above). He seemed indifferent when Dinah, his daughter by Leah, was sexually violated. When his sons by Leah took bloody revenge on Dinah's behalf, Jacob despised them for it. Now here the text states bluntly, "Israel loved Joseph more than any of his other sons," (37:3) and he apparently made no attempt to hide the favoritism. He gave Joseph a richly ornamented robe, which was probably a longer robe with more striking colors than normally worn, and may have been the type of robe more commonly reserved for royalty than for a seventeen-year-old shepherd boy.[6] The favoritism that had plagued the patriarchal family since the days when Isaac and Rebekah showed unfair preferences for Jacob and Esau (25:28) obviously continued to be the source of considerable trouble. Jealousy and sibling rivalry continued to characterize the patriarchal story.

A bad situation is made unbearable by Joseph's two dreams, and his unwise decision to tell his dreams to his family (37:5–11). The dreams portray a royal setting in which the entire family pays homage as subjects to Joseph, a scene fulfilled in Egypt (42:6; 43:26; 44:14). First, the agricultural setting portrays the sheaves of his brothers bowing down to his sheaf (vv. 5–7). Then, in the astral scene, the sun and moon representing his parents, and the eleven stars obviously representing his brothers, all bowed down to Joseph (vv. 8–9).

The dreams only intensify the hatred Joseph's brothers felt for him. This opening paragraph of the Joseph narrative is marked by the recurring phrase "they hated him" (vv. 4, 5, 8). The phrase is further modified by the observation that his brothers were unable to speak kindly to him (vv. 4, 5). The dreams, which he naively told them, only intensified their feelings against him (v. 8). Their bitter hatred of Joseph grew unchecked until their jealousy made the coming catastrophe unavoidable: "His brothers were jealous of him" (v. 11). Furthermore, the paragraph implies the problem with Joseph was contagious. In verse 2b, there appear to be only four brothers involved. In verse 4, his other brothers are implied, and in verse 10, even his father rebukes him, however mild the rebuke seems.[7] Clearly this was a family headed for disaster.

Joseph in the Pit (37:12–24)

Not recognizing the imminent danger, Jacob sends Joseph out to check on the progress of his brothers. They were grazing flocks some fifty miles away in Shechem. Upon arriving in Shechem, the unsuspecting Joseph is unable to locate his brothers. When the text portrays him "wandering around in the fields" (v. 15), Joseph seems like a young and helpless child in need of parental guidance. The suspense builds as Joseph learns his brothers have moved on, even farther from his father's protection. An unidentified stranger ("a certain man," NKJV) informs Joseph that his brothers have moved on to Dothan, another fourteen miles farther north.

There is a scene shift at verse 18, when Joseph reaches his brothers. Suddenly the narrative is given from the brothers' perspective. As he drew near to them, his brothers saw Joseph from a distance. We know from later in the narrative that Joseph was wearing his kingly robe on this journey (v. 23), and the sight of their younger brother arriving in that infuriating cloak with the assignment of taking back a report to their father was too much for them to bear. Before he arrives, they plot to murder him. But Reuben, for reasons that are not stated in the text, decides to rescue Joseph. Instead of murdering him, they pounce on him, strip him of the loathsome robe, and dump him in a dry pit. At least they will not be guilty of bloodshed.

Joseph in Potiphar's House (37:25–36)

Joseph's brothers callously sat down for a meal after having dumped him into the dry cistern. These events took place near Dothan, which was close to the Via Maris,

levirate marriage

the main trade route through Syria–Palestine leading to Egypt (see map IV.11.1). While they were eating, they noticed a caravan of merchant Ishmaelites (also known as Midianites) on their way to Egypt with their goods. Then they devised a plan whereby they could avoid the guilt of actual bloodshed, be done with Joseph permanently (they thought!), and gain a handsome financial profit all in one swift action. Young male slaves were valuable, and they could sell Joseph to the merchants for a considerable amount. The Ishmaelites would no doubt take him away to Egypt, and they would never have to hear his dreams or see his royal robe again!

The firstborn among them, Reuben, had planned to retrieve Joseph later and bring him back safely to Jacob (v. 22b). But, again, for reasons the narrator does not explain, Reuben is away during this point of the action. There is no one to protect poor Joseph, and he appears destined to a life

Joseph looked for his brothers who were grazing their flocks near Shechem. When he found them, they had moved on to Dothan, which was near one of the major trade routes to Egypt. Out of their jealous hatred for Joseph, they sold him to merchants traveling to Egypt.

of degradation and shame in far-off Egypt. His brothers dipped Joseph's coat in goat's blood, and offered it to their father as proof that Joseph had been slaughtered by a wild animal. Jacob naively accepted this explanation and was left to his own unbearable grief. The narrative appears to end, except for the curious concluding comment, which suggests that we have not heard the last of Joseph: "Meanwhile, the Midianites sold Joseph in Egypt to Potiphar, one of Pharaoh's officials, the captain of the guard" (v. 36). Joseph survived the trip to Egypt. He and his dreams are still alive.

The Judah Interlude (38)

The placement of the Judah and Tamar episode in Genesis 38 appears inexplicable at first sight. The Joseph narrative has only just begun and captured our attention with the horrible treatment of our young hero. The conclusion to chapter 37 left us in suspense, informing us that Joseph had been purchased by a high-ranking official in Egypt. There will certainly be more to that story! Indeed, Genesis 39:1 begins with a note that obviously resumes the events of chapter 37: "Now Joseph had been taken down to Egypt." In other words, the author has intentionally included Genesis 38 as an interlude between chapters 37 and 39. So before we return to Egypt to see what will become of Joseph, our narrator first invites us to consider the actions of Judah.

Judah and Tamar (38:1–30)

The opening paragraphs of Genesis 38 introduce us to all the leading characters of the story (vv. 1–11). Judah unaccountably—and unwisely—left his brothers to live in Adullam (v. 1). There he married a Canaanite woman, an action that has signaled trouble elsewhere in the patriarchal narratives. She gave birth to three sons: Er, Onan, and Shelah. Judah's firstborn, Er, grew to marriageable age and married Tamar, presumably also a Canaanitess. When Er died, Onan refused to fulfill his cultural and legal obligation in **levirate marriage**. This part of the narrative may

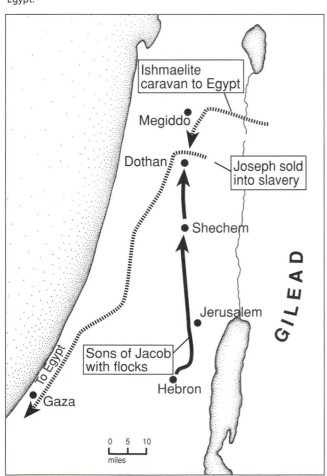

Ishmaelite caravan to Egypt

Megiddo

Dothan

Joseph sold into slavery

Shechem

Jerusalem

GILEAD

Sons of Jacob with flocks

Hebron

To Egypt

Gaza

0   5   10
miles

Ishmaelites and Midianites in Genesis 37

The appearance of both "Ishmaelites" and "Midianites" in Genesis 37 has given rise to much discussion among biblical scholars (compare vv. 25, 27, 28, and 36). Some early Jewish commentators believed Joseph was traded more than once, involving different merchants.[8] More recent scholars have taken this as evidence the narrative was composed from separate sources containing irreconcilable accounts of how Joseph was sold into Egypt. The separate sources allegedly called the wandering traders by different names, and the later editor simply chose to leave both terms in the final product.[9]

The explanation may be much simpler. A clue to the problem is found in Judges 8:24, where it is explicitly stated that the *Midianites* defeated by Gideon wore earrings, because that "was the custom of the *Ishmaelites.*"[10] Here the terms "Ishmaelite" and "Midianite" are overlapping ethnic identities. It seems likely that "Ishmaelite" was an inclusive term for all the descendants of Ishmael, the son of Abraham by Hagar (review Gn 16). The various groups of Ishmaelites were Israel's nomadic cousins, of which the Midianites were one part.

There are many examples from ancient Near Eastern sources in which interchangeable ethnic designations are used within a single document.[11]

It is difficult to be certain whether the terms reflect separate ancient sources behind the present narrative. But in light of recent scholarship on the literary unity of the Joseph narrative, it seems unlikely. It seems more probable that a single author could alternate with ease between these two designations for a variety of style, or as a means of emphasizing the point that Joseph was sold to a people outside the covenant.[12]

seem difficult to accept from a modern Christian perspective, but it was an integral element in several ancient societies, including Old Testament Israel.

When Onan also died, Judah was under obligation to give his remaining son to Tamar. His refusal left her in a situation that was socially and economically desperate for an ancient Near Eastern woman. Tamar was forced to return to "her father's house" (v. 11), which was a sad attempt to avoid a life of destitution (Lv 22:13).

The concept of levirate marriage is not the only shock awaiting the modern reader of Genesis 38. Judah's injustice to Tamar led her to disguise herself as a prostitute and trick Judah into serving as the surrogate father to her children (vv. 12–30). Thereby Judah himself unwittingly provided descendants for Er. He had acted wickedly by withholding his third son from Tamar, and now he was behaving even more wickedly. His first crime led to a second. Tamar's action shocks us, but the narrator is interested in her clever resourcefulness and the way in which she protected herself from Judah's hypocrisy. In requiring his seal, cord, and staff (v. 18),

she demanded what would be the modern equivalent to his credit cards and driver's license for identification purposes (v. 25). She was cunning, proactive, and in the right, whereas Judah was brutish, foolish, and clearly wicked. Judah was left in an undeniable position of guilt. He could only acknowledge his wrongdoing and avoid such action in the future (v. 26).

From our New Testament perspective, we certainly cannot condone what Tamar did.[14] However, as the ancient narrator makes clear at the end of the chapter, the point of the episode is that her actions were more righteous than Judah's, who has behaved abominably (v. 26). There is no condemnation of Tamar here, even faintly. A larger point is that it was through these desperate attempts on Tamar's part, and the cruel and wicked actions of Judah, that God accomplished his purposes. It is this emphasis on God's sovereign overruling in the lives of this family that we get an overall glimpse of the message of the larger Joseph story. For it is exactly this that Joseph also learns: "God moves in a mysterious way, His wonders to perform."[15]

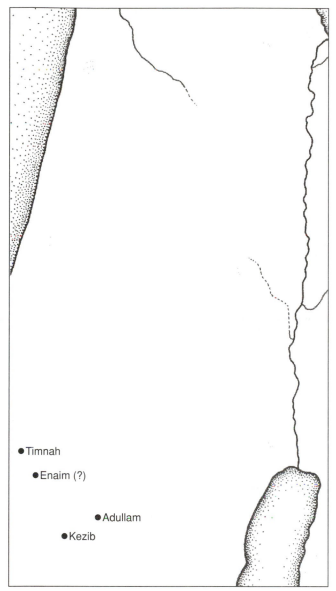

Judah's sojourn in Adullam.

- Timnah
- Enaim (?)
- Adullam
- Kezib

episode clearly plays an integral role. Before the conclusion of the Book of Genesis, we have the customary patriarchal blessings that Jacob bestowed on his sons before his death (ch. 49). Joseph and Judah received pride of place in these blessings, which also reflects their important roles in the future of Israel's history. The nation will be comprised largely of Judah in the south and the tribes of Joseph, Ephraim and Manasseh, in the north.

Moreover, the author of Genesis is always interested in the biographical sketches of his characters. The Tamar episode gives a graphic insight into Judah's character. He is a callous and rapacious individual. He had been the brother who realized that murdering Joseph was pointless when they could gain a profit by selling him (37:26–27). In Genesis 38, he fails to express any grief or show mourning for the loss of his two sons, and succinctly orders to have Tamar burned for her crime. Yet later in Genesis, Judah is a changed man. He passionately pleads Benjamin's case in Genesis 44:18–34, and offers himself as a slave in the place of his brother. It could be argued that a subplot of the Jacob *tôlĕdôt* is the transforming quality of relationship with God. Judah is clearly a changed man in later passages, and the Tamar episode helps explain the change, especially the declaration "She is more righteous than I" (38:26).[16] It is eminently fitting to recognize this emphasis on character transformation in the Jacob *tôlĕdôt*, since Jacob is the example of transformation par excellence.

More particularly, this episode also plays an important role in salvation history. Christian readers recognize God's sovereign activity in spite of the outrageous actions of Judah in a way that the original author of Genesis could not have fully grasped. This is because readers of the New Testament know the conclusion to the story. The Gospel writers included the genealogy of the Messiah, in which they drew out the full significance of the birth of Perez to this unholy union (Mt 1:3; Lk 3:33). Within the Old Testament itself, it was clear that Perez was the ancestral head of the tribe from which Boaz descended. Through the wonderful and miraculous wedding of Boaz and Ruth, the line of Judah and Perez was extended all the way to Israel's

The Place of Genesis 38

The apparent interruption created by the Judah–Tamar episode is really quite comprehensible if we remember the context of the whole. One should recall that the *tôlĕdôt* for this final section of Genesis covers "the account of *Jacob*" (37:2a). In this sense, the designation "Joseph narrative" is somewhat misleading, since Genesis 37–50 really is the history of the family of Jacob. We should not be surprised to see details from the lives of other sons of Jacob recorded here.

In addition, when one considers the narrator's overall plan, the Judah–Tamar

Levirate Marriage in the Old Testament

In Genesis 38:8, you may have been surprised by Judah's instructions to Onan, his second son: "Lie with your [dead] brother's wife and fulfill your duty to her as a brother-in-law to produce offspring for your brother." Though astonishing to us, this custom was common in Israel's day and would have seemed perfectly natural to the first readers of this text.

The institution appears to have had variations, but in general it was the obligation of the closest brother of a deceased member of the family to produce a son for the dead brother. This second marriage is known as "levirate" marriage. The term comes from the Latin *levir*, which translates the Hebrew word for "brother-in-law" *(yābām)*. The purpose of marrying a widow in the family was to guarantee

the childless woman would have children who would receive the deceased family member's inheritance. The children would also care for the woman in her elderly years.

The practice was not limited to ancient Israel. Among her neighbors, the Assyrians, the Hittites, the Hurrians of Nuzi, and the inhabitants of Ugarit are all known to have practiced some variation of this custom.[13] Levirate marriage was institutionalized formally and made a matter of Israelite law in Deuteronomy 25:5–10. Fathering additional children by one's widowed sister-in-law was apparently not often desirable, and the Deuteronomy legislation makes a provision for the individual who wants to avoid the responsibility (also illustrated probably in Ru

4:5–6). The earlier, patriarchal version of the custom (Gn 38) did not give Onan such an option. The patriarchal setting in Genesis may also imply the seriousness of Onan's refusal to continue the blessing of the covenant.

The societal requirement was for Judah to give first Onan and then Shelah to Tamar in order to raise up descendants for their deceased brother, Er. Onan's refusal to comply resulted in his own untimely demise. Judah's refusal to offer his third son led to even more intrigue and suspense in the patriarchal family. Though the practice of levirate marriage seems outlandish to modern readers, it was the expected and natural turn of events for ancient readers. The concept is an integral element of the Judah and Tamar story.

greatest king, David (Ru 4:18–22). So the story that appears so peripheral to the biblical storyline has a surprise ending, which makes Judah the ancestor of David and the Messiah himself!

Still it could be stated that Genesis 38 is literarily disruptive. The conclusion to chapter 37 would lead beautifully straight to chapter 39 without the intervening tale of Judah and Tamar. Why did the author place this account here instead of at the beginning of the Jacob *tôlĕdôt*, or near its end? First, as we have said, the narrative at the conclusion of Genesis 37 leaves us in suspense. No sooner are we informed that Joseph has been sold to Potiphar in Egypt than suddenly we are left to ponder what will become of him. The Judah–Tamar narrative is a digression that takes us, like Joseph's family, far from him and back into Canaan. Joseph is alone in Egypt, where he is left to grow up on his

own. Enough time passes for Judah to marry, raise his sons and for them to marry as well, showing just how long Joseph was left to fend for himself.

But the Judah–Tamar account points forward as well as backward. Its placement here not only leaves us in suspense about Joseph's fate at the conclusion of Genesis 37; it also creates a sharp and unmistakable contrast between Judah's character and Joseph's behavior in the next chapter, to which we now turn.

Joseph's Rise over Egypt (39–41)

This section relates Joseph's remarkable advancement in Egypt. It traces the rise of Joseph from a foreign slave in Egypt to prime minister of the entire country. At the beginning of Genesis 37 Joseph was seventeen years old. Thirteen years later, at the age of thirty, he entered the service of Pharaoh as the second most powerful ruler in Egypt (41:46). These events can only be attributed to divine guidance, as the narrator explains: "The LORD was with Joseph and he prospered" (39:2; see also 39:21, 23).

Joseph's advancement is presented in three scenes corresponding to Genesis 39, 40, and 41. The account is one of two narrative expansions in the Joseph story, and is concerned with his rise to political power.[17]

Joseph in Charge of Potiphar's House (39)

In the first scene, the author has masterfully created suspense and tension in the account by describing first Joseph's rise in Potiphar's house (39:1–6a), then an even greater fall (39:6b–20a), which is then followed by yet another advancement, this time in prison (39:20b–23).[18]

As we have said, Genesis 39:1 essentially recaps 37:36 and resumes the story of poor Joseph, sold to Potiphar in Egypt. The narrator states clearly from the outset that the Lord was with Joseph and gave him great success in all he attempted (v. 2). But one could hardly have expected him to rise to the pinnacle of power in such an important and powerful nation. God is always behind the scenes when human evil is present, and he works in the lives of those who are faithful to prosper their service. Joseph was not destined to be a successful servant! His faithfulness to God was the means of his advancement both in Potiphar's house and in prison.

Potiphar's wife was struck by Joseph's stunning good looks, which are described in much the same language as the appearance of his mother's attractive qualities (compare 39:6b with 29:17b). Joseph's quick and emphatic refusal to surrender to her sexual advances is a model for all believers on how to resist temptation. He had a clear perception of right and wrong, and he did not wait until the moment of temptation to ponder or deliberate whether it might be acceptable to sleep with her or not: "How then could I do such a wicked thing and sin against God?" (v. 9). Joseph had made his decision in advance.

He had made commitments to God (and to Potiphar), and temporary sexual pleasure would break those commitments. He refused emphatically and persistently in light of her continued requests. But when all else failed, and he was trapped by Potiphar's wife—he ran! Sometimes it is not enough to be committed and to desire to do what is right. Sometimes we simply have to avoid putting ourselves at risk. When in doubt, just walk (or run!) away.

It was precisely Joseph's refusal to have sex with Potiphar's wife that eventually landed him in prison. But there he met Pharaoh's cupbearer, who had the connections to help Joseph. So it was faithfulness to God that resulted not only in Joseph's advancement in Potiphar's house, but his disgrace and imprisonment. Obedience to God does not always mean success as the world defines success. Nevertheless, his faithfulness resulted in another advancement in prison and, ultimately, vindication in Pharaoh's court. God used the disgrace and failure of Joseph to raise him up as the vizier of Egypt, and to prepare him for even greater things in the future.

The final paragraph (vv. 20b–23) creates a perfect symmetry for the chapter. Each phrase matches almost perfectly with a corresponding phrase in the opening paragraph (vv. 2–6a). Once again the narrator states, "The LORD was with him" while he was in prison, just as he had been with him in Potiphar's house (compare vv. 20b–21 with v. 2). Joseph found favor in the sight of the prison warden, just as he had with Potiphar (vv. 21b and 4a). The prison warden put Joseph in charge of everything that went on there, just as Potiphar had placed Joseph over his entire household (vv. 22 and 4b). The Lord blessed Joseph's work and made everything he did in the prison prosper, just as he had done earlier when Joseph was in Potiphar's house (vv. 23 and 5). In light of the tragic events narrated in the intervening verses, this symmetry illustrates God's sovereign and gracious control.[19]

Pharaoh's Cupbearer and Baker (40)

The second scene in Joseph's advancement is set in the prison itself. Here he comes in contact with two formerly powerful men, Pharaoh's cupbearer and baker (vv. 1–4a). We are not told what these men had done to anger their master. What is important is they are now in Joseph's care. This is perhaps a hint as to how Joseph's fortunes may be turned around.

After a period of time, the cupbearer and baker had dreams, the significance of which they were unable to understand. Joseph successfully interpreted their dreams for them with vastly different results (vv. 4b–19). Joseph's interpretation involves a striking wordplay that seems humorous (unless you are the baker!). He explained that the dreams meant Pharaoh would lift up the heads of both men (compare vv. 13 and 19). In the case of the cupbearer, this meant Pharaoh would *symbolically* lift up his head and restore him to his previous position of honor in the royal court. For the baker, this meant Pharaoh would *literally* lift up his head by hanging him on a tree.[20] Joseph justifiably takes the opportunity to ask the cupbearer to remember him when he is restored to his position of influence in Pharaoh's court, because Joseph has been dealt a double wrong and does not belong in prison (vv. 14–15).

Three days later, on Pharaoh's birthday, the dreams as interpreted by Joseph became reality. Pharaoh lifted the heads of the chief cupbearer and the baker—one to restored honor, the other to ignoble death (vv. 20–22). We might have expected a grateful cupbearer to remember the young Hebrew prisoner who rightly interpreted his dream. But Joseph is hit with another disappointment, as the final verse of the chapter states: "The chief cupbearer, however, did not remember Joseph; he forgot him" (v. 23). Unlike the immediate rise of Joseph in the prison at the end of the first scene in Genesis 39, this scene is followed by a long delay. The next scene opens with the news that Joseph was left to languish in the prison for two long years (41:1).

The role of dreams in Genesis 40 is interesting. The two dreams that Joseph rightly interpreted remind us of the two dreams that Joseph himself had back in Genesis 37. Those dreams foretold of Joseph's rise to political power and the submission of his entire family to him. All of these dreams together point us forward to Pharaoh's two dreams of Genesis 41, which again Joseph will rightly interpret.[21] In the Joseph story, dreams serve two functions. First, they foretell and prepare the way for Joseph's rise to influence. But second, they actually become the means by which the earlier dreams are fulfilled. It was through the correct interpretation of dreams in Genesis 40 and 41 that the dreams of Genesis 37 were fulfilled.

Pharaoh's Dreams (41)

The third scene relating Joseph's rise over Egypt is set in Pharaoh's court. After two long years in which Joseph was forgotten in prison, Pharaoh had two dreams (41:1–7). The dreams portrayed seven healthy cows consumed by seven sickly ones, and seven good heads of grain consumed by seven thin ones. As with the dreams of the Babylonian king Nebuchadnezzar (Dn 2 and 4), the royal magicians of Egypt could not interpret Pharaoh's dreams (41:8). It was only then that the cupbearer remembered the wise young Hebrew in prison.

After thirteen long years of slavery and imprisonment, Joseph is suddenly released and brought to stand before Pharaoh himself (41:14). In that single moment of incredible opportunity, Joseph's true character was revealed. Pharaoh thought in terms of a highly developed and sophisticated human skill of interpretation. But Joseph knew better and could not allow this line of thought to proceed. He immediately rejected Pharaoh's approach in emphatic terms, and with a minimum of words ("I cannot do it" is all one word in Hebrew). Joseph then firmly and humbly directed attention away from himself and offered Pharaoh a new perspective on the world. It is not Joseph who can interpret these strange dreams; it is a divine gift that Pharaoh has yet to understand: "God will give Pharaoh the answer he desires" (v. 16).

Pharaoh related the dreams to Joseph, who promptly explains that they are two dreams with the same meaning. Furthermore, the dreams are of divine origin and are meant to reveal the future to Pharaoh: "God has revealed to Pharaoh what he is about to do" (vv. 25, 28). There will be seven years of plenty to be followed immediately by seven years of famine. The

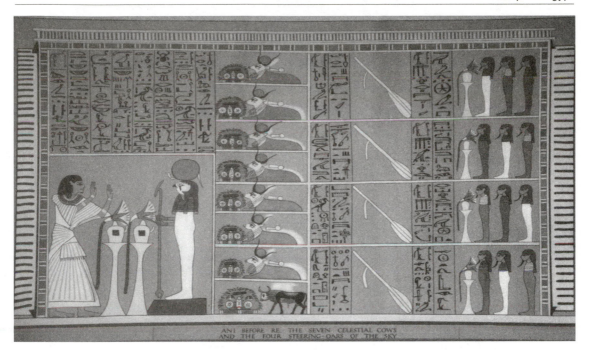

ANI BEFORE RE, THE SEVEN CELESTIAL COWS
AND THE FOUR STEERING-OARS OF THE SKY

Cows depicted in the Egyptian Book of the Dead. Cows were more than simple farm animals to the ancient Egyptians. They could symbolize Egypt itself, or one of its gods, Isis.

seven lean years will consume the abundance of the seven good years. All of these things are imminent and beyond the control of Pharaoh: "The reason the dream was given to Pharaoh in two forms is that the matter has been firmly decided by God, and God will do it soon" (v. 32).

Joseph's interpretation was at one and the same time a refutation of Pharaoh and his worldview and an undeniable confirmation of the truth of Joseph's. In Egypt, Pharaoh was accepted as a divine being, who could also influence other deities through the use of magic in order to ensure the cycle of life as the Egyptians enjoyed it (review pages 48–51, above). But Joseph presented Pharaoh with an alternate view of reality. God alone was divine, and he had revealed to Pharaoh events that were about to transpire. The only thing Pharaoh could do was to prepare himself and his nation. There was no altering the future God had set in motion. Joseph, who only a few days before had been languishing in prison, now had an opportunity to explain to the Egyptian Pharaoh how God works. Apparently the thirteen long years of painful and lonely service had prepared Joseph for this moment. He was as faithful in words to Pharaoh as he had been in Potiphar's house and in prison.

Pharaoh was much impressed with the young Joseph. Who better to store up the abundance of the seven years of plenty in preparation for the seven years of famine? Could Pharaoh find anyone in his entire kingdom like this young Hebrew, "in whom is the spirit of God" (v. 38)? In words reminiscent of both Potiphar's great confidence in Joseph and the prison warden's trust in Joseph's abilities, Pharaoh made him the second most powerful person in Egypt. "You shall be in charge of my palace ... only with respect to the throne will I be greater than you" (v. 40; compare 39:6 and 22–23). At the age of thirty, Joseph stored up huge quantities of excess grain during the seven years of plenty. Then the seven years of famine began, and it was clear that Joseph's interpretation and advice had saved the land of Egypt and prevented national crisis for Pharaoh. As the famine intensified, Pharaoh gave instructions to follow Joseph's orders. Joseph opened the storehouses and began selling grain to the hungry masses.

As with the rest of the Joseph narrative, Genesis 41 is above all about the sovereign work of God in the lives of those who serve him.[22] The chapter opened with God jolting Pharaoh out of his vainglorious self-satisfaction. In Egypt, the pharaohs viewed themselves as divine. The Egyptian king

Study Questions

1. How is the Joseph narrative both like and different from the preceding narratives in Genesis?

2. Describe how favoritism has colored the narratives in Genesis thus far, and note how this theme continues in the Joseph narrative.

3. Explain the significance of both the content and placement of the material in Genesis 38.

4. Where in the Joseph narrative do we find reference to two dreams? How are these different references related?

5. In what manner is Joseph's interpretation of Pharaoh's dreams a challenge to Pharaoh's worldview?

6. How does the entire Joseph narrative serve to emphasize the sovereignty of God?

7. What does the Joseph narrative teach us as Christians about the nature of faith?

certainly had no need to consult the word of an imprisoned Hebrew slave. But disturbing and inexplicable dreams were sometimes God's way of capsizing such prideful complacency (again, compare Dn 2 and 4). It is God who disturbs Pharaoh and jostles the memory of the cupbearer, so that he now remembers the Hebrew slave who interpreted his own dream. And God is in charge of history, so that he can grant dreams that foretell future events and inspire servants to rightly interpret those dreams. This narrative is a story about Joseph, and Pharaoh, and the cupbearer, and others. But above all it is a story about God, the great mover and shaper of history, and about his pleasure in using a single servant who is willing to submit his life to God's control.

This third and final scene relating the rise of Joseph over Egypt closes with a hint at what is to come. Joseph is distributing food to the hungry masses of Egypt because the famine has begun. But the final verse also informs us that "all the countries came to Egypt to buy grain from Joseph, because the famine was severe in all the world" (v. 57). Of course, among those to visit Joseph in Egypt will be his brothers from Syria–Palestine, who could never begin to imagine what has happened to their hapless brother during the many years since they sold him into slavery.

Key Term

levirate marriage

12 Joseph over Egypt

Genesis 42:1–50:26

And we know that in all things God works for the good of those who love him, who have been called according to his purpose.

—Paul, Rom 8:28

Supplemental Readings: Psalm 105:16–25, Acts 7:9–16, Hebrews 11:22

Outline

- **The Rationale for the Joseph Narrative**
- **The Sons of Jacob Are Reunited (42–45)**
  First Trip to Egypt (42)
  Second Trip to Egypt (43–45)
- **Settling in Goshen (46–47)**
  Vision at Beersheba (46:1–4)
  In Egypt (46:5–47:12)
  Joseph during the Famine (47:13–31)
- **The Deaths of Jacob and Joseph (48–50)**
  Jacob Blesses Ephraim and Manasseh (48:1–22)
  Jacob Blesses His Sons (49:1–28)
  The Death and Burial of Jacob (49:29–50:21)
  The Death of Joseph (50:22–26)

Objectives

After reading this chapter you should be able to

1. Comprehend and apply the truth that God uses evil and unpleasant situations to produce good results.

2. Explain why the account of Joseph takes up such a large portion of Genesis.

3. Summarize the events that occurred during the first and second journeys to Egypt by Joseph's brothers, emphasizing the guilt experienced, the test of character, and the reconciliation that ensued.

4. Identify the events in Genesis 45–47 that help bring closure to the Joseph narrative and the Jacob cycle, including the move to Egypt, Jacob's vision at Beersheba, settling in Goshen, and Joseph's leadership during the famine.

5. From Genesis 48–49, describe Jacob's blessing the sons of Joseph and his subsequent blessing of his own sons, detailing the literary, prophetic, and messianic implications of the accompanying poetic oracle.

6. Distill the theological enigma of God's sovereignty and human responsibility using the comments of Joseph to his brothers subsequent to Jacob's death and burial.

7. Contrast the burial of Joseph with the elaborate burial of Jacob, and the function of Joseph's coffin as a reminder to the Israelites that they were not home.

Why Is the Joseph Narrative Included in Genesis?

1. To explain how Jacob's family came to live in Egypt.

2. To provide in Joseph an example of holiness and faithfulness for all believers.

3. To demonstrate the partial fulfillment of the patriarchal promises.

42–45) relates the reunion of Joseph with his brothers. This unit is a powerful literary masterpiece filled with human interest and divine grace. This is followed by narratives that interweave the Joseph story with that of Jacob, and form a conclusion for the entire book (chs. 46–50). The family of Jacob moves to Egypt and settles in Goshen (chs. 46–47). Jacob blesses his sons in poetic passages that have profound implications for the rest of Old Testament history (chs. 48–49), and a final chapter (50) narrates the burial of Jacob in Canaan and the death of Joseph. All of this is tied together neatly as a conclusion to this book of beginnings.

The Bible often uses history to illustrate a truth explained more abstractly elsewhere in Scripture. Or, to put it another way, much of the Bible is poetry or letters expounding on the meaning of historical events. So the Old Testament prophetic books often elaborate on events described in the historical books, and the New Testament Epistles clarify the significance of events related in the Gospels and the Book of Acts. Different sections of the Bible are meant to complement each other in this way. The truth of history confirms and proves by example the truth of doctrine.

This final section of Genesis beautifully illustrates the truth of the apostle Paul's statement that God is always behind the scenes (and sometimes more visibly *in* the scene), working through and in the circumstances of life to accomplish his purposes for his people. Paul taught the Roman Christians that God causes all things to work for the ultimate good and spiritual well-being of those who respond to him in love. No circumstances in life—even the most unimaginable—are beyond God's control. And he often turns them around and uses such circumstances for the ultimate good of his people. Joseph is the perfect illustration of this biblical principle. God used the bad things that happened to Joseph to accomplish his purposes. But most people today associate only the good things that happen in life with God. It is up to us as readers of Genesis to learn to trust him in the "all things" of our lives.

Genesis 42–50 is a diverse combination of materials intended to wrap up all the themes of the book. The first section (chs.

The Rationale for the Joseph Narrative

As we saw in the previous chapter, the Joseph narrative is in many ways a continuation of the Jacob cycle. It could be said that the entire second half of Genesis (chs. 25–50) is really about the family of Jacob. This extended section (chs. 37–50), normally called the Joseph narrative, is really part 2 of the two-part Jacob narrative.[1]

But we have also said the Joseph narrative has noticeable differences when compared to the Abraham and Jacob cycles of narrative. We should add to this that Joseph is not included in later lists of the great fathers of Israel's faith (Ex 2:24; 3:6, etc.), and later Jewish tradition also limited the "patriarchs" (technically defined) to Abraham, Isaac, and Jacob.[2] This is probably because Joseph does not stand in the direct line of the Messiah. Genesis is composed around the special family line, starting with Adam and tracing through to the twelve sons of Jacob.[3] Specifically, the book calls attention to the "seed" of this lineage, which will become numerous and eventually possess the land of Canaan, according to the patriarchal promises. But the book further highlights one particular line of "seed" that will become a royal dynasty. It is the line of Judah that will eventually give rise to the kings of Israel, and ultimately the Messiah.

Since Joseph is not technically a patriarch, we could ask why the author of Genesis included so much material about him.

Heilsgeschichte

He does not stand in the line of the Messiah, yet we have more material devoted to him than to Isaac or Jacob. Consider also that the author of Genesis only gave us two chapters on creation, but thirteen on Joseph! Why is the Joseph narrative included in the Bible at all? Why is so much material devoted to this narrative?

First, on a purely historical level, the Joseph story is important as an explanation of how Jacob's family came to be living in Egypt in the first place. At the beginning of Exodus (arguably the beginning of the story of national Israel), the family of Abraham, Isaac, and Jacob is living outside the Promised Land in exile in Egypt. The Joseph narrative at the conclusion of Genesis explains why. Jacob's family had fled to Egypt to escape famine, and Joseph was used by God to deliver them and many others as well.

Second, beyond the purely historical level, the Joseph narrative plays an important role on another level. Perhaps more than any other Old Testament figure, Joseph is an example of holiness and faithfulness for all believers of every generation. Only Daniel near the end of the Old Testament period, and of course, Jesus in the New Testament match Joseph in terms of character. Perhaps we could criticize Joseph in Genesis 37 for pride, and for impudently relating his dreams to his family. But that could be dismissed as childish naiveté and innocence. In reality, the author wants us to see him as a victim of his circumstances, not only in Canaan with his brothers, but in Potiphar's house and in Pharaoh's prison. But in each setting, Joseph is exemplary in his faithful service to God and to those around him. Thus he is an example for all of us who seek to be faithful to our calling before God, but who often find ourselves in trying circumstances.

Finally, the Joseph narrative is included in Genesis because of its contribution to the themes of the book and to those of the Pentateuch overall. Specifically, the patriarchal promises, so very central to the message of Genesis, are carried further in the Joseph story. The promises made to Abraham in Genesis 12:1–3 and developed throughout the patriarchal narratives find gradual fulfillment in the Joseph narrative. The descendants of Abraham begin

to prosper and are miraculously preserved during the terrible famine. But, God also blessed the nations through these children of Abraham. He used Joseph as the viceroy of Egypt to save the lives of a great multitude of people (Gn 50:20).

In this way, the Joseph narrative makes a significant contribution to the *Heilsgeschichte*, or the salvation history, of the biblical storyline. The theme of the Pentateuch is the partial fulfillment (which implies also the partial nonfulfillment) of the patriarchal promises.[4] God promised Abraham that he would become a great nation (Gn 12:2). In the Joseph narrative, the patriarchal family grew from twelve to seventy (Gn 46:26–27), which was a partial fulfillment of the promise to Abraham. When Jacob blessed his children before his death, he foresaw that each of them would become a great tribe of people (Gn 49). At the end of the Pentateuch they had indeed become "as numerous as the stars in the sky" (Dt 10:22). The Joseph narrative partially fulfills the patriarchal promises also in that "all peoples on earth" began to "be blessed through" Abraham's family (Gn 12:3b). Joseph's faithfulness resulted in the salvation of "all the countries" who came to Egypt to buy grain (Gn 41:57; and see 45:5 and 50:20).

But these are still only partial fulfillments. At the end of Genesis, the patriarchal family has grown and become a blessing to other nations. But they are living outside the Promised Land, and there remains much to follow before the promises to Abraham are fulfilled. The Joseph narrative moves the story forward, but when it is finished, it is clear that "Genesis requires a sequel."[5]

The Sons of Jacob Are Reunited (42–45)

These four chapters of Genesis narrate the reunion of Joseph with his brothers. Due to the severe famine, the sons of Jacob make two journeys down to Egypt to acquire food. These trips are masterfully narrated in Genesis 42 and 43–45. The author delayed the revelation of Joseph's true identity, building up the tension and heightening the suspense leading to Genesis 45.[6]

First Trip to Egypt (42)

As you read this chapter, you probably noticed that the author revealed what Joseph knew and what his brothers did not know. Joseph recognized them immediately (v. 7), but they did not recognize him (v. 8). Much had changed. Joseph had grown up, and he now spoke and dressed like an Egyptian. But he could not help but wonder if his brothers had really changed. His last memory of them was the horror he experienced when they sold him to slave traders who carried him to Egypt. Had they changed at all, or were they still as traitorous and wicked as they had been twenty years before? Joseph decided to put them through a few tests to find out their character. He decided to detain Simeon as a hostage, while they returned to Canaan in order to bring his full brother, Benjamin, to Egypt.

The scene described in verses 21–24 is particularly moving. Joseph could speak the Hebrew dialect they were using, but he spoke only Egyptian with them and used an interpreter (v. 23).[7] When he announced that one of them would have to stay in Egypt in prison until they returned with Benjamin, they began discussing it among themselves in Hebrew. They did not realize he could understand them. Jacob's sons concluded they were being punished because of their sin against Joseph, whom Reuben presumed must be dead by now. This was all happening to them because of their guilt and their refusal to answer Joseph when he had pled for his life (a detail omitted in Gn 37). The passage of twenty years could not dull the memory of their sin against their brother, nor ease their sense of guilt. Their confession deeply moved Joseph, and he turned away and wept (42:24).

Second Trip to Egypt (43–45)

This is one of the most beautiful and moving stories of the Bible. Reconciliation between brothers once alienated is in itself a powerful theme. But in this case, the offended brother (Joseph) was totally innocent of any wrongdoing. On the other hand, his treacherous brothers are now wracked with the pain of guilt, and have long since assumed Joseph was dead. Furthermore, the narrative is written in such a way as to heighten the suspense and build to the dramatic moment in which Joseph revealed his true identity to his brothers.

These three chapters relate the second trip of Jacob's sons to Egypt. Jacob had not wanted to send them again because he would be forced to allow Benjamin to go along. He was willing to leave Simeon in prison in Egypt rather than risk losing his beloved Benjamin, his last son by Rachel. But the famine was so severe, Jacob was forced to allow his sons to return (43:1). When Joseph saw them returning with his full brother, Benjamin, they were escorted to his home for a feast at midday. When Joseph met with them, he was deeply moved at the sight of Benjamin. He retired to his private chambers until he gained control of his emotions (43:30). His brothers were amazed to realize they had been seated for the meal according to their ages, from the firstborn to the youngest, and Benjamin's portion was five times bigger than the others.

The incident of the silver cup was again a test of their character (44:1–17). Joseph's chalice was symbolic of his authority. Many thought such goblets could be used to predict the future, and that they had supernatural powers. Joseph himself had learned many years before that God revealed to him the future in the form of dreams. The drama unfolding before him was in fact the fulfillment of those dreams, since his brothers had already bowed before him several times as his dreams had predicted (37:5–9). Joseph certainly did not need the silver cup. But to steal such a goblet was a serious crime. Joseph's trick would reveal once and for all if his brothers would betray Benjamin as they had once betrayed him, and whether his brothers had actually changed during the intervening years.

When confronted with the prospect of losing Benjamin, it was Judah who took a stand (44:18–34). His speech is the longest and perhaps the most moving in Genesis. He mentioned Jacob his father fourteen times, which illustrates the central point of the speech. He acknowledged that Jacob's life, rightly or wrongly, was totally absorbed in the life of his youngest son, Benjamin. Because of Jacob's advanced age and frail condition, Judah doubted he would survive the loss of Benjamin. Judah could not bear to see his father suffer, and feared it would result in his father's premature death.

Ironically it was Judah who sold a younger brother (Rachel's firstborn, Joseph) into slavery twenty-two years earlier (37:26–27). He no doubt stood by silently while his father grieved bitterly for Joseph's life. Now it was Judah who was willing to do anything to prevent his father from suffering like that again. He offered himself as a slave in order to free another young brother (Rachel's second son, Benjamin), in order to spare his father from sorrow. Judah was clearly a changed man, when compared to his actions in earlier episodes. The change appears to have begun with his declaration "she is more righteous than I" (38:26).

Judah's speech was more than Joseph could bear. He had heard too much about the weakness of his father, and he was overcome with worry and love. Unable to control his emotions, Joseph sent the Egyptian attendants away, leaving him alone with his brothers (45:1). Suddenly Joseph revealed his true identity to his brothers: "I am Joseph" (v. 3)! His question, "Is my father still living?" is more an exclamation than an inquiry, showing that his concern was for his father's health.[8] This had been brought on by Judah's repeated mention of his aging father.

The revelation that this powerful Egyptian potentate was in reality their long lost brother was irrefutable for two reasons. First, up to this point, Joseph had been using Egyptian and communicating with his brothers through an interpreter (42:23). But now he is alone with them, and undoubtedly switches to Hebrew.[9] The revelation of his true identity in their native language, and no doubt in their own particular dialect and accent, made it impossible to deny that it was true. This was certainly Joseph, and there was no getting around it.

Second, Joseph then reminded them of how they had betrayed him: "I am your brother, the one you sold into Egypt" (45:4). This was information so personal and private that some members of their own family were unaware of it. They had carefully carried the secret of what they had done to Joseph for twenty-two years.

Only Joseph himself could have known the sordid truth. Now he had spoken words they never expected to hear, and none of his brothers could deny the reality of that terrible crime so many long years ago. This was Joseph, and there was no escaping the fact.

Little wonder Joseph's brothers were dumbfounded. After the initial shock, Joseph had said "come close to me" (v. 4), which was probably the last thing their instincts told them to do. Joseph was now a very powerful man, and he had the ability to punish them unmercifully for what they had done to him. What course of action would he take? Would he imprison them, execute them, enslave them?

Joseph immediately calmed their fears: "And now, do not be distressed and do not be angry with yourselves for selling me here, because it was to save lives that God sent me ahead of you" (v. 5). The words "you sold me … God sent me" (NRSV) offer one of the Bible's greatest statements of the sovereign love and care of God. In the biblical worldview, one needs to look at both aspects of every event: the human dimension, which is often skewed and misshapen, and the divine dimension, which graciously works for our good. Faith makes it possible to fix our attention on the latter and live our lives in the confidence that even the worst things that happen to us are used by God for our good.[10] Joseph went on to emphasize three times that it was not they who sent him to Egypt, but God (vv. 5, 7, 8).[11] And his purpose was clear: to preserve the lives of many nations, and particularly of the descendants of Abraham. Their wicked actions had been used by God to preserve his work through Abraham, Isaac, and Jacob, and indeed, to move toward the fulfillment of his promises to them. Now the way was prepared for the beginning of the history of Israel, a story that continues in the Book of Exodus.

Settling in Goshen (46–47)

The remarkable revelation of Joseph's identity had been followed by a tearful reunion between brothers (45:14–15). Pharaoh had commissioned Joseph to

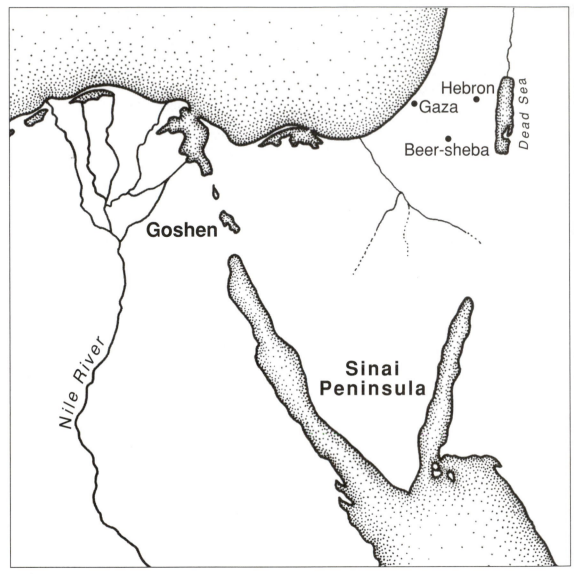

Jacob moves to Egypt.

send his brothers home to bring Jacob to Egypt, where the family would live securely on the best of the land and be safe during the famine. Jacob had been stunned by the news that Joseph was alive after all these years (45:26). But the rich gifts sent by Joseph and the carts intended to carry him to Egypt were enough to convince Jacob it was true. He resolved to go with the entire patriarchal family to Egypt, and there he would finally be reunited with his son (45:28).

The conclusion of the Joseph narrative now begins to intersect with the conclusion of the Jacob story, and ultimately with the conclusion of the patriarchal narratives in general.[12] The rest of Book of Genesis brings together issues that relate to the past and future of the patriarchal family. Chapters 46–47 bring closure to the past by relating the move of the family to Egypt and their settlement in the land of Goshen. Chapters 48–50 bring further closure on the patriarchal family by narrating the deaths of Jacob and Joseph. But this last section also addresses the future by preserving the patriarchal blessings on each of the sons of Jacob, the future tribes of Israel.[13]

Vision at Beersheba (46:1–4)

Genesis 46 and 47 relate the third and final journey to Egypt. This time the entire patriarchal family moved there and settled in the land of Goshen in the north. On the journey to Egypt, Jacob stopped at Beersheba and offered sacrifices to God. There, in a night vision, God appeared to Jacob in the only divine vision in the Joseph narrative.

Beersheba had been Isaac's base, and this act of worship may have risen from Jacob's desire for assurance that the move to Egypt was the right thing. In the vision, God reassured Jacob: "Do not be afraid to go down to Egypt, for I will make you into a great nation there. I will go down to Egypt with you, and I will surely bring you back again" (vv. 3–4).

For an indefinite period of time, God's people would live in Egypt, outside the Promised Land. But in his timing, he would bring them out of Egypt and they would reenter Canaan as a mighty nation (review Gn 15:13–16). The author of Genesis knew that Jacob's family was in fact leaving the land of promise in order to enter a land of slavery. But ultimately, this too would work to accomplish God's purposes, just as the many injustices to Joseph had been used to God's glory. The Israelites would eventually escape Egypt because of God's mighty acts, and by his grace they would enter Canaan as a mighty nation.

In Egypt (46:5–47:12)

The list of family members who settled in Egypt (46:8–27) is important because it shows what God was about to accomplish. When Jacob's family settled in Goshen, they were only "seventy in all" (v. 27), but "they acquired property there and were fruitful and increased greatly in number." Centuries later, the land was "filled with them" (Ex 1:7; and see Ps 105:24). Just as in Joseph's life, the Israelites thrived and prospered under cruel and unjust circumstances.

After a tearful reunion between Joseph and his father (46:29–30), the children of Jacob were comfortably settled in the land of Goshen. The exact location of Goshen is uncertain, but it was generally in the eastern Nile Delta (see map on page 160). This region was well situated for flocks and herds, and remained the home of the Israelites until the exodus.[14]

Joseph during the Famine (47:13–31)

At first glance, Joseph's policies during the worst years of the famine may seem

cruel. But in reality, the Egyptians themselves understood his actions as merciful: "You have saved our lives" (47:25). This is because Joseph's policies allowed the Egyptians to retain something of value. He gave them rations of grain for their money, food for their cattle, and seed for their land. When they were forced to pledge servitude to Pharaoh, Joseph allowed them to retain 80 percent of their harvests while submitting only 20 percent to Pharaoh.[15] Joseph's arrangement made it possible for Pharaoh and the Egyptians to survive the famine, all the while increasing Pharaoh's wealth and power. Jacob himself twice blessed Pharaoh (47:7, 10) and Joseph's administrative wisdom made it possible for the nation to endure the hard times. The author of Genesis seems to understand all of this as partial fulfillment of the promise "all peoples on earth will be blessed through you" (12:3b).

The Deaths of Jacob and Joseph (48–50)

These final chapters of Genesis form the conclusion to the Jacob story, which began in chapter 25, and the Joseph narrative, which began in chapter 37.[16] Though the passage narrates the death and burial of both Jacob and Joseph, it is not primarily focused on the past. On the contrary, both Jacob and Joseph insist that they may live and die in Egypt, but Egypt is not their home. Jacob makes his sons bury him in Canaan (47:29; 49:29–32), and Joseph's final wish is to be carried back to Canaan whenever the children of Israel return there (50:25). In both cases, the hope of a future for the children of Abraham is a continuation of the theme of Genesis. The patriarchal promises are partially fulfilled, but Israel's future is in Canaan and not Egypt.

Jacob Blesses Ephraim and Manasseh (48:1–22)

This chapter explains the elevation of Joseph's two Egyptian sons to the status of full Israelite tribes along with Joseph's brothers. Jacob in effect adopted Ephraim and Manasseh as his own sons, "just as Reuben and Simeon are mine" (v. 5). Thus in future lists of the twelve tribes of Israel, Ephraim and Manasseh are normally included in the place of Joseph. The tribe of Levi became a priestly tribe and therefore did not inherit land in Canaan, bringing the number of landed tribes to twelve (Nm 26:1–51; Jos 15:1–19:51).

This chapter also explains the reversal of the order of priority, the younger Ephraim taking precedence over the older Manasseh. Joseph carefully placed the older son on Jacob's right hand in order that he, Manasseh, would receive the priority blessing (48:13). But Jacob was well experienced at the way God often does the unexpected, and this is a reminder that Jacob himself had been the younger twin who received the older son's blessing (review 27:1–40). This time, however, there was no trickery or deception. Jacob quietly and reverently bestowed the greater blessing on the younger son, which is an Old Testament theme. We have no way of knowing exactly why this reversal took place, or how Jacob knew to enact it.[17] But remarkably this simple act was highlighted by the author of the New Testament Book of Hebrews as Jacob's outstanding action of faith (11:21).

Jacob Blesses His Sons (49:1–28)

This is the last of the deathbed oracles of Genesis, and is the first sustained piece of Hebrew poetry in the Old Testament.[18] The use of an extended section of poetry at the conclusion of a long narrative unit is characteristic of the Pentateuch in general. The final compiler or author of the Pentateuch used poetic speech followed by a short epilogue to conclude each major narrative section. So the Joseph story was concluded in general with Jacob's blessings of Ephraim and Manasseh (48:15–16, 20), followed by the brief narrative epilogue (48:21–22). Likewise on a larger structural scale, the Book of Genesis is concluded with a larger poetic text (Jacob's blessings for his twelve sons in ch. 49), followed by the narrative epilogue in chapter 50.[19]

Many scholars over the years have debated whether Jacob's deathbed oracles contribute anything to the Joseph narrative. But recent literary studies have made it possible to see this passage as the peak of both the Joseph story and the whole Book of Genesis. This is true because the poetry provides a glimpse of the future nation of Israel in germinal, embryonic form. Jacob is prophetically describing the future of the tribes of Israel, even giving the Judah and Joseph tribes pride of place (in the south and north, respectively), which is in fact what happened in later Israel.[20] In this sense, Jacob's deathbed blessing reiterates the book's major theme. Humankind lost the blessing of God through sin and rebellion in the Garden of Eden. But God will restore his blessing through the seed of Abraham.

Jacob's deathbed pronouncement is also very specific about one aspect of God's restoration of blessing. The saying concerning Judah (vv. 8–12) is matched in length only by that of Joseph (vv. 22–26). But in particular, Jacob refers to the coming Davidic line of royalty from the tribe of Judah. In one of the most important verses (and one of the most hotly debated) of the Bible, Jacob predicts the rise of the Davidic monarchy, the establishment of the Israelite empire, and perhaps even the coming of the Messiah himself:

> "The scepter shall not depart from Judah,
>   nor the ruler's staff from between his feet,
> until tribute comes to him;
>   and the obedience of the peoples is his." (49:10, NRSV)

Thus at the conclusion of the Book of Genesis, Jacob's vision of future Israel foresees also the means by which God will restore the blessing to all humankind.

The Death and Burial of Jacob (49:29–50:21)

The final narratives of Genesis record the deaths of Jacob and Joseph. Jacob stated again his desire to be buried in Canaan, in the cave of Machpelah, where Abraham and Sarah, Isaac and Rebekah, and Leah were all buried (49:29–31; and review Gn 23). Joseph was faithful to the last, burying his father with great pomp and ceremony in the patriarchal tomb in the land of promise (50:1–14).

After the burial of Jacob, there was again trouble in the patriarchal family. Joseph's

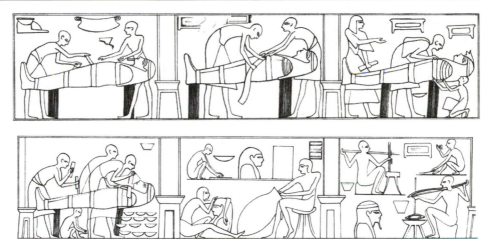

Drawing from an Egyptian tomb showing the process of mummification.

brothers were afraid they had received mercy and forgiveness from their brother only for the sake of their aged father. Now that Jacob was dead, they fully expected punishment from Joseph. Attempting first to deceive and cajole (50:16–17), they finally resorted to falling at Joseph's feet and offering to become his slaves (50:18). His reassuring words contain one of the classic statements of Scripture and provide the key to understanding the Joseph narrative: "Don't be afraid. Am I in the place of God? You intended to harm me, but God intended it for good to accomplish what is now being done, the saving of many lives. So then, don't be afraid" (50:19b–21a).

God had made both good and evil possible in the Garden of Eden at the beginning of the Book of Genesis. Now at its conclusion, we learn that in his grace and mercy, he works to accomplish his good through even the sinful actions of human beings (compare the similar statement in Gn 45:5–8). "Even where no man could imagine it, God had all the strings in his hand."[21]

The book offers no explanation of how God turns evil to good on our behalf. But implicit here is the intimate relationship between divine sovereignty and human responsibility. We can never fully understand how both are held together, yet both are clearly affirmed in Scripture. Any attempt to emphasize one at the expense of the other will result in misunderstanding how we relate to God. So, for example, to emphasize divine predestination to such a degree that you and I are not really re-

sponsible for our actions is to put too much emphasis on sovereignty. Likewise, to assert our human freedom in a way that implies any of our actions are outside God's control is to misunderstand our responsibility before God. The Joseph narrative beautifully illustrates that both are true and both must be held in balance. Joseph's life experiences taught him well. His brother's evil betrayal, Potiphar's wife's lies, the cupbearer's negligence, all had taught Joseph that God can overrule the evil of humans to accomplish good for those who serve him.

The Death of Joseph (50:22–26)

After a full and prosperous life, Joseph's departing words related to the fulfillment of God's patriarchal promises.[22] Twice in his dying words he asserted that "God will surely come to your aid" and predicted that God would deliver the future Israelite nation from Egypt in order to bring them into the land promised to Abraham, Isaac, and Jacob (vv. 24–25). Thus the driving force of the patriarchal narratives since the call of Abraham (12:1–3), and indeed the concepts of restoration and blessing that have been the concern of the Book of Genesis from the beginning, come again into focus at the end.

Joseph's last words conclude the Book of Genesis, but they are eminently forward-looking. So confident is he the Israelites will be temporary residents that he gave specific instructions that his body be taken back to Canaan: "then you must carry my bones up from this place" (v. 25).

Study Questions

1. Why is Joseph not listed among the patriarchs?

2. Give three reasons why the author of Genesis gives so much attention to the story of Joseph.

3. In what ways does the story of Joseph represent partial fulfillment of God's promises to Abraham?

4. Why does Joseph initially conceal his identity from his brothers? How do the "tests" he puts his brothers through reveal their characters?

5. Explain how there became only twelve landed tribes in Canaan in spite of the fact that Joseph's two sons were adopted by Jacob.

6. Throughout Genesis, we have seen how younger children often take precedence over older children. How is this present in at least two ways in the Joseph narrative, and where else in Genesis is this present?

7. How may it be said that "Genesis requires a sequel"?

8. Describe how the life of Joseph can serve as an example of faithfulness amid trials.

Key Term

Heilsgeschichte

He was thus embalmed and placed in a coffin in Egypt. Coffins were characteristic of Egyptian burial practices, and they are not referred to again in the Old Testament.[23] The text had related the elaborate mourning and burial ceremonies for Jacob (50:1–14). By contrast, Joseph was summarily stuffed away in a box and preserved for a greater day. His bones in the coffin would be a constant reminder to the Israelites that Egypt was not their home. And some great day, the time of deliverance would dawn in the work of one especially prepared for that event, Moses. In the meantime, Joseph's faith would serve as an example of how the Israelites were to live in a foreign land (Heb 11:22).

Genesis, like the Old Testament as a whole, ends on a note of expectation. On the one hand, it is a self-contained and complete book in that all the themes are neatly tied together. With the death of Joseph, the story of the patriarchal family is concluded, and the themes of blessing and promise are amply developed. But, on the other hand, Genesis is also incomplete in that it requires a sequel. Joseph's bones in the Egyptian coffin remind us that the patriarchal promises are only partially fulfilled. There will come a future day when the promises will be entirely fulfilled and the peace of the Garden of Eden will be restored. That story continues in the Book of Exodus and extends through the rest of the Bible.

Part

5

Encountering the Authorship of Genesis

The grass withers and the flowers fall, but the word of our God stands forever.

—Is 40:8

13 Evidence for Authorship

[Moses] was in the assembly in the desert, with our fathers and with the angel who spoke to him on Mount Sinai; and he received living words to pass on to us.

—Stephen, Acts 7:38

Primary Readings: Exodus 24:4a, Deuteronomy 31:9, 24–26

Outline

- **Evidence on the Authorship of the Pentateuch**
  Biblical References
  Jewish and Christian Tradition
  Grammatical Evidence
  Sociopolitical Evidence
  Manuscript Evidence
  Redactional Evidence
  Ancient Near Eastern Parallels
  Theological Perspective
- **Requirements of the Evidence**
  A Word about Words
  What Is the Most That Could Be Said?
  What Is the Least That Could Be Said?
- **Possibilities of the Evidence**
  Moses, the Yahwistic Innovator
  Moses, the Delegator of Authority
  Moses, the Fountainhead of Prophecy
  Scribes of Israel's Monarchy
  The Role of the Exilic Community

Objectives

After reading this chapter you should be able to

1. Discuss the relationship between the authorship issues of Genesis in comparison with the authorship of the entire Pentateuch.
2. Construct plausible arguments for authorship based on evidence from the Bible, tradition, the grammar of the text, cultural changes, available manuscripts, redactional theory, parallels with other ancient literature, and theology.
3. Using the evidence available, describe the necessary delimitations that are required regarding Mosaic authorship, as well as the possibilities that are allowed.
4. Define the roles of Moses, the levitical priests, scribes of the monarchy era, and the exilic community in the authorship, revision, and preservation of Genesis and the Pentateuch.

Now that you have encountered the contents of Genesis, it is time to encounter as well some important questions about the Book of Genesis. Unlike most modern literature, ancient Near Eastern literature in general and biblical books in particular do not often come with full bibliographical information, such as the author's name, place of publication, and date of publication. Modern scholars devote much time and energy to interpreting the meaning of these texts, which often also involves an attempt to determine who wrote the materials, when they were written, and to whom they were written.

As you know by now, the Book of Genesis has a deliberate and carefully crafted structure. It is a self-contained book that can stand on its own right. On the other hand, it has an intimate relationship with the rest of the Pentateuch, which is likewise deliberate and highly intentional. Not only does Genesis anticipate and prepare for the next four books of the Bible, but it depends on them for completion and fulfillment.[1] For this reason and others, it is impossible to consider questions of authorship without including evidence from the entire Pentateuch as well. In this next section you will be asked to consider what the text of the Pentateuch has to say about its own composition, with particular attention given to the Book of Genesis. In chapter 14, we will examine how modern scholarship has interpreted this evidence.

Evidence on the Authorship of the Pentateuch

We begin by asking what the Bible itself has to say about the authorship of Genesis and the rest of the Pentateuch. We will then consider some of the evidence available for addressing this question, including Jewish and Christian tradition, linguistic and historical evidence, and others.

Biblical References

Genesis itself contains no explicit references to the author, who has chosen to remain in the background. The rest of the Pentateuch, on the other hand, offers sev-

eral interesting glimpses. On more than one occasion we are told that Yahweh instructed Moses to write something down (Ex 34:27). The written document then may serve as a memorial for future generations (Ex 17:14). Significantly, in Exodus 24:4 the text notes that Moses wrote "all the words of the Lord" (NKJV). Near the end of Deuteronomy, it is stated that Moses wrote "the law" (31:9, 24), presumably referring to the legal core of the Book of Deuteronomy,[2] and the song of Moses (31:19, 22). On another occasion we are told that Moses recorded the travel diary of the tribes of national Israel (Nm 33:2). In addition to these explicit references, there are others in the Pentateuch that imply Mosaic writing activities (see Ex 25:16, 21–22).

These references in the Pentateuch suggest first of all that Moses could write. It may seem unnecessary to state such an obvious proposition, but it is often assumed that Moses, if he was historical at all, was probably illiterate. These references would argue against such a position. Second, these references indicate that Moses himself had a hand in the composition of certain blocks of material in the Pentateuch. Namely, it appears from these statements that Moses wrote *at least* the so-called Book of the Covenant (Ex 20–23) and a majority of the Book of Deuteronomy. In addition, we are told that other parts of the Pentateuch were given to Moses by Yahweh, though we are not quite sure of the full implications of this (see Ex 25–40, minus chapters 32–34, and most of the Book of Leviticus).

Jewish and Christian Tradition

Given these many references, it is not surprising that Jewish and Christian tradition has been unequivocal in the assumption that Moses wrote the Pentateuch. There are many other references in the Old Testament besides these from the Pentateuch that assume some connection between Moses and the materials in the Bible's first five books.[3] In fact, the Old Testament assumes in a most general way that Moses was ultimately responsible for the law, David for the hymnic literature, and Solomon for the wisdom literature. Later Jewish tradition continued along this assumption, referring to the first five books of the Bible as "the Books of Moses."[4]

The earliest Christian assumptions about the origins of Genesis and the rest of the Pentateuch are obvious from numerous references in the New Testament, such as "Has not Moses given you the law?" (Jn 7:19).[5] Though such statements appear often in the New Testament, they are of minimal help in our search for insight into the precise nature of the composition of the Book of Genesis. They do, however, illustrate the early Christian connections between the legal materials of the Pentateuch and Moses.

Grammatical Evidence

By grammatical evidence, I refer specifically to the spelling (orthography) and internal structure and forms of words (morphology) used in the Hebrew text of Genesis. Such evidence cannot, of course, provide much insight into the authorship of ancient texts. However, in light of our growing knowledge about these topics, they are helpful in suggesting the temporal limits of the text. In other words, such evidence establishes the earliest possible date for the text (that is, the *terminus a quo*).

Archaeologists have collected numerous inscriptions written in ancient Hebrew and other languages closely related to Hebrew (Phoenician, Aramaic, Moabite, etc.) dating to the tenth century B.C. and later. Comparisons between the Hebrew text of the Old Testament and these other inscriptions have increased our knowledge of early Hebrew spelling and morphology. These investigations have revealed certain features of Hebrew grammar that make it possible to date the present Book of Genesis no earlier than approximately the tenth century B.C., thereby establishing a *terminus a quo*. This is not to say the materials in Genesis could not have been written prior to that date, but only that the *present* text of Genesis could not have been produced prior to that date. This type of evidence also puts limits on how late the text may have been produced. Orthographic features of the present text of Genesis reflect the Persian period and could not have come from later than Israel's postexilic period.[6]

It is impossible to explain the significance of this evidence without a detailed discussion of Hebrew grammar. But perhaps it would be useful to describe in the most general terms a few of these observations. For example, the history of Hebrew orthography is instructive, specifically in the way Hebrew developed a spelling system to mark vowels. Until the tenth century B.C., northwest Semitic in general (the language family of which Hebrew was a part) represented only consonantal sounds. During the ninth century, Hebrew and other languages of this group developed a means by which the most common vowels could be marked.[7] But these markers were usually reserved for the vowels at the ends of words. Then in the mid-eighth century, the vowel letters began to appear in the middle of words.[8] Since Genesis uses these vowel markers regularly throughout (both in the middle of words and at the end) this evidence alone is enough to demonstrate that the present text of Genesis (and indeed of the rest of the Old Testament) reflects the revisioning and normalization of the late preexilic period, that is, after the mid-eighth century B.C.[9]

In terms of morphology, a single example may suffice. The true relative pronoun for early Hebrew was *zû*, as is clear from ancient Phoenician inscriptions and the archaic Hebrew poetry preserved in the Old Testament. But this was replaced in Hebrew around the tenth century by the term *ʾăšer*, which is commonly used in all Old Testament narrative, including the Book of Genesis.[10]

Such observations do not provide definitive evidence for authorship and date. However, they illustrate that the text has gone through some significant grammatical revisioning and literary updating, and these observations provide time markers for when those changes were made. An author or compiler of Genesis may have finished the work centuries before these changes in the language occurred. But the text itself continued to need revisions.

Remember, these minor grammatical revisions had no detrimental effect on the inspired truth of the text. God's inspiration of the Bible has preserved his truth faithfully (2 Tim 3:16; 2 Pt 1:19–21). As sovereign God, he has superintended the entire process of inscripturation, including grammatical updating. The situation is not completely unlike the proliferation of new English translations of the Bible in our day. The truth of the ancient authors has not changed, but we are in constant need of freshening our translations in order to match the changing English language.

Sociopolitical Evidence

When one compares Old Testament Israel with other Semitic nations of the ancient Near East, there are certain similarities that are noticeable.[11] Besides the general comparisons made by anthropologists about the way different cultures develop around the world, it is possible to see repeatable trends in ancient Semitic cultures as well. These generally progress through a period of tribalism in a pre-state context to statehood over many centuries. After a period of imperial strength, the nation usually succumbs to internal decay and eventual ruin.[12]

It was during the periods of greatest political strength that most of these cultures preserved and produced their literature. Periods of politically enforced peace provided the only times in which kings and scribes were afforded the luxury and resources necessary for the production of literature. In some cases, new forms of historiographic literature were developed and the older venerated literature of that culture was collected and deliberately preserved.

Israel certainly reflected this sociopolitical pattern. Her period of political strength, the united monarchy of David and Solomon, was painfully brief, though later generations of Israelites always esteemed it as the ideal time in their history (1 Kgs 4:25). The Bible hints that the kingdoms of David and Solomon devoted resources to the scribal arts. For the first time in Israelite history, we read of officials whose specific task it was to record events or details of monarchic life. These court historians were the "recorder, chronicler" (*mazkîr*, 2 Sm 8:16; 20:24; 1 Kgs 4:3) and the "scribe, secretary" (*sôpēr*, 2 Sm 8:17; 20:25; 1 Kgs 4:3). Though it is impossible for us to know the exact function these officials served in the royal court, their titles imply they either recorded daily activities of the court or preserved the sacred literature of Israel's past, or both. It is possible that Israel's united monarchy produced humankind's first historiographies.

This may also confirm the Bible's portrayal of David and Solomon as patrons of the literary arts, especially hymnic and wisdom literature. If this is a fair comparison, then just as certain Assyrian and Babylonian kings preserved the ancient literature of their cultures,[13] so David and Solomon preserved materials already viewed as ancient and sacred at the time of Israel's united monarchy. This would presumably have included the ancient Mosaic traditions now preserved in the Pentateuch, as well as the creation and patriarchal traditions of Genesis.

Statements in Genesis That Appear to Come from the Period after Moses

Genesis 11:28, 31

"Ur of the Chaldeans"

The Chaldeans had not entered Mesopotamia at the time of Moses, so Ur could not have been known as "of the Chaldeans" until much later.

Genesis 14:14

"as far as Dan"

The city of Dan was known as Laish until after Moses. It was given the name "Dan" during the period of the judges (Jgs 18:29).

Genesis 36:31

"before any Israelite king reigned"

This statement suggests that the passage was updated during the monarchic period.

Such sociopolitical comparisons accent the role of the united monarchy in the preservation of pentateuchal traditions. This emphasis explains several individual references in the Pentateuch that seem to have come from the period after Moses. For example, the list of Edomite kings and sheikhs included at the end of the Esau *tôlĕdôt* (36:31–43) is likely a piece of post-Mosaic material. The statement that these individuals ruled "before any Israelite king reigned" (36:31) makes it seem likely that this was an insertion from the monarchic period of Israel's history.

In addition to this list from the monarchy, there are several briefer comments that appear to have come into the text later in Israel's history. The designation of the homeland of Abram as Ur "of the Chaldeans" (11:28, 31, and elsewhere) is probably a later gloss. The Chaldeans do not appear in texts from the ancient Near East until the first millennium B.C., when they apparently first entered Mesopotamia. The city of Ur in southern Babylonia could not have been known as "of the Chaldeans" until much later. Since this passage in Genesis is not a predictive prophecy, we should assume the designation of the city is a later insertion to distinguish it from another city of the same name.[14]

There are other such examples from elsewhere in the Pentateuch. But perhaps one more from Genesis will suffice here. In 14:14, we are told that Abram pursued Lot's captors "as far as Dan." But the city of Dan was given that name in the judges period (Jgs 18:29), and was formerly known as Laish. It seems likely, then, that this is another example of revisioning, or updating an early Israelite tradition from a monarchic perspective. If we are correct that the royal scribes of the united monarchy had a significant role in copying and editing these Genesis traditions, such slight revisions would be no more unusual than the subtle changes in English Bible translations.

Manuscript Evidence

Besides the standardized Hebrew text of the Pentateuch, we also have ancient translations in several other languages, as well as a paleo-Hebrew form known as the Samaritan Pentateuch. Together these serve as valuable witnesses to the relative date for the composition of the Pentateuch. Using these sources, it is possible to establish the *terminus ad quem* (or finishing point), being the latest possible date at which the Pentateuch could have been formulated as we have it today.

The Greek translation known as the **Septuagint** together with other Jewish sources from ancient Qumran (i.e., the Dead Sea Scrolls) were using editions of the Pentateuch that were in basic agreement with the text as we have it in the standardized Hebrew text. This observation demonstrates that the text of the Pentateuch has been handed down in its present form since at least the third century B.C.[15]

But we can go even further back than this. In a way that has not been fully appreciated by modern scholarship, the Samaritan Pentateuch also establishes the antiquity of the Pentateuch. Detailed studies of the Samaritan Pentateuch and its relationship with the Septuagint, the Dead Sea Scrolls, and other ancient Jewish sources reveal the existence of a pentateuchal text type in ancient Palestine already in the fifth century B.C. The earliest forms of the Samaritan Pentateuch were being revised and modernized as early as about 450 B.C., which testifies to the existence of a complete text of the Pentateuch at that time.[16] This confirms that the Pentateuch itself must be older than the fifth century B.C. Such an early date is confirmed by the need for the scribes of the time of Ezra (mid-fifth century B.C.) to modernize and interpret the Pentateuch in order to make it understandable to the people of their day (Neh 8:8, 13).

Redactional Evidence

As we shall emphasize in chapter 15, Genesis serves as an important prologue for the rest of the Pentateuch. However, it is much more than a mere historical and geographical prelude. Many of the episodes and ideas detailed here anticipate the rest of the Pentateuch. There is an intimate theological connection between Genesis and Exodus–Deuteronomy created by literary parallels between the Primeval History and patriarchal narratives on the one hand, and the events and institutions of the Mosaic period on the other. All of this appears to have been quite intentional and must have been in the mind of the author of Genesis from the start. The Book of Genesis has been redacted (or "edited") intentionally from a Mosaic perspective, and therefore has implications for the date of the composition of Genesis.

I offer here only a couple of examples. Already in Genesis 1 the author carefully constructed the creation account with the Sinai covenant in mind. The idea of Sabbath rest is as old as creation itself (Gn 2:2–3). Yet the way in which the seven days of creation prepare for the fourth commandment at Sinai is unmistakable (Ex 20:9–11). The reason for keeping Sabbath is in fact the ideal that the Israelites should imitate the Creator's example: "For in six days the LORD made the heavens and the earth, the sea, and all that is in them, but he rested on the seventh day. Therefore the LORD blessed the Sabbath day and made it holy" (Ex 20:11). The creation account in Genesis 1:1–2:4a appears to have been redacted with the Sinai covenant in view.

In Genesis 12:10–20, the author related how severe famine forced Abraham to flee to Egypt, where God protected and cared for him (review pages 73–74, above). That account also has been intentionally edited so as to prefigure the later experience of the Israelites. Like Abraham, the children of Jacob were forced to Egypt by famine (the Joseph narrative). Like their great forefather, the Israelites acquired wealth from the Egyptians when they left (Ex 12:35–36). In both accounts, God sent plagues on Egypt in order to liberate first Abraham,

This tablet is an example of ancient Mesopotamian writing.

then Moses and the Israelites (Gn 12:17 and Ex 7:14–12:36). There are other parallels, but this is sufficient to demonstrate that the Genesis account has been intentionally edited with the Mosaic era in mind.[17]

The date of Moses and the exodus is of course still a moot question. Most of those scholars who assume the events of Exodus–Deuteronomy are historical place them in the Late Bronze Age (1550–1200 B.C.), specifically in either the fifteenth century B.C. or the thirteenth century B.C. The fact that Genesis was edited in the light of the rest of the Pentateuch implies it could not have been put in its present literary form *prior* to the Mosaic period. On the other hand, the editorial additions referred to above from the united monarchy would suggest that the book was in something similar to its present form by the time of David and Solomon.

Ancient Near Eastern Parallels

Besides the general sociopolitical comparisons with other Semitic cultures of the ancient Near East, it is helpful to review again the literary parallels from Israel's ancient neighbors (see pages 46–48, above). As we have seen, the most striking parallels to the early chapters of Genesis, and to a lesser extent the patriarchal narratives, come from Mesopotamia. Genesis frequently addresses similar topics in an outline comparable to that of the Mesopotamian sources. But the actual names and details are often quite different. It appears there was definite Mesopotamian influence on the traditions of Genesis, though somewhat indirect. If we could determine the approximate time when such influence took place, we might have additional clues as to when the traditions of Genesis took their present form.

We know that Mesopotamian culture spread throughout Syria–Palestine in the mid-second millennium B.C.[18] But after the arrival of the Sea Peoples around 1200 B.C., the normal flow of international cultural interchange was disrupted. The ancient Israelites were not likely to have been influenced by Mesopotamian culture for centuries afterwards. Against the views of many modern scholars, it is even more unlikely that the Jews of the **Babylonian exile**

in the sixth and fifth centuries B.C. would have incorporated features of Babylonian mythology in their ancient traditions, even after stripping such myths of pagan and polytheistic elements. The Jewish leadership was too adamantly opposed to such Babylonian influence, and materials received under such pagan influence would not likely have found a place in their sacred Scriptures.

Instead, the oblique Mesopotamian influence on Genesis is more likely to have been the result of cultural contact much further back in Israel's history. The only likely time Mesopotamian literary influence could have had such an impact on Genesis seems to be the first half of the second millennium B.C.[19]

Religious Perspective

We have observed that the faith expressed in the patriarchal narratives best reflects the first half of the second millennium B.C. (2000–1500 B.C., review pages 87–88, above). In addition, it can be stated that the author(s) or editor(s) of the Pentateuch highly valued the religious traditions of the patriarchal narratives in spite of the many features that seem to be at odds with the form of Yahwism defined in Exodus–Deuteronomy.

The compiler of the Pentateuch has gone to considerable length to associate the faith of the patriarchs with that of Mosaic Yahwism. He has accurately depicted actual patriarchal beliefs and practices, even when those beliefs and practices seemed to conflict with normative Yahwism. He has been faithful to the patriarchal traditions handed down to him, without suppressing or extracting those features that were so different from the faith of Moses.

Some modern scholars have argued that the patriarchal traditions were contrived by first-millennium authors who speculated about hypothetical ancestors of Israel's past—Abraham, Isaac, and Jacob. But if this were so, we might expect such a late author to make the patriarchal traditions conform to the accepted Yahwism of the Israelite monarchy. Instead, the patriarchal traditions were accepted as genuine traditions from an ancient period of Israel's history, and were included as a theological predecessor to the Yahwism defined by

Moses.[20] It is not likely that a late author could have created fictitious patriarchs who had certain religious ideas in common with later Canaanite Baalism (see below), nor could such a late author accurately reflect the early-second-millennium traditions of Genesis 12–50. The following observations lend credibility to the argument that the theological perspective of the patriarchal traditions has been accurately preserved in Genesis and incorporated into the Yahwism of the Mosaic period.

The details of this kind of evidence are complex. They have been summarized recently around the issue of holiness.[21] This concept of holiness (Hebrew *qādôš*) becomes central in Mosaic definitions of Yahwism from Exodus 3:5 on, where God says to Moses, "Take off your sandals, for the place where you are standing is holy ground." Thus the holiness of Yahweh requires religious expression that is exclusivistic, regulated by legal stipulations, mediated by a priest or prophet, and based at a central sanctuary, which became Jerusalem in later Israelite Yahwism. By contrast, the term for holiness does not occur in the patriarchal narratives.[22] The absence of terminology for the concept of holiness illustrates the contrasts between Mosaic Yahwism and patriarchal religion, which does not appear to have been exclusivistic at all. In contrast to Moses, Abraham and his family had a faith that was unstructured, unmediated, and did not elevate one particular place as more sacred for divine worship over others.

The contrast can be seen in certain other details. The frequent use of El (the Hebrew generic word for "God") in the patriarchal traditions is significant, both in the names for God (see page 87, above) as well as in the names for people and places, such as the compound names Israel, Ishmael, and Bethel. Given the central importance of some of these names, we may assume they arose prior to the constitutive expression of Yahwism in the rest of the Pentateuch. In other words, since Yahweh was the God of Israel, we would have expected compound names such as Isra-Yah, or Beth-Yah in these traditions. The only explanation is that these patriarchal traditions arose prior to the Mosaic period.[23]

Certain cultic practices also illustrate the contrast. In general, patriarchal religion seems completely unmediated, requiring no one to intercede between the worshiper and God. Abraham and Jacob talk with God and interact with him freely. Later Israelite faith required prophets and priests to mediate the relationship between people and God.

The role of trees (12:6–7; 13:18; 21:33) and pillars (28:18, 22; 31:13, 45–46; 35:14) in patriarchal worship seems particularly foreign to the faith of later Israelite Yahwism.[24] Such customs were intimately related to later Canaanite fertility cults, and were given a resounding prohibition elsewhere in the Pentateuch (Ex 23:24; 34:13; Lv 26:1; Dt 16:21–22). Rather than suppress or conform these traditions to convictions of a later period, the editor of Genesis clearly views them as vestiges of religious expression from an earlier age, and includes them without explanation. They appear to reflect a genuinely ancient patriarchal tradition—ancient, that is, to the editor of the Pentateuch.

Finally, it is important to notice that of the three great religious observances of the Pentateuch and later Israelite faith, only one is mentioned at all in the patriarchal narratives.[25] Circumcision becomes an important sign of God's covenant with Abraham (Gn 17), and is accepted as fundamental to Yahwism elsewhere in the Pentateuch. But the other two observances of the Pentateuch (Sabbath observance and dietary restrictions) are completely absent in the patriarchal narratives. Again, this is presumably because the editor of these Genesis materials who combined them with the rest of the Pentateuch already considered the patriarchal narratives to be of great antiquity and to accurately reflect the religious expression of the ancestors of Israel's faith.

Canaanite religion changed significantly sometime around the middle of the second millennium B.C. The chief god El was replaced by Baal as the supreme deity of the Canaanite pantheon, and a religion that had been somewhat compatible with patriarchal religion was replaced by a radical fertility cult that could never exist comfortably alongside Israelite Yahwism. The use of El-type names became less prevalent than before, now being replaced by Baal names. This change from El to Baal brought other innovations in Canaanite religion. The uses of trees and stones took on an entirely different connotation, one of sexual fertility and divine sexual activity. Such practices could never be tolerated by Mosaic Yahwism. The rest of Old Testament history is largely the story of Israel's failure to resist compromises of their orthodox Yahwism with Canaanite Baalism.

In conclusion, the cumulative effect of the various religious traditions in the patriarchal narratives is clear. Patriarchal faith reflects a period of time before Mosaic Yahwism received its constitutive expressions in the rest of the Pentateuch. The editor(s) of the Pentateuch intentionally equated patriarchal faith with Yahwism without suppressing non-Yahwistic elements because the traditions were already venerated as sacred and ancient, and they therefore accurately reflect the situation in the first half of the second millennium B.C. These Genesis traditions were adapted by the compiler of the rest of the Pentateuch as part of the constitutive religious heritage of ancient Israel.

Requirements of the Evidence

Having surveyed the evidence available for the authorship of Genesis and the rest of the Pentateuch, it will now be our task to summarize what this evidence demands of us. This brief discussion will explore the parameters of the evidence in order to determine the maximum and minimum conclusions possible in light of that evidence. In other words, we seek now to answer the questions, "What is the most that could be said about the authorship of Genesis on the basis of this evidence?" and "What is the least that could be said?"

A Word about Words

Before proceeding, we need to define an important term: "authorship." The term as used here deals not so much with the mechanical process of writing or recording, as we usually mean when we apply the term to the production of modern literature. With regard to ancient books such as Genesis, we can only use the term to refer to the fundamental substance of the content. This is true partly because ancient books do not come with a complete set of bibliographical data, as we said at the beginning of this chapter. But also the nature of the evidence we have just surveyed makes it impossible to discern the precise relationship between the substance of a book and the actual mechanical process of writing.

More often than not, it is impossible for modern scholarship to determine the relationship between the origin of an ancient book's substance and the actual act of recording. Not only is most ancient Near Eastern literature anonymous; the concept of "author," where it is present, tends to indicate someone who is a preserver of the past, someone who builds on earlier versions and adapts traditions for a new day.[26] This is complicated even further by the ancient use of oral traditions and our inability to trace the history of such traditions. So by "author" and "authorship" we seek to discern the source or the origin of the materials of Genesis, which may or may not have a relationship with the actual process of recording.

What Is the Most That Could Be Said?

In general, the Bible, and all of Jewish and Christian tradition credit Moses as the author of the Pentateuch. None of the other types of evidence makes this unfeasible, though the Pentateuch must have been a malleable and adaptable text that went through later revisions and updates. This would reasonably mean Moses inherited the traditions of the Primeval History (Gn 1–11) and the patriarchal narratives (Gn 12–50) from Israel's ancestors and incorporated them as a one-book introduction for the Pentateuch. Whether he received them in written or oral form is beyond our ability to determine. Whether he was the one responsible for the current structure of Genesis is also impossible to determine.

In addition, the evidence also requires that Moses is responsible for the pentateuchal law, which with many insertions covers roughly Exodus 20–Deuteronomy 26. Thus the heart of the Pentateuch has a Mosaic self-claim, which should not be missed. Much of this material is said to be material that the Lord spoke to Moses (as in Ex 25:1 and Lv 1:1), or the very "words Moses spoke to all Israel" (Dt 1:1). More specifically, the text states that Moses actually wrote down an account of the battle against Amalek (Ex 17:14), the so-called Book of the Covenant (Ex 24:4), a section known as "the code of festivals" (Ex 34:27), the desert itinerary (Nm 33:2), and at least portions of the Book of Deuteronomy (31:9, 19, 22, 24).

Since none of the other evidence available precludes these textual claims, this is the most that we can say on the basis of our present knowledge. Moses is the author or originator of the Pentateuch in general, and he personally was involved in the mechanical composition of certain sections as defined by the statements in Exodus, Numbers, and Deuteronomy.

What Is the Least That Could Be Said?

On the other hand, it should also be observed that the evidence does not require that Moses drafted the Pentateuch, either in its entirety or in its present five-book formation. Many of the traditions and teachings that he handed down to the later Israelites may have been oral in nature and may not have taken literary shape until later. The least that can be said is that Moses was involved in the composition of parts of the Pentateuch and was ultimately seen by later Israelites as responsible for the gist of the whole, though the current five-book format may have been decided later.

Possibilities of the Evidence

The previous section explored what the evidence *demands* of us regarding the authorship of the Pentateuch. Now we will consider what the evidence *allows*. Keeping all the evidence in mind, this brief section will suggest a feasible model for the composition of the Pentateuch in general and the Book of Genesis in particular.

Moses, the Yahwistic Innovator

First, we know from Exodus 3:13–15 and 6:2–3 that Moses was the "Yahweh innovator" of Israel's religion. The precise interpretation of these important passages is a matter of enormous scholarly debate and need not detain us here. The point for our discussion is that Moses ushered in a Yahwistic innovation in Israelite religion. He received patriarchal traditions that appear to have referred to God consistently as El, "God," or with El-type names (Elohim, El-Shaddai, El-Elyon, and the like). But from Moses' time forward, God would be known primarily by his intimate name, Yahweh, which reveals more of his character. The more generic term "El" reveals *what* he is (God); the name "Yahweh" reveals *who* he is.

The specific phraseology of Exodus 3:15 is instructive on this point: Elohim said to Moses, "Say to the Israelites, 'The LORD [i.e., Yahweh], the God [i.e., Elohim] of your fathers—the God of Abraham, the God of Isaac and the God of Jacob—has sent me to you.' This is my name forever, the name by which I am to be remembered from generation to generation." This statement intentionally associates God's new name with the ancient patriarchal traditions.

The patriarchal traditions in Genesis 12–50 have been preserved in Yahwistic framework, which anticipates and prepares for the materials in the rest of the Pentateuch. As we have seen, the Genesis materials are more than a mere historical introduction, tracing the origins of Israel and explaining how the children of Jacob came to be in Egypt. The book is a theological prologue for the exodus and Sinai covenant. Genesis is fundamentally and intimately tied to Exodus–Deuteronomy in a way that has been intentional throughout its editing process, a process that was distinctively Yahwistic in nature.

Moses, the Delegator of Authority

In Exodus 18:13–27, Moses learned from his father-in-law how to delegate responsibility to those who were trustworthy and able. It is clear from a few references in the Pentateuch that Moses entrusted the preservation of the legal materials, and in some cases even the responsibility for writing those materials, to the priesthood. The most important of these is Deuteronomy 31:9: "So Moses wrote down this law and gave it to the priests, the sons of Levi, who carried the ark of the covenant of the LORD, and to all the elders of Israel." Moses thus entrusted the safekeeping of the document itself to the levitical priesthood, and he gave the responsibility of seeing that the nation actually lived according to its instruction to the elders of Israel. This added further to the role of the levitical priests, who were in charge of the ark of the covenant with its copy of the Ten Commandments. In verses 24–26, Moses further instructed the priests concerning their role in preserving the written copy of the legal material.[27]

In ancient Near Eastern treaties, it was customary to make two copies of the agreement, one for the sanctuary of each party entering into the agreement's obligation.[28] But in Israel's unique covenant with God, there was but one sanctuary for the written form of the treaty. So the written law was entrusted to the care of the levitical priests who were also caretakers of the ark of the covenant, which served as the receptacle for the tables of law. It appears that Moses delegated responsibility for the law to the priests.

The Pentateuch contains a few other hints about the role of the priests in preserving

the law. Moses gave instructions for all future kings of Israel to keep a copy of the law ever before them, making a royal copy from the official and sanctioned version preserved by the priests (Dt 17:18). On occasion, the priests were to be consulted about specific legal requirements, which they were said to teach the Israelites according to the details of what Yahweh "commanded them" (Dt 24:8). On another occasion they were actually given the responsibility for preserving a specific legal rite in written form (Nm 5:23–24). Later in Israelite history it appears there were priestly scribes who specialized in preserving legal material through writing (Jer 8:8).[29]

The full significance of these references has not often been appreciated. We cannot be precise about the role played by the levitical priests in the composition and preservation of the Pentateuch in general. But it seems clear that they were deeply involved. Perhaps the levitical priests were an extension of Moses' work on the Pentateuch. He may have officially sanctioned them to use their own authority in protecting, preserving, and even composing sections of the pentateuchal law.[30]

Moses met with God on Mount Sinai.

Moses, the Fountainhead of Prophecy

There can be no doubt that Moses stands at the head of Israel's literary traditions as the great lawgiver. He can be said to be the fountainhead of all Israelite prophecy.[31] In this light, the deposition of the written form of the law into the ark of the covenant is significant (Dt 31:24–26). It is likely that other documents that contributed to the understanding of Israel's covenant relationship with Yahweh also began to be compiled and collected along with this basic constitutive document of Israel's religion and nationhood. As we have seen, the priests may have had a significant role in the actual preservation of such documents. But ultimately, it was only Moses who had authority to determine the contents of what was preserved in the ark and what was excluded. This would have been the beginning of the canonical process for ancient Israel's Scriptures. Future documents would have authority in the community only if they complemented Israel's understanding of the covenant with Yahweh.

So we suggest a picture of a growing body of religious traditions centering around the Mosaic covenant of Mount Sinai and preserved by the priesthood, perhaps even contained along with the Ten Commandments in the ark of the covenant.[32] These would have included the materials that ultimately made up the Book of Genesis (i.e., the traditions of the Primeval History and the patriarchal narratives), the legal materials, and other types of materials all sanctioned by Moses as appropriate expressions of the covenant. In this way, the sacred writings from the time of Moses were preserved in the Israelite sanctuary for well over two centuries, at least until the united monarchy was established.

Scribes of Israel's Monarchy

As we have said, evidence suggests that the earliest literature of an ancient Semitic culture is systematically studied for the first time, collected, and preserved for future generations during the height of that culture's imperial strength (see sociopolitical evidence above). The biblical references to the scribes and recorders in the royal court of David and Solomon seem to confirm such a picture for ancient Israel. It seems likely that scribes of the united monarchy formally devoted themselves to the study and preservation of the ancient texts related to the Sinai covenant.

This explains the obvious post-Mosaic material present in Genesis, such as the designation of Abraham's hometown as "Ur of the Chaldeans" and the presence of the Edomite king list (36:31–43, see discussion above). The scribes of the united kingdom would no doubt have updated and modernized the texts for their own readers. It is possible these scribes were even the ones who arranged the materials in the present five-book format, which would explain the editorial intentionality with which Genesis prepares for Exodus–Deuteronomy.

The Role of the Exilic Community

After Jerusalem fell to Nebuchadnezzar in 586 B.C., most of the leaders were taken into exile in Babylonia. The exile officially ended in October 539 B.C., when Babylonia was captured by the Persians and the Jews were released and permitted to return to the ruins of Jerusalem. Scholars have often speculated about the role these exilic and postexilic communities might have played in the production of the literature of the Old Testament (see ch. 14, below).

It is certainly true that Israelites of the monarchic period (i.e., before the fall of Jerusalem and the loss of the monarchy) did not have a "static" view of these texts. In other words, ancient texts were not standardized, but were rather more fluid than we tend to view them today.[33] Such a standardized or static view of the text was certainly a later Jewish development and was not characteristic of Israelite times. The preeminent scribe of the postexilic period, Ezra, found it necessary to clarify and interpret the meaning of the text as he read it to the people, which implies he modernized the text as he taught (Neh 8:8).

The Jewish practice of standardization explains the Hebrew text as we now have it. It has without doubt gone through significant grammatical revisions and spelling updates, which is what we would expect from this period. "A principle

Study Questions

1. What do orthography and morphology contribute to a discussion regarding the date of the Pentateuch? What can these issues *not* determine for us?

2. Explain the importance of the monarchical period when discussing the dating of the Pentateuch. What textual anachronisms suggest that textual editing took place during this period?

3. Define "redaction." How is it apparent a significant redaction of Genesis took place during or after the Mosaic era?

4. Describe how the theological perspective of the patriarchs differs from that of the Pentateuch as a whole. What do these differing theological perspectives reveal?

5. What can be confidently confirmed in response to the statement, "Moses wrote the Pentateuch"?

6. Comment on the possible roles of priest, scribe, Moses, and the exilic community in the preservation and transmission of the Genesis material.

7. What issues have captured your attention during this discussion of dating and authorship? What areas and arguments would you like to explore further?

which must never be lost sight of in dealing with documents of the ancient Near East is that instead of leaving obvious archaisms in spelling and grammar, as later became the fashion in Greece and Rome, the scribes generally revised ancient literary and other documents periodically."[34]

I offer the following general statement as a conclusion to this brief survey of the evidence on the authorship of Genesis. On the basis of the internal features of Genesis and other types of evidence surveyed here, the materials compiled in the book appear to have originated in their various features during the Mosaic era. They were preserved by the priests and scribes of early Israel, until they were finally organized in their current format, probably during the united monarchy. The text continued to be revised and updated well into the exile and beyond.[35]

Above all, we should rejoice in the knowledge that the entire process of inscripturation was providentially superintended, so that Genesis, like the rest of the Bible, is true and certain. We do well to give it our closest attention, "as to a light shining in a dark place, until the day dawns and the morning star rises in [our] hearts." For as the New Testament apostle explains, no portion of Scripture is a product of human effort or will. Rather, the Bible came to us from people who spoke from God under the direction of the Holy Spirit (2 Pt 1:19–21).

Key Terms

Septuagint
Babylonian exile

14 Interpretations of the Evidence

In those days Israel had no king, so the people did whatever seemed right in their own eyes.

—Jgs 17:6; 21:25 (NLT)

Outline

- **Nature of Biblical Criticism**
- **Survey of the Methods**
  Textual Criticism
  Source Criticism and Redaction Criticism
  Form Criticism and Tradition Criticism
  Historical Criticism
  Literary Criticism
  Canonical Criticism
- **Survey of Scholarship on the Book of Genesis**
  Eighteenth Century
  Nineteenth Century
  Conservative Responses
  Early and Mid-twentieth Century
  Recent Developments
- **Conclusions**

Objectives

After reading this chapter you should be able to

1. Describe eight methods of criticism used by modern Bible scholars.
2. Recount the history of biblical criticism as it relates to the Book of Genesis, the Pentateuch, and the Old Testament in general.
3. Summarize Wellhausen's Documentary Hypothesis and similar, related approaches that preceded it.
4. Identify recent modifications and corrections to the Documentary Hypothesis perspective that make use of archaeological evidence and ancient Near East studies.
5. Begin to develop a method of biblical interpretation that affirms a high view of Scripture and makes use of archaeological evidence, Near Eastern studies, and the critical methodologies in ways that are compatible with a holistic supernatural worldview.

lower criticism

higher criticism

autographs

As in any field of endeavor, there is a great variety of opinions among Old Testament scholars about the evidence we considered in the preceding chapter. However, the situation is even more complicated than one might expect. The author of the Book of Judges assessed the moral and political climate of his own day as one of chaos and turmoil. His assessment is not inappropriate to describe the field of Old Testament studies today. No single theory or scholarly consensus rules the day, so chaos prevails.

In this chapter, I will give a brief introduction to the methodologies used by modern biblical scholars. This will be followed by a survey of the scholarship on Genesis and the Pentateuch in general, which will in essence be an overview of how modern scholarship has interpreted the evidence surveyed in chapter 13. The ideas outlined here are exceedingly complex, and you should bear in mind that this chapter can only introduce you to the many issues involved.

Nature of Biblical Criticism

In its broadest sense, biblical criticism is the search for truth through the application of the laws of reason to an investigation of the biblical text.[1] It has the unfortunate sound of something negative and distasteful because of the primary meaning of "criticism" as the act of passing judgment on the merits of something or someone, a judgment that is usually unfavorable. You may be asking, "Who would dare criticize the Bible?" But criticism also designates the "science which deals with the text, character, composition, and origin of literary documents."[2] As such, it is a strictly neutral term, neither negative nor positive. And, as such, it is something we all do! It is in fact impossible to read the biblical text without also considering the questions of authorship and date of composition.

So biblical criticism seeks truth by applying the laws of reason to the biblical text.[3] One of the tasks of modern criticism has been to develop appropriate rules for such investigation, which has in turn led to the development of several distinct methodologies. These have sometimes been subdivided into "**lower criticism**" and "**higher criticism**," though these terms are not as common as they once were because of their derogatory implications. Lower criticism refers to textual criticism, which seeks to reconstruct the original wording of the texts from the various manuscripts currently available. Higher criticism refers to all other forms of biblical criticism, which seek to answer questions regarding the Bible's composition and origins. Since the Enlightenment (seventeenth and eighteenth centuries A.D.), biblical criticism has given rise to a number of distinguishable but interconnected methodologies, to which we now turn.

Survey of the Methods

This overview will introduce you to the most commonly used methods of biblical criticism. A few will receive only brief mention though they are no less important in the task of interpreting the Bible.

Textual Criticism[4]

No original copies (called "**autographs**") of any books of the Bible have survived to the present day. Textual critics therefore seek to reconstruct as completely as possible the original wording of the text based on the existing manuscripts available. This involves the examination of ancient medieval Hebrew manuscripts (the Masoretic Text), as well as the early Greek translations (the Septuagint and various ancient editions), and translations in many other languages, including Latin, Coptic, Ethiopic, and Aramaic. In addition, archaeologists found hundreds of manuscripts and manuscript fragments in eleven caves along the northwestern coast of the Dead Sea between 1947 and 1956 (the so-called Dead Sea Scrolls). These scrolls written in Hebrew, Aramaic, and Greek (a few) antedate by almost a thousand years the previously known earliest manuscripts of the Old Testament. The Dead Sea Scrolls have had great impact on Old Testament studies in general and textual criticism in particular, largely confirming the reliability of the text as we have it.

All of these manuscripts were copied by hand since they were produced before the age of the printing press. Therefore errors of the eye and ear were inevitable. The textual critic works to discover these errors and restore the original text as much as possible. This task may appear to be an exceedingly frustrating one. Without the benefit of any original manuscripts, how can textual critics ever know if they have reconstructed the text correctly? So many years removed from the autographs, is textual criticism an exercise in futility resulting in nothing more than educated guesswork?

Actually there is a remarkably high percentage of agreement among the numerous manuscripts available. The work of textual critics illustrates the reliability of the text without the need for a perfect witness to it. We may use as an illustration the standard yard at the Smithsonian Institution in Washington, D.C.[5] Few of us have ever actually seen the perfect standard of measurement by which we all are accustomed to measuring objects. Many of us never even realized it existed. Yet we routinely use our rulers, scales, and tape measures without the need to consult the pristine standard in Washington. These approximate measures derive their value from that standard, and are true and dependable because they have the true standard behind them. Nor would the loss or destruction of the standard yard significantly affect us. The numerous copies of the standard in our possession would enable us to continue with our lives as normal. Likewise, the loss of the biblical autographs is not really significant for textual critics. They seek to compare the copies in order to preserve the standard as carefully as possible.

Finally, it should be noted that the number of variants in the Old Testament text that change the way we interpret a given passage are exceedingly small. None of the variants that would actually alter our interpretation of a passage have any significant bearing on the great doctrinal truths of the church.

Source Criticism and Redaction Criticism

The role of **source criticism** in Old Testament studies is to discover the literary patterns of the text. These patterns in turn enable the critic to speculate about, and possibly isolate, various sources used in

The Dead Sea Scrolls, found in these caves, have had a significant impact on Old Testament textual criticism

Tasks of the Form Critic

1. Analyze the structure of the genre.

2. Define the text as an example of one genre or another.

3. Identify the social setting that produced and maintained the genres.

4. Determine the intention of the genres.

the composition of the text.[6] Often the source critic relies on a combination of several types of criteria to distinguish the sources. In pentateuchal studies, these include the different names for God, repetition or parallel accounts of single events, apparent contradictions, style, and theology. I will only introduce the various criteria used for source analysis here. You will see them again below when we survey the results of source critical work on Genesis.[7]

First, we have seen how the opening chapters of Genesis use both the general word "God" (Elohim) and the sacred name for God, usually translated "the Lord" (Yahweh). Sometimes we even encountered the two together: "the Lord God." We have also observed that the patriarchal narratives use El-type names for God with much more frequency than the otherwise widespread use of Yahweh. Scholars working on Genesis since the 1750s have accepted the two divine names as a fundamental criterion for source distinction in Genesis and elsewhere in the Pentateuch.

Second, we have also observed that the author of Genesis records parallel events on a number of occasions. For example, both Abraham and Isaac lie to foreign kings about their relationship to their wives (12:14–20; 20:1–18; 26:1–11). There seem to be two namings of Beersheba (21:22–34; 26:26–33), and two occasions when Bethel is given its name (28:10–22; 35:13–15). Similarly, there are two passages explaining the change of Jacob's name to Israel (32:22–32; 35:10). Source critics have often assumed such duplications and trip-

lications of incidents are separate traditions of a single event.

Third, source critics sometimes assume that apparently contradictory statements in Genesis reflect different sources behind the text. For example, in the flood story, Genesis 6:20 instructs Noah to bring into the ark one pair of every kind of animal, whereas 7:2 says for him to bring in seven pairs of clean animals.[8] Likewise certain statements that seem inconsistent in the creation accounts of Genesis 1 and 2 are often used as evidence for separate sources, as are disagreements between the legal sections of Exodus and Deuteronomy.

Variety in style and vocabulary is often accepted as a fourth criterion for source analysis. Source critics frequently assume that a source will have a consistent way of expressing ideas that is not necessarily present in other sources. This includes not only distinctive words or phrases that a particular source uses, but also the general level at which the prose narrative is written. Some prose narratives are lofty and grandiose, possessing a certain poetic quality, while other bits of prose can be dull and repetitious. Such differences are often used by source critics to distinguish between sources.

Fifth, sometimes source critics rely on religious and theological concepts as a criterion for source division. Certain sources, it is assumed, have a stilted and transcendent view of God, while others portray him in a more personal and intimate manner.

The validity of these five criteria for source distinction has been challenged on various grounds. The last two criteria discussed here (style and theology) are the most subjective and least reliable. But source critics believe that the cumulative effect of all five criteria together make it possible to distinguish the ancient sources used by the editor of the Pentateuch. Once the sources are identified primarily through the use of the first three of these criteria, it is believed the use of style and theology is further confirmation of the results of the study. I will have more to say later about the validity of these criteria, but for now it is enough to point out that source analysis in ancient texts can be quite subjective. The Pentateuch does not use cross-references or any other

Redaction
criticism

form criticism

Sitz im Leben

method to reveal the nature of its sources. The fact is we have little objective evidence for sources behind the present text of the Pentateuch.

The historical books refer more frequently to their sources, with express mention of *The Book of Jashar* (or *Book of the Upright,* Jos 10:13, 2 Sm 1:18), *The Book of the Annals of Solomon* (1 Kgs 11:41), *The Book of the Annals of the Kings of Israel* (1 Kgs 14:19; 15:31; and others), and *The Book of the Annals of the Kings of Judah* (1 Kgs 14:29; 15:7; and others). The later historical books obviously relied on traditional Israelite sources, some of which have survived in the Bible (see Ezr 1:2–4, and the use of Samuel and Kings by the author of 1 and 2 Chronicles). But with the sole exception of the mention of *The Book of the Wars of Yahweh* in Numbers 21:14, such explicit references to sources are not used in the Pentateuch.

These were real sources that the authors of the Old Testament had before them, but which perished over the course of history. The source critic seeks to go beyond this point by reconstructing those sources that were *unnamed* by the biblical authors. If the source critical approach is valid at all, it must always be a tentative endeavor because of the impossibility of verification, and any conclusions reached through source critical analysis should be held open to constant scrutiny and reevaluation.

Redaction criticism is related to source criticism and is tied to its conclusions. The term "redaction" refers to the editorial activity in which received materials have been arranged in a definite literary form. The tasks of the redaction critic are sometimes defined differently, but they usually involve analyzing the manner in which the sources were edited together, in which case it assumes the results of source criticism and agrees with its findings. Redaction critics also attempt to uncover the theological perspectives of the individual editors of biblical sources by analyzing the editorial techniques and choices used in shaping and framing the written sources available to him. They study the literary tapestry of a text in order to learn about the ancient editor who created it. In this way source criticism and redaction criticism are complementary endeavors.

Form Criticism and Tradition Criticism

The role of **form criticism** in Old Testament studies is to analyze and interpret the literature of the Old Testament through a study of its literary types or genres.[9] This approach assumes that ancient literature usually began as oral tradition, and Old Testament form criticism likewise starts by assuming that most of Israelite literature arose as folk literature, which went through a long and complicated oral prehistory. Although these oral genres were a constant for much of the Old Testament period, there was also a certain flexibility and change that can be detected in their development. Each genre or form is believed to have originated in a particular historical setting (or *Sitz im Leben*, "situation in life") in the history of the Israelite people. The form critic believes this original setting can be recovered through a study of the form itself.

Thus form criticism attempts to go beyond the work of source criticism, which has tended to view the sources of the Pentateuch as literary products of individual personalities, rather than as a collection of the literary traditions of the people. The form critic's methodology traditionally has four steps, involving the form's structure, genre, setting, and intention.[10]

First, the form critic analyzes the *structure* of the genre. This usually involves an investigation of the beginning and concluding formulas, or other conventional patterns of communication in an attempt to isolate the original speeches or stories that were later combined into the larger unit of written text. After the smaller divisions have been determined, the form critic studies the structure or outline of the specific unit.

Second, the form critic defines and describes the text as an example of one or another *genre* or type. The goal here is to locate the most appropriate literary category for the unit in question. The genres or forms are greatly varied, but they can include such examples as the announcement of a child's birth, the naming of a city, a prophetic judgment speech, or an individual psalm of thanksgiving. These forms are never rigid but contain a great deal of flexibility, and one of the important ob-

tradition criticism

historical criticism

literary criticism

canonical criticism

servations at this stage of the study is the way in which a particular example of a genre differs from other examples in the Old Testament.

Third, the form critic attempts to identify the social *setting* that produced and maintained the various genres. This study involves an investigation into the national life of ancient Israel in an attempt to locate the precise historical situation, or *Sitz im Leben*. These historical locales out of which Israel's literature arose often come from religious and worship practices, legal institutions, education, family life, or customs of the royal court.

Fourth, the form critic seeks to determine the *intention* of the genre, and offers an explanation of its purpose and function. Form criticism assumes that each genre of the Old Testament arose from its historical situation in order to fulfill some specific purpose in the life of national Israel, and it survived because it continued to meet that need. The task at this point is to ask about both the purpose of the genre in Israel's history in general and the purpose of the particular unit under investigation in particular.

Both source and redaction criticism deal in particular with *literary* stages of Old Testament literature. The emphasis of form criticism on the *preliterary* oral stages gave rise to yet another methodology, **tradition criticism**. The designation "tradition criticism" has been used in a variety of ways. But in general it attempts a comprehensive analysis in order to tell the whole story. It brings together the results of both source criticism and form criticism in order to construct a history of Old Testament literature through both its preliterary and literary stages.[11] It assumes that both oral and written traditions played a role in the final shape of Old Testament literature. In a sense, tradition criticism lies between form criticism and redaction criticism. It is interested in all the steps from the beginning of the oral traditions (form criticism) to the last stages of the editing (redaction criticism).

Historical Criticism

Sometimes the designation "**historical criticism**" is used for the methodology that seeks to combine the results of all the other

critical approaches in an attempt to reconstruct a chronology of the history of Israelite literature. This endeavor deals with the historical setting of a document, including its date and place of composition. Historical criticism attempts a chronological narrative of events related to the composition of Israel's literature within the total picture of Israel's history in general. Its distinction from the other methods is one of emphasis, since historical criticism is interested in the history of Israel in general, including the history of the production of Israelite literature.[12]

Literary Criticism

In the past few decades, a new methodology has risen in biblical studies known as **literary criticism**.[13] This approach in general seeks to analyze a biblical text not in light of who composed it or when it was written. Rather, the literary critic is interested in the intention of the author and the way in which the author has created meaning through the various component elements of the structure of the text itself. Thus the literary critic begins not with the who and when, but with the why and how of a text. The results of this approach have included a new appreciation for the literary artistry of the biblical text. Many literary critics have also challenged the findings of the older and more established conclusions of source and form criticism.

Canonical Criticism

Another relatively new approach is the so-called **canonical criticism**, which may refer to a number of approaches sharing a similar interest in the nature, function, and authority of the biblical canon. The term "canon" itself refers to the authoritative collection of biblical books that have been accepted as the rule of faith and practice (Greek *kanon*). Canonical criticism attempts to study the received form of the Old Testament and to expose its theological message. This approach is less concerned with particular editorial levels and more interested in the final product. It also seeks to discern the interpretive techniques used in different communities of faith by which the ancient traditions were adapted.

While not rejecting the findings of the documentary approaches, scholars using canonical criticism seek to study the final form of the Bible, since this is what has authority for the religious community.[14] They are less concerned with how the text arrived and more concerned with the internal and theological message of the canon. This approach provides a helpful corrective to the atomizing tendencies of its critical predecessors.

Survey of Scholarship on the Book of Genesis

The Book of Genesis has been at the center of pentateuchal research for well over two hundred years. There are a number of reasons for this, but among them is the fact that Genesis is foundational for the rest of the Pentateuch, and the issues involved in source and form critical analysis first come to the surface in its opening chapters. Therefore scholarly work on Genesis has set the stage for the great variety of views on the authorship of the Pentateuch.

This section will survey the major developments of research that have dominated and controlled work on Genesis in particular and the Pentateuch in general in modern critical scholarship. These developments involved hundreds of scholars around the world, and we can only highlight the events here in brief summary.[15]

Eighteenth Century

The seeds for modern science were sown during the Enlightenment, when human beings elevated the significance of human reason and began to interpret the world from a purely humanistic and, in most cases, nontheistic worldview. It was inevitable that the authority and reliability of the Bible would come to be questioned, since the concept of divine revelation and supernaturalism in general were being rejected.

Jean Astruc

The beginnings of a source critical approach to the Pentateuch are usually traced to Astruc, though he had less illustrious predecessors. Astruc was a French student of medicine who in 1753 published anonymously an inductive investigation of the Pentateuch. His work is usually acclaimed as the beginning of pentateuchal source criticism proper. Astruc established the divine names "Elohim" and "Yahweh" as the basic criterion for identifying and distinguishing the sources used by Moses in the compilation of Genesis. He concluded that Moses used one source referring to God primarily as Elohim (Astruc's source A) and one referring to him as Yahweh (source B). Astruc developed other criteria, which he used to further divide the sources for the rest of the Pentateuch.

Astruc never questioned Mosaic authorship or the authority of the Pentateuch. His approach was naive in that he assumed he could approach ancient Near Eastern literature with the same assumptions one might use for modern Western European literature. Yet his primary emphasis on the divine names as a criterion for source analysis paved the way for future source critics of the Pentateuch.

Johann G. Eichhorn

Eichhorn produced a three-volume introduction to the Old Testament (1781–83), in which the term "introduction" designated a thorough scholarly treatment of the higher critical issues for the entire Old Testament. He is sometimes called the "Father of Old Testament Criticism."

In his treatment of Genesis, Eichhorn followed Astruc's lead by accepting the divine names "Elohim" and "Yahweh" as the basic criterion for separating the main sources. He used "E" to designate the Elohim document (Astruc's A source), and "J" for the Yahweh document (Astruc's B).[16] But Eichhorn also admitted there must be other sources for Genesis, since it was evident that some materials did not harmonize with the J and E documentary approach. He speculated about other criteria, such as style and content as means to understand the original sources better. Eichhorn also applied this approach to the rest of the Pentateuch, and he eventually rejected Mosaic authorship altogether.

Eichhorn's early documentary hypothesis quickly became popular because it seemed to supply the most satisfying explanation of how the Pentateuch was composed. But there were unanswered questions about his conclusions and the next one hundred years of European scholarship on the Old Testament were devoted to answering two questions: How does one explain the obvious unity of the Pentateuch in light of the diverse documents used in its composition? What were the basic characterizing features of each of the documents themselves?

At the end of the eighteenth century, scholars continued Eichhorn's investigations. The period was one of unrestrained confidence and optimism, even arrogance. Some scholars claimed to have isolated as many as seventeen different sources in Genesis alone! K. D. Ilgen was the first to divide E into two separate documents, E^1 and E^2, and grouped the numerous different sources of Genesis into three basic documents: J, E^1, and E^2.

Nineteenth Century

In the early part of the nineteenth century, the two- or three-document hypothesis began to lose favor. Several scholars began to advocate a "fragmentary" hypothesis of pentateuchal composition. In this approach the Pentateuch had been produced by combining a mass of fragments rather than documents. Some scholars believed these original fragments were woven together by a redactor (or editor) in the period of Solomon. Others claimed to have discovered as many as thirty-eight or more fragments for the Pentateuch, and felt they were edited together during the exile.

W. M. L. de Wette

De Wette was among the early fragmentary proponents, suggesting that a group of J fragments and E fragments was behind the present Pentateuch. But his views were criticized by Heinrich Ewald, and by 1840 de Wette changed his position to a supplementary hypothesis (see below).

However, the most important proposal made by de Wette had to do with the Book of Deuteronomy, and left a lasting impact on Old Testament studies in general. He revived Jerome's initial suggestion that Deuteronomy was the law book found by Josiah's officials in 622 B.C. (read 2 Kgs 22–23). Jerome's original observation is quite possible since Deuteronomy

had been deposited in the temple at Solomon's dedication (see Dt 31:26 and 1 Kgs 8:1–4). It had no doubt been neglected during the reigns of Manasseh and Amon. But de Wette went further by suggesting that Deuteronomy was in fact a pious fraud. He argued that the book was not an ancient document long neglected, but a new document written in Josiah's day to support the Josianic religious reforms. Deuteronomy's anonymous author had intentionally written the book so that it would only appear to be from Moses. Rather than a book from the time of Moses (Late Bronze Age), Deuteronomy came be seen as a late-seventh-century composition.

Heinrich Ewald

Early in his career, Ewald emphasized the unity of Genesis in an attack on the fragmentary theories. In 1823, he suggested a "supplementary" hypothesis, in which a single core E document was supplemented by J and strands from the Book of Deuteronomy.

However, Ewald's supplementary theory did not account for all the material in the Pentateuch. The legal sections especially did not belong to any of the three documents, J, E, or D. So twenty years later he proposed his complicated "crystallization" hypothesis, in which numerous narrators and editors participated in the composition of the Pentateuch plus Joshua. Ewald joined those scholars who preferred to speak of a **Hexateuch** (the first six books of the Bible) rather than a Pentateuch. His crystallization approach suggested that each of the first six books contained cores or centers around which other parts clustered. These materials went through an elaborate editorial process until the whole reached final form around 600–500 B.C. This hypothesis never gained wide acceptance.

Wilhelm Vatke

Like all of us, these scholars were influenced by the philosophical ideas of their day. At this point in our survey, it is necessary to discuss Vatke and the influence of Georg W. F. Hegel's idealism, because of its great importance for the rest of our story. Hegel's famous dialectic (or logical) philosophy was one of the most important philosophies of the nineteenth century and had great influence on historians, theologians, economists, and scientists. The dialectic was based on the concept of the contradiction of opposites (thesis and antithesis) and their continual resolution (synthesis). An idea (or thesis) comes into conflict with its opposite (antithesis), but eventually converges with it in a new synthesis. The new synthesis will likewise eventually come into conflict with its own antithesis, and the process continues onward. The phenomenon of conflict, combination, and development has manifested itself in nature, history, and religion throughout human history.

The impact of Hegel on Old Testament studies is undeniable.[17] Beginning with Vatke, scholars of the nineteenth century forced the religious history of ancient Israel into the Hegelian model. Vatke argued that Israel's religion was primitive and naturalistic during the judges period and the early monarchy (thesis). The antithesis of this came during the later monarchy and the age of the prophets, when Israel's religion emphasized a more personal and spiritual God. The postexilic period provided the synthesis of these by institutionalizing and legislating Israelite faith. This approach to Israel's religion combined with nineteenth-century evolutionary thought became a powerful influence on later Old Testament scholars. This is particularly true of Julius Wellhausen, who said he learned "best and most" from Vatke.[18] But more about him later.

Vatke's developmental and evolutionary approach led him to an innovative suggestion concerning Israelite law and the legal sections of the Pentateuch. He concluded that the law of the Old Testament appeared at the *end* of Israel's religious heritage rather than the beginning, as the Bible claims. Vatke's argument that the legal regulations of the Pentateuch were actually composed during the exilic and postexilic periods did not meet with instant approval. But this feature of his work would eventually become the linchpin for the source critical approach to the Pentateuch.

Herman W. Hupfeld and Eduard Riehm

In the mid-nineteenth century, these two scholars made adjustments in the documentary approach that would eventually win wide acceptance. In 1852, Hupfeld argued for the presence of three self-contained documents behind the Pentateuch, E^1, E^2, and J. The framework of the whole was provided by E^1, which was the foundational document for the others. J was a continuous document that had been woven together with E^2. In 1853, Riehm identified Deuteronomy as a self-contained, independent source. Thus the four main sources—E^1, E^2, J, and D—for the Pentateuch were established, though the sequence would change.

K. H. Graf and Abraham Kuenen

Initially Graf agreed with the Hupfeld sequence of the documentary sources (that is, E^1, E^2, J, D). But he eventually became convinced by the arguments that the law came late in Israel's history. In 1865, he used the fixed date of D (622 B.C., following de Wette) and effectively convinced the scholarly world that E^1 was exilic, thus establishing the sequence E^2JDE^1. He suggested a significant role for Ezra in the exile who supposedly compiled the priestly and legal materials in E^1, and later combined them with E^2, J, and D to form E^2JDE^1, the Pentateuch. Because of the effective way in which Graf argued for the lateness of the priestly-legal materials of the Pentateuch, the Documentary Hypothesis that won the day is often known as the Graf-Wellhausen Hypothesis.

Subsequently, Kuenen reversed the sequence of the first two sources, arguing that the Yahwist (or J author) was the earliest of the four authors. He established the sequence JE^2DE^1. By attempting to date the composition of the individual sources, Graf and Kuenen elevated source criticism beyond its earlier attempts and began to move in the direction of historical criticism. This would further set the stage for Wellhausen, whose synthesis of previous work and whose articulation of the Documentary Hypothesis would make him the most important Old Testament scholar of the century.

Julius Wellhausen

We have said that since Eichhorn's day European Old Testament scholars had been concerned with two main questions: How does one explain the unity of the Pentateuch in light of the sources it used?

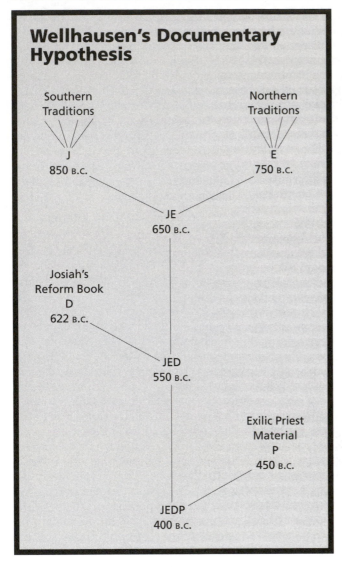

Wellhausen's Documentary Hypothesis

Southern Traditions

J
850 B.C.

Northern Traditions

E
750 B.C.

JE
650 B.C.

Josiah's Reform Book
D
622 B.C.

JED
550 B.C.

Exilic Priest Material
P
450 B.C.

JEDP
400 B.C.

Kuenen with skillful historical criticism in a way that appeared to explain the unity question. Now the source hypothesis had the unity it needed. Within a few decades of his work, the Graf-Wellhausen Hypothesis had swept the scholarly world, and remains with us today as one of the leading theories of pentateuchal origins.

Wellhausen accepted the consensus built over the previous century concerning the nature and sequence of the four self-contained documents behind the Pentateuch. He accepted the late date for the legal material of E^1 and changed its siglum to P in order to emphasize the document's priestly origins. Now the sources were JEDP.[19]

J was composed according to Wellhausen around 850 B.C. in Judah and used the divine name "Jehovah," or "Yahweh." In a simplistic narrative style, this document presented God in anthropomorphic terms. Angels appear in this document occasionally, but usually God deals directly with humans face to face. The E document was written around 750 B.C. as a corrective to the J document (its antithesis). This document uses the less intimate word "Elohim" ("God"), and avoids anthropomorphic terminology. E presents the northern perspective in a prose style more stilted and formal than that of J.

Sometime after the Assyrians conquered the northern kingdom of Israel (722 B.C.), a redactor or editor (known as R^{JE}) combined J and E into a new document, JE. This new document reflected the theological convictions after the historical crisis. Accepting de Wette's hypothesis about Deuteronomy, the D document was written around 622 B.C. to reinforce the cultic purity of Judah's worship. This new source stressed the importance of worshiping the Lord God (often combining "Yahweh" and "Elohim") at a central shrine, Jerusalem. The D document was the antithesis of JE, since it corrected and updated the less precise and older document. Early versions of the Documentary Hypothesis limited D to Deuteronomy 5–26 and 28. This document used a sermonic style, often expressing its theology in exhortations.

The redactor (R^D) put D together with JE around 550 B.C., after the fall of Jerusalem to the Babylonians in 586 B.C. But the new JED document neglected the

What were the basic characterizing features of each of the documents themselves? After a century of scholarship, most believed the latter question had been answered. The JE^2DE^1 analysis of Graf and Kuenen was widely accepted as self-evident for most scholars near the end of the nineteenth century. But the problem of unity remained. Given the differences in style, vocabulary, theological conceptions, and so on, how does one explain the obvious unity of the present arrangement of the Pentateuch?

It was into this atmosphere of optimistic scholarly endeavor that Wellhausen arrived on the scene. With exceptional acumen and clarity, he was able to combine the prevalent source theory of Graf and priestly concerns of the postexilic community. At some point during the middle of the fifth century BC, the P document (formerly E^1) was written to address this deficiency. Wellhausen believed the P document contained legal material concerning priests, Levites, and the various types of sacrifices (e.g., Lv 1–7). P also emphasized the transcendence and awesomeness of God. Around 400 B.C., these two final documents (JED and P) were combined by another redactor into a JEDP complex of materials that comprise the Pentateuch as we know it today. Further modifications and editorial changes were added until around 200 B.C., when the Pentateuch as we know it was completed.

Wellhausen believed that the law, and indeed the concept of monotheism, were late developments in Israelite history. Any references to a central sanctuary with exclusive worship of God at Jerusalem had to be later than 622 B.C., when Josiah's reforms were enacted and D was composed. Religious material from the late postexilic period was read back into the ancient history of Israel. There was thus almost no historical veracity in the Pentateuch. Wellhausen's reconstructions were dominated by antisupernaturalism and by the evolutionary thought so prevalent in the nineteenth century. The theory made no allowance for divine intervention in history, or for unique divine revelation.

The influence of Hegelian thought on Wellhausen is obvious. The JE document stemmed from the period of early Israel's nature religion, in which worship arose freely from the circumstances of the cycles of nature and the agricultural calendar. The Deuteronomic emphasis on central worship was antithetical to the freedom of the nature religion (the D document). The JED document was a synthesis between these positions. The P document with its priestly concerns completed the "denaturing" process in ancient Israel by legalizing the religious guild and creating a rigid and legalistic tradition. The Pentateuch as we know it was thus a synthesis between JED and P.[20]

Wellhausen had brilliantly united the results of source criticism with the nineteenth century's understanding of historical and religious institutions in ancient Israel. It seemed that all the questions had been answered. Wellhausen's presentation was compelling and persuasive. By the turn of the century, the Graf-Wellhausen Hypothesis had convinced the scholarly world, including scholars in England and America.

Conservative Responses

From the very beginning of the source critical endeavor, there had been many scholars who questioned the assumptions and presuppositions of its proponents. They challenged the results of source criticism on several grounds, including internal biblical evidence and the growing body of archaeological evidence from the ancient Near East. We can only mention a couple of these early opponents here, but it is significant to realize that the church was not left without a voice in the debate. Unfortunately, few people were listening.

Ernst Wilhelm Hengstenberg

The leader of the conservative wing of European biblical scholarship was without question Hengstenberg. In the mid-nineteenth century, Hengstenberg argued against the antisupernatural presuppositions of Vatke, de Wette, and others. He believed the sequence and deliberate arrangement of materials in the Pentateuch presupposed the authenticity of the Bible's message. His arguments were in many ways never satisfactorily answered and are still valuable in today's ongoing debate about the origins of the Pentateuch. Hengstenberg influenced many other German authors, most notably Karl Friedrich Keil, who collaborated with Franz Delitzsch to produce a series of commentaries on the Old Testament from a conservative perspective. Published in the mid- and late-nineteenth century, the English translation of their commentaries is still widely used by conservative scholars.

James Orr

The often repeated claim that no serious alternative was ever offered by conservative scholars for the Documentary Hypothesis is patently untrue. In 1906, Orr, a leading conservative scholar of the day, offered a scorching criticism of the Wellhausen school and suggested his own hypothesis. He defended Mosaic authorship and the historicity of the Pentateuch, while using a keen critical approach to offer his own solution. He admitted the presence of a variety of writers, but rejected the J and E distinction. Most of the materials in the Pentateuch are Mosaic or immediately post-Mosaic, including Deuteronomy and the P document, which provided a framework for the materials usually taken as J or E. Genesis itself is almost entirely pre-Mosaic. Orr also admitted that the Pentateuch did not reach its final form until the exilic or postexilic period, perhaps under Ezra's supervision.

Orr's criticisms were enough to show that it was not the methods being used by Old Testament scholars that were flawed. The critical approaches themselves (that is, source, form, and historical criticism) had not caused the vitiating results of the past one hundred years of scholarship. Instead the negative conclusions were due to the antisupernatural and rationalistic presuppositions of the scholars who were using the critical methodologies. Orr's penetrating critique, like that of Hengstenberg, was never answered by proponents of the Graf-Wellhausen Hypothesis.

Early and Mid-twentieth Century

Despite the stringent criticisms of Hengstenberg, Orr, and others, the Graf-Wellhausen Hypothesis became an unquestioned assumption in most scholarly circles within a few decades. Old Testament scholars in Germany, France, Great Britain, and America accepted the source hypothesis as something other than just that, a *hypothesis*. As has happened at other times in the human endeavor to understand the world, a mere theory used to explain reality gained such wide acceptance that it became established dogma, appearing above challenge or question.[21] But theories need constant reexamination and reconsideration, and the widespread acceptance of a given hypothesis does not guarantee its truth. Truthfulness is not decided by the collective opinions of those who seek it.

Old Testament scholarship during the first half of the twentieth century is characterized for the most part by modifications and variations of the Documentary Hypothesis. After a brief comment about the significance of ancient Near Eastern research during this period, we shall survey a few of the most significant developments of the early twentieth century. But none will wander too far from the basic tenets of the Graf-Wellhausen hypothesis.

Archaeology and the Ancient Near East

It is interesting to note that just as the source critical approach was finding its definitive shape in the Graf-Wellhausen theory during the last half of the nineteenth century, an entirely new field of research was developing. Egyptian hieroglyphics and Mesopotamian cuneiform were deciphered, and thousands of written documents from the ancient Near East began yielding their secrets. Though ancient Near Eastern research has since developed into a scientific field of study in its own right, its relationship with Old Testament studies is clear. The world of the ancient Near East is the world of the Old Testament, and the Hebrew books of the Old Testament are products of that ancient culture.

Yet the emergence of ancient Near Eastern studies has produced a distinct tension with Old Testament studies. The ancient world that emerged from the new data tends to agree and confirm the structure and integrity of the Old Testament documents as they have been transmitted to us. But this is often in contrast to the reconstructions of nineteenth-century Old Testament scholarship.[22] Already in the nineteenth century, the findings of the new disciplines of Assyriology and Egyptology were challenging the results of source criticism. One distinguished proponent of the source critical position, Oxford professor A. H. Sayce, abandoned his support of the Wellhausen reconstruction as a result of a serious consideration of the archaeological data. The facts emerging from ancient Egypt and Mesopotamia seemed to him to confirm the basic historicity of the biblical text.[23]

But the material available to Sayce in 1904 was nothing like the virtual explosion of data from the ancient Near East that occurred in the twentieth century. At the turn of the century, archaeologists first discovered the famous law code of Hammurapi from approximately 1750 B.C., but which actually preserves much older legal customs. With the discovery of Hammurapi's law code, archaeology revealed an ancient Semitic legal system centuries

---

Archaeological Discoveries of the Early Twentieth Century

1901 Law Code of Hammurapi
Revealed an ancient legal system several centuries older than Moses

1906 Hittite Civilization
Revealed that references to Hittites in the Pentateuch were plausible

1920s Ur in Southern Babylonia
A city more sophisticated than previously thought

1930s Mari
Revealed documents that portray a culture parallel to patriarchal life in Genesis

1930s Ugarit
Revealed the nature of polytheistic religion in Syria-Palestine

---

older than Moses, which shared many features with Mosaic law. Rather than a late exilic or even postexilic Jewish phenomenon, ancient Semitic laws appear to have originated early in ancient Near Eastern culture, and presumably early in Israelite history as the Bible attests.[24]

In 1906, German excavators began working in Asia Minor and eventually revealed an entire culture previously unknown, the Hittites. Prior to this point, scholars assumed the pentateuchal references to the Hittites were historically worthless because we had no extrabiblical evidence of their existence. Now, however, we know of an elaborate Hittite civilization, with two periods of imperial strength in which the Hittites were one of the most powerful kingdoms of the ancient world. We know enough about their language to write a modern dictionary, and to study their prayers, political treaties, and concepts of history.[25]

I offer here a few other examples of important archaeological finds illuminating the ancient Near East, though space does not permit me to elaborate in great detail. In the 1920s and 1930s, the ancient city of Abraham, Ur of the Chaldeans, came to light. Archaeological research there revealed an ancient city far more sophisticated than previous Old Testament scholars could have imagined. Writing was shown to be common hundreds of years before Moses; perhaps even Abraham had been able to read and write. The Mesopotamian site of Nuzi was a burgeoning city

in the mid-second millennium B.C. It was also uncovered in the late 1920s and yielded legal documents from private homes that contained parallels with social customs reflected in the patriarchal narratives of Genesis.

Another large city along the Euphrates, Mari, was excavated in the 1930s and produced thousands of letters and other documents. Most come from the first half of the second millennium B.C., and portray a culture in many ways parallel to patriarchal life as described in Genesis. The port city Ugarit along the Mediterranean coast of Syria was excavated during 1929–37, and has continued to have periodic excavations since 1948. The many documents discovered have thrown light on the nature of polytheistic religion in Syria–Palestine during the fifteenth and early fourteenth centuries B.C. Beyond its obvious importance as a source for the study of ancient Israelite religion, the Ugaritic language has also proven to be close to biblical Hebrew. Much from the Ugaritic documents parallels the writing style, vocabulary, and forms of Old Testament Hebrew.

There are dozens of other important archaeological discoveries that I could mention. This discussion has not included the important finds in Egypt, or the more recent finds at Ebla and Emar in Syria–Palestine, or even the importance of the Dead Sea Scrolls for the later biblical periods. But this is enough to illustrate that the first half of the twentieth century was a remarkable period of archaeological discovery, and the

193

fields of Assyriology, Egyptology, and Syro-Palestinian archaeology came of age.

William F. Albright

The application of these new disciplines to Old Testament studies was most evident in the prodigious works of William F. Albright and his many students in the United States. Albright was an individual of immense gifts and talents who made significant and lasting contributions to the study of ancient languages, archaeology, and ancient Near Eastern history in general. His continuing influence on Old Testament studies in particular makes him perhaps the most significant scholar in this field in the twentieth century.[26]

It is not accurate to say that this great mass of new information somehow proved the Bible right, or confirmed the Mosaic authorship of the Pentateuch. In fact, rare is the ancient Near Eastern discovery that has any *direct* connection with an Old Testament event or person. But the first half of the twentieth century saw a burgeoning new field, ancient Near Eastern studies, which at last provided an external, objectifiable check on the needless speculations of earlier Old Testament scholars. Exponents of the Graf-Wellhausen Hypothesis believed that the authors of Genesis had simply created a world that did not exist. The age of the patriarchs portrayed in Genesis merely disappeared as a historical period. But archaeology and ancient Near Eastern studies provided hard facts, objective evidence of an ancient world very much like the one described in Genesis.

Unfortunately, Old Testament scholars were not always paying attention, especially those working in Europe. While archaeology may have been providing an external check on the whimsical theories of the nineteenth century, many scholars in the first half of the twentieth century continued developing or modifying the Documentary Hypothesis.

Hermann Gunkel

One important development that could have benefited from closer attention to ancient Near Eastern materials was the rise of form criticism, which attempted to trace the fundamental ideas of the ancient Israelites back to their original oral forms (see discussion above). The pioneering

scholar who helped give definition to form criticism was Gunkel, who wrote several important works on Genesis.[27] Though Gunkel accepted the basic Documentary Hypothesis as defined by Wellhausen, his approach implied a fundamental criticism of Wellhausen as well. He believed that behind the J and E sources of Genesis were collections of sagas preserved orally for centuries, instead of relatively late writings of a few great individual authors. Gunkel was in many ways closer to the fragmentary hypothesis of the early nineteenth century. Since many of these sagas were preserved accurately, they may in some cases preserve historical kernels of truth. In some ways, the new form criticism was affirming in a different way what the growing body of evidence from the ancient Near East was showing.

Gunkel and his many followers failed to utilize fully the ancient Near Eastern data. The smaller biblical units that eventually comprised Genesis were not accepted as reflecting actual historical events, but were rather the products of fruitful human thinking and cultural speculation. Ultimately the final text and its meaning became less important to form critics than the oral stages or the situation behind the text. In addition, the whole question of an extended period of oral transmission has been challenged on all sides. Conservative scholars have consistently objected that there is no evidence in the Bible or the ancient Near East supporting the idea that biblical materials had a long oral prehistory prior to being committed to writing.[28] Other scholars who can hardly be labeled as conservatives have also challenged the possibility of an extensive preliterary stage of pentateuchal materials.[29]

Albrecht Alt and Martin Noth

Gunkel's form critical approaches were continued in the first half of the twentieth century in the influential works of Alt and Noth. They applied form critical techniques to the text in an attempt to discern the nature of Old Testament law, the social organization and religious beliefs of the early Israelite tribes, and biblical history in general. Much of their reconstruction of patriarchal and premonarchic Israel has not withstood the test of time. But their form critical investigations did succeed in reclaiming the early historical traditions of the Israelites, much of which had been rejected by adherents of the Graf-Wellhausen Hypothesis as unreliable.

Gerhard von Rad

Another important German scholar of the early twentieth century was von Rad. Of his numerous works, several used form critical and redaction critical approaches, still assuming the basic validity of the Graf-Wellhausen Hypothesis. Von Rad believed Israel had preserved her basic history in the form of "ancient credos," or short historical creeds still apparent in certain passages of the text (particularly Dt 6:20–24; 26:5b–9; Jos 24:2b–13). These creeds were preserved because they were used for centuries in liturgical affirmations of faith in public acts of worship. Von Rad believed he could trace the redactional history of these creeds. He concluded that the author of the J document (the Yahwist) had inherited the basic historical outline of God's actions on Israel's behalf, and filled it out with materials from local and tribal sources. The Yahwist was thus the one who gave the Pentateuch its rudimentary form.

The various works of von Rad have had a tremendous impact on Old Testament studies, and many of his insights have lasting value. However, a few caveats need to be mentioned. The creeds identified as such by von Rad omitted any reference to the Sinai covenant, so von Rad assumed this element of the Pentateuch had been edited into the whole by J at a later date. But it is obvious from only a cursory reading of the rest of the Pentateuch that the Sinai covenant is central to the whole. Furthermore the reconstruction of the history of these creeds is extremely subjective, as is the role of the Yahwist in editing these materials.

Recent Developments

The works of Noth and von Rad oddly enough had emphasized the historical dimensions in the early Israelite traditions. They did not often agree with the Bible's self-claims, but at least their form critical investigations allowed some degree of basic historicity behind the oral and written traditions of ancient Israel. Developments of the later twentieth century would challenge even these conclusions.

Thomas L. Thompson and John Van Seters

Critical investigation of the early Israelite traditions preserved in Genesis reached a turning point in the mid-1970s, when two important books were published just a year apart. Thompson's work published in 1974 refuted the archaeological evidence for a patriarchal age in Israel's history.[30] His was an attack on the widely accepted argument that archaeology and ancient Near Eastern evidence support a second-millennium B.C. setting for the Abraham narratives. Thompson emphasized the patriarchal narratives as literary creations. Instead of traditions that preserved even the smallest trace of reliable history, they were theological stories from later times reflecting an unhistorical worldview. The patriarchal stories were used in the J document toward the end of the tenth century or during the ninth century B.C. They contained nothing of historical value whatsoever from Israel's earlier periods.

Likewise, Van Seters also denied the second-millennium setting for the Abraham narratives.[31] In Van Seters' view, everything in the Abrahamic cycle is responding to the exilic situation. The Yahwist was an actual author in the exile rather than an editor of oral and written traditions from early in Israel's history. Abraham was a fictional figure, created for theological reasons. Van Seters employed form critical methods to arrive at his conclusions, and then supported them with archaeological evidence from the first millennium B.C. He denied the validity of any second-millennium archaeological connections. In a sense, Van Seters has revived a supplementary hypothesis, since the exilic J document was then supplemented by a postexilic P document. He questioned the existence of the E source as defined by the Graf-Wellhausen school.

Rolf Rendtorff

A major criticism of the Documentary Hypothesis appeared in the 1970s, when Rendtorff offered a new approach to the production of the Pentateuch.[32] Rendtorff felt the tradition-critical approaches of his predecessors in Germany, especially Noth and von Rad, were incompatible with the classical expression of the Graf-Wellhausen Hypothesis. He argued that their method of moving from the smallest units of the text through the larger complexes of tradition and ultimately to the final form of the text left no room for independent literary sources such as J, E, and P. Therefore the Documentary Hypothesis must be abandoned.

Instead, Rendtorff argued that the Pentateuch was comprised of large strands of material that have been joined end to end. The Primeval History (Gn 2–11), the Exodus history (Ex 1–15), the Sinai materials (Ex 19–24), and the various cycles of patriarchal narratives were brought together during the time of Solomon. Unlike Thompson and Van Seters, Rendtorff assumed the various blocks of materials in the Pentateuch reflected a level of actual historical events, and he valued the ancient Near Eastern control data more seriously. Rendtorff suggested a P and eventual D redaction of the whole, but in general he argued against the classical source analysis of JEDP and its tendency to atomize the text.

Canonical and Literary Criticism

These two relatively recent developments have also been less likely to accept the classical expression of the Graf-Wellhausen Hypothesis. Canonical criticism actually employs all the various approaches we have discussed here, but tries to use them in a balanced way, avoiding the extremes of each one. While most who fit in this category would not necessarily reject the JEDP analysis, they seek to explore the theological message of the received form of the canon, rather than individual sources or literary traditions behind the text.

Recent work by literary critics has been even less accepting of the older source approaches. Literary criticism by definition is less concerned with investigating the historical evolution of the text (that is, its diachronic development), and more interested in the literary artistry of the text as it now stands (that is, its synchronic structure).[33] Of the many examples of literary critics who flatly reject the JEDP Hypothesis, perhaps the one most relevant for Genesis is the work of Gary A. Rendsburg.[34] After careful literary critical analysis of the four cycles of Genesis, Rendsburg concludes that the source distinctions in Genesis as isolated by the Graf-Wellhausen Hypothesis are untenable. His literary approach found more uniformity and much less fragmentation in Genesis than is generally assumed, and he argued that the standard source divisions (J, E, and P for Genesis) must be discarded.

Conclusions

It should be clear by now that the latter part of the twentieth century has witnessed the collapse of the older consensus on the Documentary Hypothesis. This has not been a total collapse, since there are still plenty of scholars who work on this assumption. However, it has become clear that in our day, Old Testament scholars are all doing what is right in their own eyes and no single approach or methodology seems to have the answers.

The works of literary critics together with the severe criticisms of Rendtorff have exposed the bankruptcy of the Graf-Wellhausen approach. Conservative biblical scholars on the whole have taken one of two approaches. On the one hand, many have rejected the Documentary Hypothesis altogether and leveled rather impressive arguments against it.[35] On the other hand, more and more conservatives are attempting to reclaim the genuinely useful insights of the earlier source critics, such as Astruc and Ewald, and incorporate these into a new construction of how the Pentateuch came into being.[36] This is a promising development since many of the observations of those scholars working prior to Graf and Wellhausen were legitimate and completely compatible with a high view of Scripture. It was the skeptical and antisupernaturalistic impulses of the second half of the nineteenth century that debased those observations and resulted in an approach to the Bible that is in fact incompatible with the Bible itself.

The various critical methodologies are not inherently antisupernaturalistic. Indeed, they are necessary for serious biblical studies and productive in the hands of scholars who respect the unique nature of the Bible. Christian scholars will always embrace the concept of divine intervention, which must also be brought together with the intellectual achievements of modern Western civilization. A Christian approach to the biblical text will be a wholistic view, which means it will never appropriate only that portion which can be squeezed into a

Study Questions

1. Define "criticism," and distinguish between "lower" and "higher" criticism.

2. List and explain five criteria by which source critics identify sources in the narrative of the Pentateuch.

3. Compare and contrast source criticism and form criticism. How does tradition criticism relate to source criticism and form criticism?

4. What is distinctive about historical, literary, and canonical criticism? In what way does each interpret the text uniquely?

5. Chronicle the development of the Documentary Hypothesis, and explain how this development paved the way for the work of Julius Wellhausen.

6. Outline the chronology of Wellhausen's Documentary Hypothesis. Ac-

cording to Wellhausen, when was each document composed and why?

7. How have the remarkable discoveries of the twentieth century demonstrated that one may be justified in viewing certain features of the patriarchal narratives as historically based?

8. In what ways has form criticism contributed to Old Testament scholarship?

9. Compare and contrast the recent developments in pentateuchal studies. What features do these approaches share, and what features are distinctive?

10. Describe how various approaches to biblical criticism may enhance our understanding of the text. On the other hand, how do philosophical presuppositions influence one's reading of the Scriptures?

predetermined naturalistic system. Christian scholars will apply the best of their critical skills to the text while always remaining open to divine intervention in the world and in history.[37]

Finally, it should be clear from this brief survey that a greater use is needed of the ancient Near Eastern materials as an external check on Old Testament studies in general. The enormous amount of data from the ancient Near East is continuing to accumulate, and there is no sign of abatement in the near future. Every summer, archaeological expeditions are carried out across the Middle East, and exciting finds are not uncommon. The very nature of such an enormous amount of material makes it important to involve numerous scholars cooperating across several disciplines. A careful use of the critical methodologies will produce very different results than we have seen over the past two hundred years if they are combined with two commitments: first, a commitment to the-

istic supernaturalism and second, a commitment to the use of the ancient Near Eastern parallel materials as a control over theoretical hypotheses.

Key Terms

lower criticism
higher criticism
autographs
Redaction criticism
form criticism
Sitz im Leben
tradition criticism
historical criticism
literary criticism
canonical criticism
Hexateuch

Conclusion

Genesis and Beyond

It is all so wonderful that even the angels are eagerly watching these things happen.

—1 Pt 1:12b (NLT)

Primary Readings: Hebrews 1:1–2; 1 Peter 1:10–12

Outline

- **From Paradise to the Patriarchal Promises**
  The Problem with Paradise
  The Promises to Abraham
  The Promises to Isaac
  The Promises to Jacob and Joseph
- **From the Patriarchs to Moses**
- **From Moses to Jesus**

Objectives

After reading this chapter you should be able to

1. Summarize the broad theological themes of Genesis: creation, sin, and the effects of sin in Genesis 1–11, and the patriarchal narratives that emphasize the concept of covenant in Genesis 12–50.
2. Articulate subthemes of Genesis, including suffering danger and exile for sin, the preparation for the remainder of the Pentateuch, how the righteous actions of a few can accomplish much for others, and promises of land and descendants given to Abraham, Isaac, Jacob, and Joseph.
3. Compare the relationship between the Old and New Testaments to the relationship between Genesis and the remainder of the Pentateuch.
4. Contrast Moses to the patriarchs, as well as observe important continuities between them.
5. Examine the theological concept of covenant as it relates to the conditional acquisition of the land, the implication that exile can occur due to disobedience, yet the possibility of reclaiming the homeland of Canaan and the potential for peace, a relationship with God, and living in God's presence.
6. Trace the three administrations of God's grace: the patriarchal, the Mosaic, and the messianic.

It is impossible to overemphasize the influence of the Book of Genesis on the rest of the Bible, or for that matter on world history. This concluding chapter will consider the theological connections within Genesis itself, and then relate these to the rest of the Pentateuch and the Bible as a whole. As the New Testament apostle said, even the angels in heaven long to understand the full significance of these truths.

As you know well by now, the Book of Genesis has two main sections, the universal scope of chapters 1–11 and the patriarchal narratives of chapters 12–50. The description of the universe is given in sweeping detail in the two opening chapters. Then the problem of human sin is graphically portrayed in the Garden of Eden and the rest of chapters 3–11. The problem of sin is not limited to the first human couple, but is in fact endemic to the entire human race. The entrance of sin has a devastating effect on God's perfect creation. As a result, the first human family loses its uninhibited relationship with God and human history appears to be caught up in an endless cycle of chaos, evil, and destruction.

But a significant turn occurs with the call of Abraham in chapter 12. The problem of sin finds partial resolution through covenant relationship with God. God established the covenant with Abraham, demonstrated the transformational results of the covenant through Jacob, and revealed his sovereign, providential care through Joseph. In some ways the rest of the Bible is an elaboration of these themes. God's revelation creates a people of God (Israel) who is to live in covenant relationship with him, thereby solving their own problem with evil. This covenant people is then succeeded in the New Testament period by the church of Jesus Christ.

From Paradise to the Patriarchal Promises

There is a sense in which the theme of Genesis 1–11 is also the theme of the rest of the book, and indeed the whole of the Pentateuch. No matter how drastic human rebellion was, God's grace never failed to deliver from the consequences of sin. The theme of the patriarchal narratives and for the Pentateuch as a whole is thus foreshadowed here. Abraham and the other patriarchs suffered danger and exile because of their deceitfulness and faithlessness. But God's promises of children and protection were fulfilled. Likewise, Israel suffered a generation's delay in inheriting the Promised Land because of their rebellion. Yet at the conclusion of the Pentateuch, they stand on the borders of the Promised Land ready to enter the blessed hope. Thus the first eleven chapters of the Bible foreshadow on a universal scale the same themes developed in the rest of the Pentateuch.[1]

The Problem with Paradise

As we have seen, Paradise was perfect in every way. God himself proclaimed every aspect of his creation as "good." The only problem with the Garden of Eden was that it was populated with human beings. The narrative from Genesis 3–11 illustrated graphically the nature of the human sin problem and the devastating effects it had (and still has) on the world. Once sin entered into God's good and perfect creation, it only continued to escalate with seemingly endless effects. Yet God's grace also preserved a faithful and righteous remnant who served him.

The Promises to Abraham

In this context, the appearance of the promises to Abraham may not have seemed to meet the need (12:1–3). What can the promises of land, descendants, and blessing to a single individual mean in light of the universal problems detailed in Genesis 3–11? But the text illustrates the principle that God often uses the righteous actions of a few in order to accomplish his great purposes on behalf of the many. In fact we might see this as a recurring theme in the Bible. Joseph was righteous in the face of the insidious scheming of his brothers, and later against the insurmountable odds in Egypt. Moses faced Pharaoh and the mighty Egyptian forces, and Gideon's three hundred men prevailed against the Midianite thousands (Jgs 7:1–8). The prophet Elisha verbalized this principle: "Those who are with us are more than those who are with them"

(2 Kgs 6:16). His disciple's eyes were then opened and he saw the heavenly forces supporting Elisha against the Syrian army (2 Kgs 6:8–19).

God's solution to the sin problem was contained in Abraham's response of faith to the threefold promise. The promises were gradually explained further as the Abrahamic narrative unfolded. Abraham's nephew Lot chose a certain portion of the land because of its appearance ("Lot looked up and saw . . . so Lot chose for himself the whole plain of the Jordan," 13:10–11). But of course, this was land chosen for the wrong reasons, and land that Lot would not long claim as his own. By contrast, God commanded Abraham to lift up his eyes and look north and south, east and west at all the land of Canaan. The entire land will be Abraham's and his descendants will become as numerous as the dust of the earth (13:14–17).

In this way, the two primary promises, land and descendants, become intertwined in subsequent statements. In the two sections of Genesis 15, God recommits himself to these two promises. The enormous number of descendants is the point of vv. 1–6: "Look up at the heavens and count the stars . . ." (v. 5). Here also God clarified that the coming promised child would be Abraham's own biological son, not an adopted one (v. 4). Genesis 15:7–21 confirmed the land-promise and established the covenant between God and Abraham. Consequently, the land and descendants are linked together, and both are associated with Abraham's new covenant with God.

Genesis 17 is significant as the passage in which God places the marks of the covenant upon Abraham: the name change and circumcision. The chapter is striking for its emphasis on the covenant, as we observed earlier because of its use of the term "covenant" thirteen times. But this chapter also builds on the promises of the covenant ("You will be the father of many nations," v. 4b), and the name change itself illustrates Abraham's fatherhood of a great multitude ("I have made you a father of many nations," v. 5b). The two promises of land and descendants are linked further when God promises to give "the whole land of Canaan" to Abraham *and* to his offspring (v. 8).

After the binding of Isaac, God again restated the promises to Abraham: "I will surely bless you and make your descendants as numerous as the stars in the sky and as the sand on the seashore" (22:17). This account of the offering up of Isaac as a sacrifice on Mount Moriah reveals the Old Testament perception that a man's children were extensions of his own value and significance.[2]

The Promises to Isaac

In the brief narrative dealing with Isaac, all three promises—land, descendants, and blessing for the earth—which were given originally to Abraham are restated this time for Isaac (26:2–5). There is, however, a new element here. This time the divine land-promise is expanded to include the presence of God: "Stay in this land for a while, and I will be with you and will bless you" (v. 3). For the first time in the patriarchal narratives, we begin to see the Garden of Eden principle again: life in the land given by God means life in God's presence as well (see also "for I am with you" in 26:24). This implies of course that the land can be lost if God's presence is driven away.

The Promises to Jacob and Joseph

A central part of Jacob's stairway dream at Bethel is the reaffirmation of the patriarchal promises in Genesis 28:13–15. As with Isaac, all three promises made at the beginning to Abraham are included here. As with Isaac before him, the reaffirmation of the promises to Jacob also involved a promise of God's presence: "I am with you and will watch over you wherever you go, and I will bring you back to this land. I will not leave you until I have done what I have promised you" (28:15).

The strongest reaffirmation of the patriarchal promises to Jacob occurred in the second Bethel theophany (35:11–12). Again the land and descendants are tied together: "I will give this land to your descendants after you" (v. 12). This statement of the covenant promises further contains a promise that kings will come from Jacob's line (v. 11). This element of the patriarchal promises had not been heard since the days of Abraham (17:6, 16), and foreshadows the coming Messiah.

When the aged Jacob took his family to Egypt due to famine, God again comforted him and restated the basic patriarchal promises. He spoke of a multitude of descendants ("I will make you into a great nation"), his own guiding presence ("I will go down to Egypt with you"), and the certainty of a return to the Promised Land ("I will surely bring you back again," 46:3–4).

As we have seen, the Joseph narrative is different from the patriarchal narratives proper. But even here the patriarchal promises find reverberations. The narrative itself carries forward the story of the patriarchal family in a general way. The presence of God as a feature of the promises to Isaac and Jacob plays an integral role in the Joseph narrative as well. The section devoted to the rise of Joseph in Egypt repeats the refrain "the LORD was with Joseph" (39:2, 21, 23). More specifically, Jacob spoke from his deathbed to Joseph of the all important divine promises given to his fathers and to him personally at Bethel (48:3–4). As for Joseph himself, his final wish may demonstrate that he had learned his lessons well: "I am about to die. But God will surely come to your aid and take you up out of this land to the land he promised on oath to Abraham, Isaac and Jacob" (50:24). He was about to die in Egypt. But he understood that he did not belong in Egypt, even though he had made his home there for many years. Ultimately, Joseph knew that God would visit his descendants and lead them out of Egypt to the Promised Land. That confidence led him to declare that, on that great and glorious day, he did not want his bones to be left behind in Egypt.

From the Patriarchs to Moses

The patriarchal narratives of Genesis 12–50 relate to the rest of the Pentateuch in a way that is familiar to Christian readers. The best analogy is the relationship between the Old and New Testaments.[3] As the New Testament complements and fulfills the Old, so the Mosaic covenant relates to that of Abraham. As the New Testament teaches that Jesus Christ fulfills divine promises from the Old Testament, so the exodus from Egypt and the revelation in Exodus to Deuteronomy fulfills the promises to the patriarchs in Genesis 12–50.

In neither case has the new revelation superseded the old. Mosaic Yahwism did not replace patriarchal religion any more than the New Testament makes the Old Testament outdated or obsolete. Rather, they are both mutually illuminating.[4] A famous quote from Saint Augustine states that "the New is in the Old concealed, the Old is in the New revealed."[5] This sentiment emphasizes that the truths of the New Testament exist in germinal form in the Old Testament, and those of the Old Testament are made clearer in the New.

But the reverse of this quotation is just as true: the Old is in the New concealed, and the New is in the Old revealed. In other words, the revelational truth of the Old Testament is hidden in Jesus Christ, just as yeast is hidden in dough.[6] It is through the reading of the Old Testament that the true character and person of Jesus becomes clear. For the Christian reader, the two Testaments need each other to such an extent that either one will be misunderstood without the other. The New Testament is incomprehensible without the Old, and the Old Testament is incomplete without the New.

The relationship between Abraham and Moses is very much like the mutual illumination between the Testaments. The theological dependency between the patriarchal narratives and the rest of the Pentateuch is abundantly clear in the little paragraph at Exodus 2:23–25. Moses had fled from the turmoil in Egypt and sought a new life in the land of Midian (Ex 2:11–22). The children of Israel still needed rescuing from their bondage, but Moses had turned his back. But the cry of the Israelites rose up to God, and he heard their groaning, he saw their pain and was determined to do something about their bondage to the Egyptians. This paragraph prepares the reader for the conflict between God and Moses in Exodus 3 and 4. Moses is determined to put Egypt behind him and forget the horrible suffering of his people. But God is just as determined to send Moses back as a means of salva-

> The New is in the Old concealed,
> the Old is in the New revealed.
>
> Saint Augustine

tion. The conflict at the burning bush was inevitable because of God's gracious persistence and Moses' stubborn rebellion. God and Moses were on a collision course.

One little phrase in Exodus 2:24 reveals God's motives, and gives a glimpse into the heart of God. What was it that made him determined to save the Israelites? It was his covenant relationship with the patriarchs: God heard the groans of the Israelites in Egypt, and "he remembered his covenant with Abraham, with Isaac and with Jacob." This reveals the connection between the patriarchal promises of Genesis 12–50 and the deliverance described in Exodus. Theologically, all that transpires in Exodus, the call of Moses, the plagues, the escape from Egypt and crossing of the Red Sea, and the tabernacle instructions in the wilderness, all of it is the result of God's love for Abraham, Isaac, and Jacob!

Another important passage theologically is Exodus 6:2–8. This passage is significant for any study of Old Testament theology for a number of reasons. Perhaps central among them is the emphasis on the switch from patriarchal El-type religion to Mosaic Yahwism.

> God also said to Moses, "I am the Lord [Yahweh]. I appeared to Abraham, to Isaac and to Jacob as God Almighty [El Shaddai], but by my name the Lord [Yahweh] I did not make myself known to them." (6:2–3)

Scholars often debate whether this means the patriarchs knew the name Yahweh at all. Regardless of the outcome of that debate, the passage clearly makes a distinction between Moses and the patriarchs, a distinction that can justifiably be compared to the differences between the Old and New Testaments.

Yet in some ways Exodus 6:2–8 is more remarkable for tying Moses *to* the patri-

archs than it is for distinguishing *between* them. The paragraph goes on to remind Moses that God made a covenant with the patriarchs to give them the Promised Land in which they were living as aliens (v. 4). Furthermore, the Israelites have groaned under their heavy bondage in Egypt, and God states laconically, "I have remembered my covenant" (v. 5). This is followed by a list of things God intends to do for the Israelites: he will bring them out and free them from their slavery, he will redeem them, and make them his people (vv. 6–7). Finally he will bring them to the land he swore on oath to give to Abraham, to Isaac and to Jacob, and it will become their possession (v. 8).

The passage is certainly aware of the distinction between patriarchal history and religion on the one hand, and the time and faith of Moses on the other. But the point is they are related, despite their differences. Moses and the exodus event (Exodus–Deuteronomy) are natural results of the Abrahamic covenant (Genesis 12–50). They flow one from the other and they need each other for mutual interpretation. They are not mutually exclusive but mutually illuminating. So theologically and literarily, the rest of the Pentateuch flows from Genesis 12–50. And historically, Moses and the exodus occurred as a result of the relationship between God and the patriarchs.[7]

At the end of the Pentateuch, there is one further reference that ties Exodus–Deuteronomy together and relates the whole to Genesis 12–50. Just before the death of Moses, the Lord showed the whole of the promised land to Moses and stated, "This is the land I promised on oath to Abraham, Isaac and Jacob . . ." (Dt 34:4). Thus all of the events of Moses' life—the plagues, the exodus, the building of the tabernacle—the events recorded in Exodus–Deuteronomy have happened as a result of the patriarchal promises and are theologically dependent on them. Israel's possession of the land was due to God's promises to the patriarchs.

However, contained also in these patriarchal promises and in Mosaic law is the possibility of exile. As horrible as this prospect was for the Israelites, the Pentateuch was clear that later Israel could lose the land and be driven from its borders.

Mosaic law had established Israel as God's people. But they did not yet inhabit God's land. So the constitutive nature of the relationship between God and Israel was covenant faithfulness, not physical possession of Palestine. The Mosaic law itself does not relate the giving of the land, which is reserved for the Book of Joshua. The essential element of the relationship between God and Israel is law, not land.

As long as the covenant relationship was maintained, the land was secure. Yet Deuteronomy emphasized that the land would be given to Israel as a gift and as the natural result of Israel's relationship with God. Acquisition of the Promised Land was conditioned upon Israel's continued faithfulness to God's covenant relationship (Dt 28:36, 64).

In this respect, the rest of the Pentateuch looks both backward to the Garden of Eden and forward to Israel's future. Adam and Eve also inherited the land (the Garden of Eden) and were charged with preserving the created order and living in relationship with God. Like Israel, their life in Paradise was conditioned on their continued relationship with God. When they broke that relationship, they lost the garden. Likewise with Israel, their life in Palestine was conditioned on their covenant with Yahweh. Deuteronomy could quite naturally predict the loss of the land and an exile of the Israelite people if they failed to guard their most precious possession: their covenant relationship with God.

The reverse was also true. For Adam and Eve, blessed peace and security was theirs simply by living in harmony with God. The patriarchal promises included the lasting presence and protection of God as a consequence of their relationship with God. So with later Israel. The presence of God was related to the temple in Jerusalem. The Holy of Holies inside illustrated God's presence with his people. But God's presence was not somehow guaranteed by that physical structure. The temple itself could be torn down and the people driven away from the Promised Land. This was in fact what Jeremiah and other prophets warned would happen if Israel refused prophetic calls to repentance. But continued enjoyment of his blessed presence was possible for Israel as long as they lived in harmony with God and kept his covenant.

From Moses to Jesus

As we have seen, the patriarchal promises of Genesis 12–50 are foundational for the rest of the Pentateuch. God's covenant with Abraham, Isaac, and Jacob was the first administration of God's grace, which came to fruition in another administration, that of Mosaic Yahwism. Thus Moses developed, modified, and perpetuated the covenant promises to Abraham.

But the significance of the patriarchal promises is not limited to the law of Moses or the internal structure of the Pentateuch. Indeed, the basic elements of the promises continue to be central for the rest of the Old Testament, and therefore for the New Testament as well. It is possible to speak of *three* administrations of God's grace, the patriarchal, the Mosaic, and the messianic.[8] Though there are significant differences in each, God's commitments to Abraham at the beginning of salvation history carry through the rest of Scripture in a way that adds continuity and consistency to the whole. In this final section I want to illustrate only a few of the many ways in which this is so.

Immediately after the Pentateuch closes, the next chapter is intended to show the continuity between Moses and Joshua. Israel's new leader is the legitimate successor to the great lawgiver. The Lord candidly informed Joshua that Moses his servant was dead, and charged him with the responsibility of leading the people of Israel into the promised land: "Now then, you and all these people, get ready to cross the Jordan River into the land I am about to give to them" (Jos 1:2). The Israelites are certain to meet with success because of the land-promise, which has now become Moses' promise as much as it was the patriarchs': "I will give you every place where you set your foot, as I promised Moses" (1:3, 6).

But as we have seen, the land-promise in the patriarchal narratives was broadened to include more than just possession of the physical land, but included life in God's presence. So also God assured Joshua of his abiding presence: "As I was

Study Questions

1. How are the themes of the first eleven chapters of the Bible continued throughout the Pentateuch?

2. Describe how God's promises to Abraham are experienced and partially fulfilled in the lives of Abraham's descendants.

3. How may we say that Genesis looks forward to the rest of the Pentateuch as the Old Testament looks forward to the New Testament?

4. In what way does all that transpires in Exodus testify to God's love for the patriarchs?

5. How does Exodus 6:2–8 tie Moses to the patriarchs?

6. Explain how Jesus fulfills certain Old Testament expectations.

7. How has this study of Genesis enhanced your understanding of God? What new insights have you gained as you have walked through Genesis? In what tangible ways will these insights affect your walk of faith?

with Moses, so I will be with you; I will never leave you or forsake you" (Jos 1:5b; and see also 1:9b). Just as God assured Moses at the burning bush that he would not be alone when he returned to Egypt (Ex 3:11), so now he assures Joshua of his protecting presence as Joshua leads the Israelites into the Promised Land. Centuries later, the magnificent temple in Jerusalem would be the Holy Place where God's presence would abide with the children of Israel (1 Kgs 8:12–13), as had been predicted by Moses (Ex 15:17, and see Ps 132:14).

In a sense, the rest of the Old Testament is the story of God's relationship with the children of Abraham, Isaac, and Jacob. The plot is filled with twists and turns in which they at first lived in the presence of God in the Promised Land, but ultimately failed to keep the covenant. Like Adam and Eve in the Garden of Eden, they eventually drove God's presence from the land and were themselves driven from the land into exile. The temple, symbol of God's abiding presence, was torn down as a painful reminder that God was no longer blessing this land.

But along the way there were also hints of a new administration of God's grace. The coming king who would restore peace to the land was called "Immanuel," meaning "God with us" (Is 7:14). The prophets also spoke of a restoration of the people to the land, and even of a rebuilt temple (Ez 40–43), with a new outpouring of God's spirit on his people (Ez 37; Jl 2:28–29). Though the children of Israel had sinned and failed to live to the level of their covenant with God, his divine promises to the patriarchs were sure. Fulfillment awaited the future.

In a way that is far more complex than we can possibly go into here, it is clear that the New Testament authors saw Jesus and the rise of the Christian church as the fulfillment of those Old Testament expectations. In a real sense, the patriarchal promises find their ultimate fulfillment in the church. The divine promises to the patriarchs pointed to a royal descendant who would be the instrument of God's blessing to all nations of the earth (Gn 17:6; 35:11; 49:8–12). The New Testament authors share the conviction that Jesus Christ is the Son of David, the expected Messiah who fulfills those patriarchal promises.[9]

Notes

Before You Begin . . .

1. The *tôlĕdôt* device introduces in most cases what happens in that patriarch's family rather than to the patriarch himself. This means that most of the information about the person named in the *tôlĕdôt* phrase often appears *before* the phrase itself, leading some scholars to believe the *tôlĕdôt* phrase was a summarizing formula at the end of each unit rather than an introductory catchword. See P. J. Wiseman, *Ancient Records and the Structure of Genesis: A Case for Literary Unity*, ed. Donald J. Wiseman (Nashville: Thomas Nelson, 1985 [1936]) and R. K. Harrison, *Introduction to the Old Testament* (Grand Rapids: Eerdmans, 1969), 543–47.

2. The *tôlĕdôt* clause is repeated in 36:1a and 9a. Some prefer to divide Esau's material into separate sections, giving Genesis eleven panels plus the prologue, for a total of twelve.

3. There is strong literary evidence to support this four-part structure. See Gary A. Rendsburg, *The Redaction of Genesis* (Winona Lake, Ind.: Eisenbrauns, 1986). Walter Brueggemann relates the four sections of Genesis to the call of God: (1) the sovereign call of God, (2) the embraced call of God, (3) the conflicted call of God, and (4) the hidden call of God (*Genesis*, Interpretation [Atlanta: John Knox, 1982]).

Chapter 1: *The Grandeur of God's Perfect Creation*

1. Claus Westermann, *Genesis 1–11*, trans. John J. Scullion, Continental Commentary (Minneapolis: Fortress, 1984), 22.

2. Gordon J. Wenham, *Genesis 1–15*, Word Biblical Commentary 1 (Waco, Tex.: Word, 1987), 6; Westermann, *Genesis 1–11*, 84–85; and Victor P. Hamilton, *Handbook on the Pentateuch: Genesis, Exodus, Leviticus, Numbers, Deuteronomy* (Grand Rapids: Baker, 1982), 19–20.

3. Victor P. Hamilton, *The Book of Genesis: Chapters 1–17*, New International Commentary on the Old Testament (Grand Rapids: Eerdmans, 1990), 125; Derek Kidner, *Genesis: An Introduction and Commentary*, Tyndale Old Testament Commentary (Downers Grove: InterVarsity, 1967), 45–46; Allen P. Ross, *Creation and Blessing: A Guide to the Study and Exposition of the Book of Genesis* (Grand Rapids: Baker, 1988), 104; and Wenham, *Genesis 1–15*, 6–7.

4. David Toshio Tsumura, *The Earth and the Waters in Genesis 1 and 2: A Linguistic Investigation*, Journal for the Study of the Old Testament—Supplement Series 83 (Sheffield: JSOT, 1989), 17–43.

5. Gerhard von Rad, *Genesis: A Commentary*, trans. John H. Marks, rev. ed., Old Testament Library (Philadelphia, Westminster, 1972), 62.

6. Bill T. Arnold, "רֵאשִׁית," in *New International Dictionary of Old Testament Theology and Exegesis*, ed. Willem A. VanGemeren, 5 vols. (Grand Rapids: Zondervan, 1997) 3:1025–26.

7. Ross, *Creation and Blessing*, 718–23.

8. Von Rad, *Genesis*, 47.

9. Wenham, *Genesis 1–15*, 11–13.

10. Raffaele Pettazzoni, "Myths of Beginnings and Creation-Myths," in *Essays on the History of Religions*, trans. H. J. Rose (Leiden: E. J. Brill, 1967), 24–26.

11. For details on what follows and beginning bibliography, see Pattle P. T. Pun, "Evolution," in *Evangelical Dictionary of Theology*, ed. Walter A. Elwell (Grand Rapids: Baker, 1984), 388–92.

12. Used again in 1:21, 27 (three times); 2:3; 5:1–2 (three times); 6:7; and elsewhere in the Old Testament.

13. Kenneth A. Mathews, *Genesis 1–11:26*, New American Commentary 1A (Nashville: Broadman, 1996), 128–29.

14. Christoph Barth, *God with Us: A Theological Introduction to the Old Testament*, ed. Geoffrey W. Bromiley (Grand Rapids: Eerdmans, 1991), 9–11.

15. For details on what follows, see Hamilton, *Genesis 1–17*, 132–34, and Eugene H. Merrill and Alan J. Hauser, "Is the Doctrine of the Trinity Implied in the Genesis Creation Account?" in *The Genesis Debate: Persistent Questions about Creation and the Flood*, ed. Ronald F. Youngblood (Nashville: Thomas Nelson, 1986), 110–29.

16. John H. Sailhamer, *The Pentateuch as Narrative: A Biblical-Theological Commentary* (Grand Rapids: Zondervan, 1992), 95–96.

17. Gerald Bray, "The Significance of God's Image in Man," *Tyndale Bulletin* 42, no. 2 (1991): 224–25.

Chapter 2: *The History of the First Human Family*

1. *On the Duty of Civil Disobedience* (1849).

2. Derek Kidner, *Genesis: An Introduction and Commentary*, Tyndale Old Testament Commentary (Downers Grove: InterVarsity, 1967), 58.

3. Kenneth A. Mathews, *Genesis 1–11:26*, New American Commentary 1A (Nashville: Broadman, 1996), 183–84; and Gordon J. Wenham, *Genesis 1–15*, Word Biblical Commentary 1 (Waco, Tex.: Word, 1987), 49–50.

4. Though it occurs over twenty times elsewhere in the Old Testament. See Victor P. Hamilton, *The Book of Genesis: Chapters 1–17*, New International Commentary on the Old Testament (Grand Rapids: Eerdmans, 1990), 152–53.

5. Wenham, *Genesis 1–15*, 60.

6. Kidner, *Genesis*, 60.

7. On the literary use of names in the Primeval History, see Richard S. Hess, *Studies in the Personal Names of Genesis 1–11*, Alter Orient und Altes Testament 234 (Kevelaer/Neukirchen-Vluyn: Butzon & Bercker/Neukirchener, 1993), 107–55.

8. Ephraim A. Speiser, *Genesis*, Anchor Bible 1 (Garden City, N.Y.: Doubleday, 1964), 18; Wenham, *Genesis 1–15*, 32 and 115; and Hess, *Personal Names of Genesis 1–11*, 14–19, 59–65, 131.

9. Wenham, *Genesis 1–15*, 90–91.

10. Some have said there was only one tree at the center of the garden (and the narrative), and that the appearance of two is the result of subsequent conflation of traditions (Claus Westermann, *Genesis 1–11*, trans.

John J. Scullion, Continental Commentary [Minneapolis: Fortress, 1984], 212–14; and Gerhard von Rad, *Genesis: A Commentary,* trans. John H. Marks, rev. ed., Old Testament Library [Philadelphia, Westminster, 1972], 78–79). But this does an injustice to 3:22.

11. For a summary of the views and of this discussion, see Hamilton, *Genesis 1–17,* 163–66, and Wenham, *Genesis 1–15,* 63–64.

12. Mathews, *Genesis 1–11:26,* 174

13. Kidner, *Genesis,* 67.

14. Donald G. Bloesch, "Sin," in *Evangelical Dictionary of Theology,* ed. Walter A. Elwell (Grand Rapids: Baker, 1984), 1013.

15. R. W. L. Moberly, "Did the Serpent Get it Right?" in *From Eden to Golgotha: Essays in Biblical Theology,* South Florida Studies in the History of Judaism 52 (Atlanta: Scholars, 1992), 1–27.

16. Etiology is a study of causes. The Old Testament often uses an ancient story to explain how a person or geographical place was named, or to explain how a custom known to the author became accepted in the society. Many modern scholars assume the presence of etiology in a narrative means it cannot be historically accurate. But this method is not necessary and does an injustice to the traditions. See Allen P. Ross, *Creation and Blessing: A Guide to the Study and Exposition of the Book of Genesis* (Grand Rapids: Baker, 1988), 54–56.

17. See for this discussion Carl Friedrich Keil and Franz Delitzsch, *Commentary on the Old Testament,* 10 vols. (Grand Rapids: Eerdmans, 1978 [n.d.]), 1:101–2; but see also the cautions of Hamilton, *Genesis 1–17,* 199–200.

18. For more on what follows here, see Hamilton, *Genesis 1–17,* 200–202, and Mathews, *Genesis 1–11:26,* 248–52.

19. Kidner, *Genesis,* 71.

20. For an overview, see Millard J. Erickson, *Introducing Christian Doctrine,* ed. L. Arnold Hustad (Grand Rapids: Baker, 1992), 198–203.

21. Kidner, *Genesis,* 74.

Chapter 3: *What's Wrong with This Picture?*

1. Bill T. Arnold and Bryan E. Beyer, eds., *Readings from the Ancient Near East: Primary Sources for Old Testament Study* (Grand Rapids: Baker, forthcoming).

2. For convenient survey of each important people group, see Alfred J. Hoerth, Gerald L. Mattingly, and Edwin M. Yamauchi, eds. *Peoples of the Old Testament World* (Grand Rapids: Baker, 1994).

3. For more on the geographical details of the ancient Near East, see Bill T. Arnold and Bryan E. Beyer, *Encountering the Old Testament: A Christian Survey* (Grand Rapids: Baker, 1999), 35-44.

4. Walter R. Bodine, "Sumerians," in *Peoples of the Old Testament World,* ed. Alfred J. Hoerth, Gerald L. Mattingly, and Edwin M. Yamauchi (Grand Rapids: Baker, 1994), 19–22.

5. Herodotus 2.5.

6. On the relationship between these two, see Keith N. Schoville, "Canaanites and Amorites," in *Peoples of the Old Testament World,* ed. Alfred J. Hoerth, Gerald L. Mattingly, and Edwin M. Yamauchi (Grand Rapids: Baker, 1994), 167.

7. For more on what follows, see John H. Walton, *Ancient Israelite Literature in Its Cultural Context: A Survey of Parallels between Biblical and Ancient Near Eastern Texts* (Grand Rapids: Zondervan, 1989), 19–44; Gordon J. Wenham, *Genesis 1–15,* Word Biblical Commentary 1 (Waco, Tex.: Word, 1987), xlvi–l; and Kenneth A. Mathews, *Genesis 1–11:26,* New American Commentary 1A (Nashville: Broadman, 1996), 86–97.

8. Excerpts in James B. Pritchard, ed., *Ancient Near Eastern Texts Relating to the Old Testament,* 3rd ed. (Princeton, N.J.: Princeton University Press, 1969), 4–6.

9. W. G. Lambert and Alan R. Millard, *Atra-hasis: The Babylonian Story of the Flood* (Oxford: Clarendon, 1969), and Isaac M. Kikawada and Arthur Quinn, *Before Abraham Was: The Unity of Genesis 1–11* (Nashville: Abingdon, 1985), 41–48.

10. Pritchard, *Ancient Near Eastern Texts,* 101–3; Walton, *Israelite Literature,* 63–65.

11. One leading scholar has isolated 433 distinctiveness passages in the Old Testament (Peter Machinist, "The Question of Distinctiveness in Ancient Israel: An Essay," in *Ah, Assyria . . . : Studies in Assyrian History and Ancient Near Eastern Historiography Presented to Hayim Tadmor,* ed. Mordechai Cogan and Israel Eph'al, Scripta Hiersolymitana 33 [Jerusalem: Magnes, 1991], 203–4, note 22).

12. Machinist, "The Question of Distinctiveness," 196–212.

13. Theodore J. Lewis, "Divine Images and Aniconism in Ancient Israel," *Journal of the American Oriental Society,* 118.1 (1998), 52–53.

14. For what follows, see G. Herbert Livingston, *The Pentateuch in Its Cultural Environment,* 2nd ed.(Grand Rapids: Baker, 1987), 129–30.

15. Bill T. Arnold, "Religion in Ancient Israel," in *The Face of Old Testament Studies,* ed. David W. Baker and Bill T. Arnold (Grand Rapids: Baker, forthcoming).

16. William F. Albright, *Archaeology and the Religion of Israel* (Baltimore: Johns Hopkins, 1942), 24. Baruch Halpern calls the religion of monarchic Israel "unselfconsciously monotheistic" ("'Brisker Pipes than Poetry': The Development of Israelite Monotheism," in *Judaic Perspectives on Ancient Israel,* ed. Jacob Neusner, Baruch A. Levine, and Ernst S. Frerichs [Philadelphia: Fortress, 1987], 88).

17. For more on the contrast between the worldviews presented here, see Yehezkel Kaufmann, *The Religion of Israel: From Its Beginnings to the Babylonian Exile,* trans. Moshe Greenberg (New York: Schocken, 1972 [1960]), 7–121; and John N. Oswalt, "The Old Testament and Homosexuality," in *What You Should Know about Homosexuality,* ed. Charles W. Keysor (Grand Rapids: Zondervan, 1979), 24–37.

18. Kaufmann, *The Religion of Israel,* 21–25.

19. In the Pentateuch alone, see the following: Exodus 22:18; Leviticus 19:26, 31; 20:6, 27; and Deuteronomy 18:10–11.

20. Mark W. Chavalas, "Magic," in *Evangelical Dictionary of Biblical Theology,* ed. Walter A. Elwell (Grand Rapids: Baker, 1996), 502.

21. Bill T. Arnold, "The Weidner Chronicle and the Idea of History in Israel and Mesopotamia," in *Faith, Tradition, and History: Old Testament Historiography in Its Near Eastern Context,* ed. Alan R. Millard, James K. Hoffmeier, and David W. Baker

(Winona Lake, Ind.: Eisenbrauns, 1994), 129–48.

22. The Pentateuch plus Joshua, Judges, Samuel, and Kings.

Chapter 4: *Sin's Contamination of Creation*

1. In the famous Sumerian King List, the reigns of certain ancient kings are fantastically long, the longest being 72,000 years. See Thorkild Jacobsen, *The Sumerian King List* (Chicago: University of Chicago, 1939).

2. For more on these questions, see Carl Friedrich Keil and Franz Delitzsch, *Commentary on the Old Testament,* 10 vols. (Grand Rapids: Eerdmans, 1978 [n.d.]), 1:123–24, Derek Kidner, *Genesis: An Introduction and Commentary,* Tyndale Old Testament Commentary (Downers Grove: InterVarsity, 1967), 82–83, and Gordon J. Wenham, *Genesis 1–15,* Word Biblical Commentary 1 (Waco, Tex.: Word, 1987), 130–34.

3. For interpretive options in this paragraph, see Kidner, *Genesis,* 83–85; Wenham, *Genesis 1–15,* 139–40; and F. B. Huey Jr. and John H. Walton, "Are the 'Sons of God' in Genesis 6 Angels?" in *The Genesis Debate: Persistent Questions about Creation and the Flood,* ed. Ronald F. Youngblood (Nashville: Thomas Nelson, 1986), 184–209.

4. Angels apparently do not marry or reproduce (Matt. 22:30).

5. Kidner, *Genesis,* 85.

6. Steven A. Austin and Donald C. Boardman, "Did Noah's Flood Cover the Entire World?" in *The Genesis Debate: Persistent Questions about Creation and the Flood,* ed. Ronald F. Youngblood (Nashville: Thomas Nelson, 1986), 210–29.

7. Claus Westermann, *Genesis 1–11,* trans. John J. Scullion, Continental Commentary (Minneapolis: Fortress, 1984), 398–406; and Kenneth A. Mathews, *Genesis 1–11:26,* New American Commentary 1A (Nashville: Broadman, 1996), 98–101.

8. Westermann, *Genesis 1–11,* 400–401.

9. See James B. Pritchard, ed., *Ancient Near Eastern Texts Relating to the Old Testament,* 3rd ed. (Princeton, N.J.: Princeton University Press, 1969), 93–97.

10. For an excellent survey, see David Toshio Tsumura, "Genesis and Ancient Near Eastern Stories of Creation and Flood: An Introduction," in *"I Studied Inscriptions from before the Flood": Ancient Near Eastern, Literary, and Linguistic Approaches to Genesis 1–11,* ed. Richard S. Hess and David Toshio Tsumura (Winona Lake, Ind.: Eisenbrauns, 1994), 44–57, and other articles in the same volume.

11. A. Heidel, *The Gilgamesh Epic and Old Testament Parallels* (Chicago: University of Chicago, 1946), 268. It is possible that there is no literary dependence at all between Genesis and the Babylonian parallels, but that we have here "two literary perspectives on a single actual event" (Walton, *Israelite Literature,* 40).

12. On Noah's and Ham's actions, see Wenham, *Genesis 1–15,* 198–201.

13. Kidner, *Genesis,* 103.

14. Ibid., 110.

15. Walter Brueggemann, *Genesis,* Interpretation (Atlanta: John Knox, 1982), 97.

16. The author has presented his material in a fashion that highlights the promised line. He listed and discussed first the families that branched off the main line that led to Abraham, and after he satisfactorily placed those families aside, he returned to pick up the main line in more detail. Thus the line from Adam to Seth to Noah to Terah and Abraham is clear. See Keil and Delitzsch, *Commentary,* 1:37.

17. For more on what follows, see David J. A. Clines, "Theme in Genesis 1–11," in *"I Studied Inscriptions from before the Flood": Ancient Near Eastern, Literary, and Linguistic Approaches to Genesis 1–11,* ed. Richard S. Hess and David Toshio Tsumura (Winona Lake, Ind.: Eisenbrauns, 1994), 285–309.

Chapter 5: *The Beginning of Our Faith Heritage*

1. The difference between his two names, Abram and Abraham, will be explained later. He is Abram until Genesis 17, when his name is then changed to the more familiar Abraham.

2. Gordon J. Wenham, *Genesis 1–15,* Word Biblical Commentary 1 (Waco, Tex.: Word, 1987), 281–82.

3. On the chronological difficulties here, see Victor P. Hamilton, *The Book of Genesis: Chapters 1–17,* New International Commentary on the Old Testament (Grand Rapids: Eerdmans, 1990), 366–68.

4. Victor P. Hamilton, *Handbook on the Pentateuch: Genesis, Exodus, Leviticus, Numbers, Deuteronomy* (Grand Rapids: Baker, 1982), 87.

5. Gerhard von Rad, *Genesis: A Commentary,* trans. John H. Marks, rev. ed., Old Testament Library (Philadelphia, Westminster, 1972), 159.

6. With the definite article in the Hebrew, unlike the KJV and NKJV, "to a land that I will show you."

7. Nahum M. Sarna, *Understanding Genesis* (New York: Schocken, 1970 [1966]), 100.

8. Hamilton, *Handbook,* 95.

9. The older assumption that Abram's actions were also related to a Hurrian wife-sister custom is now largely rejected. See John H. Walton, *Ancient Israelite Literature in Its Cultural Context: A Survey of Parallels between Biblical and Ancient Near Eastern Texts* (Grand Rapids: Zondervan, 1989), 57–58.

10. Claus Westermann, *Genesis 12–36,* trans. John J. Scullion, Continental Commentary (Minneapolis: Fortress, 1985), 159–68.

11. John H. Sailhamer, *The Pentateuch as Narrative: A Biblical-Theological Commentary* (Grand Rapids: Zondervan, 1992), 141–43.

12. Derek Kidner, *Genesis: An Introduction and Commentary,* Tyndale Old Testament Commentary (Downers Grove: InterVarsity, 1967), 118.

Chapter 6: *Tracking Abram and His Family*

1. Bill T. Arnold, "Babylonians," in *Peoples of the Old Testament World,* ed. Alfred J. Hoerth, Gerald L. Mattingly, and Edwin M. Yamauchi (Grand Rapids: Baker, 1994), 57.

2. Claus Westermann, *Genesis 12–36,* trans. John J. Scullion, Continental Commentary (Minneapolis: Fortress, 1985), 139–40. See also Victor P. Hamilton, *The Book of Genesis: Chapters 1–17,* New International Commentary on the Old Testament (Grand Rapids: Eerdmans, 1990), 363–65, and Gordon J. Wenham, *Genesis 1–15,* Word Biblical Commentary 1 (Waco, Tex.: Word, 1987), 272–73.

3. Eugene H. Merrill, *Kingdom of Priests: A History of Old Testament Israel* (Grand Rapids: Baker, 1987), 25–26, especially note 13.

4. We cannot discuss every geographical reference. Certain places mentioned in the Abrahamic narrative are omitted: Dan, Hobah, and Damascus, for example (14:14). But we will survey the most important locations for Abraham's travels.

5. The so-called Execration Texts from the first two centuries of the second millennium shed light on the cities of Syria–Palestine at that time. Yohanan Aharoni, *The Land of the Bible: A Historical Geography,* trans. Anson F. Rainey (London: Burns & Oates, 1979), 144–47.

6. Derek Kidner, *Genesis: An Introduction and Commentary,* Tyndale Old Testament Commentary (Downers Grove: InterVarsity, 1967), 115.

7. Wenham, *Genesis 1–15,* 280.

8. Ibid., 281.

9. Westermann, *Genesis 12–36,* 181.

10. Ephraim A. Speiser, *Genesis,* Anchor Bible 1 (Garden City, N.Y.: Doubleday, 1964), 147–48.

11. Julius Wellhausen, *Prolegomena to the History of Israel,* trans. J. Sutherland Black and Allan Menzies (Atlanta: Scholars, 1994 [1885]), 320.

12. Alan R. Millard, "Abraham," in *Anchor Bible Dictionary,* ed. David Noel Freedman, 6 vols. (New York: Doubleday, 1992), 1:35–41.

13. Millard, "Abraham," 37–40.

14. For more on what follows here, see Bill T. Arnold and Bryan E. Beyer, *Encountering the Old Testament: A Christian Survey* (Grand Rapids: Baker, 1999), 44–59; and Amihai Mazar, *Archaeology of the Land of the Bible, 10,000–586 B.C.E.* (New York: Doubleday, 1990), 174–231.

15. For more on what follows, see John J. Bimson, "Archaeological Data and the Dating of the Patriarchs," in *Essays on the Patriarchal Narratives,* ed. Alan R. Millard and Donald J. Wiseman (Winona Lake, Ind.: Eisenbrauns, 1983), 53–89.

16. David N. Freedman, "The Real Story of the Ebla Tablets: Ebla and the Cities of the Plain," *Biblical Archaeologist* 41 (1978): 143–64.

17. William F. Albright, *Yahweh and The Gods of Canaan: An Historical Analysis of Two Contrasting Faiths* (Winona Lake, Ind.: Eisenbrauns, 1990 [1968]), 64–73.

18. Bimson, "Archaeological Data," 54–58.

19. Roland de Vaux, *The Early History of Israel,* trans. David Smith (Philadelphia: Westminster, 1978), 58–64, 263–66.

20. De Vaux, *Early History,* 200–209, and Mazar, *Archaeology,* 224–26.

21. See especially Cyrus H. Gordon, *Introduction to Old Testament Times* (Ventnor, N.J.: Ventnor, 1953), 100–119.

22. Martin J. Selman, "Comparative Customs and the Patriarchal Age," in *Essays on the Patriarchal Narratives,* ed. Alan R. Millard and Donald J. Wiseman (Winona Lake, Ind.: Eisenbrauns, 1983), 91–139.

23. For a representative sample of this position, see P. Kyle McCarter Jr., "The Patriarchal Age: Abraham, Isaac and Jacob," in *Ancient Israel: A Short History from Abraham to the Roman Destruction of the Temple* (Englewood Cliffs, N.J./Washington, D.C.: Prentice Hall/Biblical Archaeology Society, 1988), 1–29.

24. John Bright, *A History of Israel,* 3rd ed. (Philadelphia: Westminster, 1981), 83–87. This is supported further by the fact that most of the personal names in the Primeval History (Gen. 1–11) can be traced to the Amorite world of the early second millennium (Richard S. Hess, *Studies in the Personal Names of Genesis 1–11,* Alter Orient und Altes Testament 234 [Kevelaer/Neukirchen-Vluyn: Butzon & Bercker/Neukirchener, 1993], 5, 103–6). Some prefer a date slightly earlier; see Merrill, *Kingdom of Priests,* 78–79.

25. There are a few exceptions in the Abramic cycles, in which both El-type names and Yahweh occur together. For an overview of these data, see Gordon J. Wenham, "The Religion of the Patriarchs," in *Essays on the Patriarchal Narratives,* ed. Alan R. Millard and Donald J. Wiseman (Winona Lake, Ind.: Eisenbrauns, 1983), 161–95.

26. John H. Walton, *Covenant: God's Purpose, God's Plan* (Grand Rapids: Zondervan, 1994), 13–14.

Chapter 7: *"Then God Gave Him the Covenant"*

1. Gordon J. Wenham, *Genesis 1–15,* Word Biblical Commentary 1 (Waco, Tex.: Word, 1987), 316.

2. Victor P. Hamilton, *The Book of Genesis: Chapters 1–17,* New International Commentary on the Old Testament (Grand Rapids: Eerdmans, 1990), 414–16, and see Eugene H. Merrill, *Kingdom of Priests: A History of Old Testament Israel* (Grand Rapids: Baker, 1987), 263–65.

3. "Bread and water" would have been daily fare, but Melchizedek offers "bread and wine."

4. Derek Kidner, *Genesis: An Introduction and Commentary,* Tyndale Old Testament Commentary (Downers Grove: InterVarsity, 1967), 121.

5. "Delivered" in 14:20 is *miggēn,* and "shield" in 15:1 is *māgēn.*

6. He had been seventy-five years old when they departed Haran; Sarai, sixty-five (Gen. 12:4).

7. Hamilton, *Genesis 1–17,* 420.

8. The older views that specific Hurrian practices (from the ancient city of Nuzi) are precisely parallel to Abram's situation are now almost universally rejected. But comparisons with ancient Near Eastern customs generally are still apropos (Wenham, *Genesis 1–15,* 328–29).

9. So justice in the Old Testament is an action, rather than an unattainable ideal. Justice is something we do rather than some absolute norm we achieve.

10. Walter Brueggemann, *Genesis,* Interpretation (Atlanta: John Knox, 1982), 145–46.

11. For an overview of the New Testament's use of this verse, see Brueggemann, *Genesis,* 146–48.

12. John H. Sailhamer, *The Pentateuch as Narrative: A Biblical-Theological Commentary* (Grand Rapids: Zondervan, 1992), 152.

13. Richard S. Hess, "The Slaughter of the Animals in Genesis 15: Genesis 15:8–21 and Its Ancient Near Eastern Context," in *He Swore an Oath: Biblical Themes from Genesis 12–50,* ed. Richard S. Hess, Philip E. Satterthwaite, and Gordon J. Wenham, 2nd ed. (Grand Rapids/Carlisle, England: Baker/Paternoster, 1994), 55–65.

14. It may be argued that the term "covenant" is not used in a conventional manner in this chapter, and that in fact it really means "binding obligation" or "solemn assurance" in verse 18. See Claus Westermann, *Genesis 12–36,* trans. John J. Scullion, Continental Commentary (Minneapolis: Fortress, 1985), 229.

15. Hamilton, *Genesis 1–17,* 430–37.

16. Brueggemann, *Genesis,* 150.

17. John H. Walton, *Ancient Israelite Literature in Its Cultural Context: A Survey of Parallels between Biblical and Ancient Near Eastern Texts* (Grand Rapids: Zondervan, 1989), 54–55.

18. Fiorella Imparati, "Private Life among the Hittites," in *Civilizations of the Ancient Near East*, ed. Jack M. Sasson, 4 vols. (New York: Scribner, 1995), 1:573–74.

19. Gordon J. Wenham, *Genesis 16–50*, Word Biblical Commentary 2 (Dallas: Word, 1994), 7–8, 12.

20. The new name may simply be a dialectical variant of the older name. See Wenham, *Genesis 16–50*, 21; and Wenham, *Genesis 1–15*, 252.

21. Though apparently not practiced in Mesopotamia, circumcision was common among most other peoples of the ancient Near East. Wenham, *Genesis 16–50*, 23–24; and see Nahum M. Sarna, *Understanding Genesis* (New York: Schocken, 1970 [1966]), 131–33.

22. Sarna, *Understanding Genesis*, 131–33.

23. And see the wonderful sermon by John Wesley entitled "The Circumcision of the Heart," *The Works of John Wesley*, third ed., 14 vols. (Grand Rapids: Baker, 1991 [1872]), 5:202–12.

24. Gary A. Rendsburg, *The Redaction of Genesis* (Winona Lake, Ind.: Eisenbrauns, 1986), 46–47.

Chapter 8: *Standing on The Promises of God*

1. *Pensées*, trans. A. J. Krailsheimer (London: Penguin, 1995), number 185.

2. This is obscured somewhat by the NIV's "Then the LORD said," which is not in the Hebrew.

3. Gordon J. Wenham, *Genesis 16–50*, Word Biblical Commentary 2 (Dallas: Word, 1994), 48.

4. This rhetorical question is taken up by Jeremiah in his discourse on God's sovereignty (32:17, 27) and again in Zechariah 8:6.

5. This is one of only eighteen ancient scribal corrections (*tiqqûnê sōpĕrîm*) of texts, made for a variety of reasons.

6. Derek Kidner, *Genesis: An Introduction and Commentary*, Tyndale Old Testament Commentary (Downers Grove: InterVarsity, 1967), 131.

7. Walter Brueggemann, *Genesis*,

Interpretation (Atlanta: John Knox, 1982), 164.

8. Wenham, *Genesis 16–50*, 55, 63.

9. Since Gerar is not "between Kadesh and Shur" (20:1) it is often assumed that the author was confused geographically. But it seems quite plausible that Gerar was his base camp while Abraham was traveling in the southland (Victor P. Hamilton, *The Book of Genesis: Chapters 18–50*, New International Commentary on the Old Testament [Grand Rapids: Eerdmans, 1995], 59).

10. The term "mocking" is literally "Isaac-ing," a play on Isaac's name. The precise nature of Ishmael's taunt is not known.

11. The people of this area are also called "Philistines" in Genesis 26. The better-known Philistines of the Iron Age did not enter Syria–Palestine until around 1200 B.C. (see Judges and 1–2 Samuel). The Middle Bronze Philistines of the patriarchal period were probably also newcomers from the Aegean, and therefore the term seemed wholly appropriate for the author of Genesis. See Sidebar 9.1, below.

12. Gerhard von Rad, *Genesis: A Commentary*, trans. John H. Marks, rev. ed., Old Testament Library (Philadelphia, Westminster, 1972), 238.

13. Wenham, *Genesis 16–50*, 95.

14. Hamilton, *Genesis 18–50*, 101.

15. For more on this, see Wenham, *Genesis 16–50*, 105; and Nahum M. Sarna, *Understanding Genesis* (New York: Schocken, 1970 [1966]), 157–59.

16. Adapted from Midrash Rabbah to Genesis (Harry Freedman and Maurice Simon, eds., *Midrash Rabbah*, 10 vols. [London: Soncino, 1961], 1:486).

17. For more on the common literary mold of Genesis 12 and 22, see Nahum M. Sarna, *Genesis: The Traditional Hebrew Text with the New JPS Translation*, JPS Torah Commentary (Philadelphia: Jewish Publication Society, 1989), 150.

18. See, for example, George W. Coats, *Genesis, with an Introduction to Narrative Literature*, Forms of the Old Testament Literature 1 (Grand Rapids: Eerdmans, 1983), 161.

19. Von Rad, *Genesis*, 244.

20. Or this could be "your *precious* son whom you love." See Hamilton, *Genesis 18–50*, 97, especially note 3.

21. For more on these observations, see Wenham, *Genesis 16–50*, 117–18, and Hamilton, *Genesis 18–50*, 119–23.

22. Carl Friedrich Keil and Franz Delitzsch, *Commentary on the Old Testament*, 10 vols. (Grand Rapids: Eerdmans, 1978 [n.d.]) 1:253.

23. The materials in Genesis 23:1–25:18 are appendixes, according to Gary A. Rendsburg (*The Redaction of Genesis* [Winona Lake, Ind.: Eisenbrauns, 1986], 71–77).

24. This episode illustrates partial fulfillment of the promises as the theme of the Pentateuch. See David J. A. Clines, *The Theme of the Pentateuch*, Journal for the Study of the Old Testament—Supplement Series 10 (Sheffield: JSOT, 1978).

25. Whether this servant was the Eliezer of Genesis 15:2 is uncertain. It seems unlikely that he, as the previous presumed heir, would be Abraham's current majordomo. It also seems unlikely that a previously identified character would be unnamed in this narrative.

26. Keil and Delitzsch, *Commentary*, 1:261–62.

27. Though the phrase may mean something more like "the clans descended from Ishmael camped close to one another" (see NLT).

28. Wenham, *Genesis 16–50*, 165–66.

Chapter 9: *Jacob Struggles with His Family*

1. *Marmion*, cto.6, st. 17 (1808).

2. Remember that the *tôlĕdôt* usually introduces not what happened to a particular patriarch, but what happened in that patriarch's family. So the "account" of Isaac here introduces the Jacob narrative (25:19), just as that of Terah introduced the Abraham narrative (11:27).

3. Victor P. Hamilton, *The Book of Genesis: Chapters 18–50*, New International Commentary on the Old Testament (Grand Rapids: Eerdmans, 1995), 174.

4. There will be others—see especially David and his brothers. Bill T. Arnold, "בכר," *New International Dictionary of Old Testament Theology and Exegesis*, ed. Willem A. VanGemeren, 5 vols. (Grand Rapids: Zondervan, 1997) 1:659.

5. Gordon J. Wenham, *Genesis 16–50*, Word Biblical Commentary 2 (Dallas: Word, 1994), 169, 180.

6. Derek Kidner, *Genesis: An Introduction and Commentary*, Tyndale Old Testament Commentary (Downers Grove: InterVarsity, 1967), 152.

7. Bill T. Arnold, "בכר," in *New International Dictionary of Old Testament Theology and Exegesis*, ed. Willem A. VanGemeren, 5 vols. (Grand Rapids: Zondervan, 1997) 1:659. Ancient Near Eastern practices make it clear that the right of the firstborn could be bought and sold among brothers, though the exchange does not appear to have affected Esau's rank in the family, as illustrated by Genesis 27. On the ancient Near Eastern customs of birthright exchange, see Nahum M. Sarna, *Genesis: The Traditional Hebrew Text with the New JPS Translation*, JPS Torah Commentary (Philadelphia: Jewish Publication Society, 1989), 180–81.

8. Claus Westermann, *Genesis 12–36*, trans. John J. Scullion, Continental Commentary (Minneapolis: Fortress, 1985), 418.

9. Genesis 26 corresponds to Genesis 34, which at first sight also appears out of place. See Gary A. Rendsburg, *The Redaction of Genesis* (Winona Lake, Ind.: Eisenbrauns, 1986), 58.

10. There are proportionately more references to Abraham in this chapter than to any other in subsequent chapters of Genesis (Wenham, *Genesis 16–50*, 194).

11. Hamilton, *Genesis 18–50*, 192.

12. See discussion of the Iron Age transition above (p. 86).

13. Ephraim A. Speiser, *Genesis*, Anchor Bible 1 (Garden City, N.Y.: Doubleday, 1964), 200; and John A. Van Seters, *Abraham in History and Tradition* (New Haven, Conn.: Yale University Press, 1975), 52–54.

14. For more on this problem, see Kenneth A. Kitchen, "Philistines," in *Peoples of Old Testament Times*, ed. Donald J. Wiseman (Oxford: Clarendon, 1973), 56–57; Hamilton, *Genesis 18–50*, 94, with extensive bibliography in note 30; and David M. Howard Jr., "Philistines," in *Peoples of the Old Testament World*, ed. Alfred J. Hoerth, Gerald L. Mattingly, and Edwin M. Yamauchi (Grand Rapids: Baker, 1994), 237–38.

15. Carl Friedrich Keil and Franz Delitzsch, *Commentary on the Old Testament*, 10 vols. (Grand Rapids: Eerdmans, 1978 [n.d.]), 1:277.

16. Kidner, *Genesis*, 155; and Wenham, *Genesis 16–50*, 215–16.

17. "Paddan Aram," or the plain of Aram (28:2, 5–7), is the region around Haran in northwest Mesopotamia. This was the traditional homeland of Abraham, and was deemed the appropriate place to find a suitable patriarchal wife (Gen. 24).

18. The encounter has unmistakable Mesopotamian reference points. In particular, the stairway recalls the Babylonian ziggurats, or temple-towers, with their external ramps linking heaven and earth. The identification of the site as "the gate of heaven" (v. 17) is reminiscent of the etymology of the Akkadian name for Babylon, "gate of the gods" (Bill T. Arnold, "Babylonians," in *Peoples of the Old Testament World*, ed. Alfred J. Hoerth, Gerald L. Mattingly, and Edwin M. Yamauchi [Grand Rapids: Baker, 1994], 43–44). "The allusion is all the more suggestive when viewed in connection with Jacob's journey to Mesopotamia" (Speiser, *Genesis*, 220). See further, Nahum M. Sarna, *Understanding Genesis* (New York: Schocken, 1970 [1966]), 193.

19. Allen P. Ross, *Creation and Blessing: A Guide to the Study and Exposition of the Book of Genesis* (Grand Rapids: Baker, 1988), 489.

20. John H. Sailhamer, *The Pentateuch as Narrative: A Biblical-Theological Commentary* (Grand Rapids: Zondervan, 1992), 193.

21. Wenham, *Genesis 16–50*, 224.

22. Walter Brueggemann, *Genesis*, Interpretation (Atlanta: John Knox, 1982), 246.

23. Kidner, *Genesis*, 159.

24. Westermann, *Genesis 12–36*, 466.

25. Hamilton, *Genesis 18–50*, 262–63.

26. Rendsburg, *Redaction of Genesis*, 65–66. See also Westermann, *Genesis 12–36*, 409.

27. For more details on what follows, see Wenham, *Genesis 16–50*, 273–74; and Hamilton, *Genesis 18–50*, 291.

28. Speiser, *Genesis*, 249–51.

Chapter 10: *Jacob Struggles with God*

1. "Idee zu einer Allgemeinen Gesichte in Weltburgerlicher Absicht" (1784), quoted in Isaiah Berlin, *Crooked Timber of Humanity*, ed. Henry Hardy (New York: Knopf, 1990).

2. Derek Kidner, *Genesis: An Introduction and Commentary*, Tyndale Old Testament Commentary (Downers Grove: InterVarsity, 1967), 167.

3. Sometimes the Hebrew text has different chapter and verse numbers from English translations, most of which follow the ancient Greek translation (the Septuagint), which occasionally divides the text in different places. Here, chapter 32 in the Hebrew begins with the English verse 31:55, which means the rest of the verses of chapter 31 are also different.

4. There are several intentional verbal links between the Bethel and Mahanaim visions. See Gordon J. Wenham, *Genesis 16–50*, Word Biblical Commentary 2 (Dallas: Word, 1994), 281; and Carl Friedrich Keil and Franz Delitzsch, *Commentary on the Old Testament*, 10 vols. (Grand Rapids: Eerdmans, 1978 [n.d.]), 1:301.

5. Claus Westermann, *Genesis 12–36*, trans. John J. Scullion, Continental Commentary (Minneapolis: Fortress, 1985), 506–7.

6. Ibid., 511.

7. Wenham, *Genesis 16–50*, 291.

8. Gerhard von Rad, *Genesis: A Commentary*, trans. John H. Marks, rev. ed., Old Testament Library (Philadelphia, Westminster, 1972), 320.

9. Victor P. Hamilton, *The Book of Genesis: Chapters 18–50*, New International Commentary on the Old Testament (Grand Rapids: Eerdmans, 1995), 329; and Wenham, *Genesis 16–50*, 195, 292.

10. Joyce G. Baldwin, *The Message of Genesis 12–50*, The Bible Speaks Today (Downers Grove/Leicester: InterVarsity, 1986), 137.

11. Kidner, *Genesis*, 169.

12. Hamilton, *Genesis 18–50*, 343; and Wenham, *Genesis 16–50*, 304.

13. "Please, take my *blessing* that is brought to you . . ." (NKJV) is obscured by most modern English translations, which use "gift" or "present." But this word intentionally shows Jacob's attempt to make amends for his crimes of twenty years before. See Nahum M. Sarna, *Genesis: The Traditional Hebrew Text with the New JPS Translation*, JPS Torah Commentary (Philadelphia: Jewish Publication Society, 1989), 230.

14. Allen P. Ross, *Creation and*

Blessing: A Guide to the Study and Exposition of the Book of Genesis (Grand Rapids: Baker, 1988), 546–59.

15. John H. Sailhamer, *The Pentateuch as Narrative: A Biblical-Theological Commentary* (Grand Rapids: Zondervan, 1992), 199; and Westermann, *Genesis 12–36, 524*.

16. Wenham, *Genesis 16–50,* 308.

17. Ibid., 317.

18. Ibid., 318.

19. This may continue a parody in the Jacob narrative about the worthlessness of such strange gods (see Hamilton, *Genesis 18–50,* 375).

20. Westermann, *Genesis 12–36,* 511.

21. Baldwin, *Genesis 12–50,* 150.

22. Westermann, *Genesis 12–36,* 557.

23. Sarna, *Genesis,* 230.

24. Kidner, *Genesis,* 177.

Chapter 11: *Joseph in Egypt*

1. Gordon J. Wenham, *Genesis 16–50,* Word Biblical Commentary 2 (Dallas: Word, 1994), 345.

2. Gary A. Rendsburg, *The Redaction of Genesis* (Winona Lake, Ind.: Eisenbrauns, 1986), 79–80, and Allen P. Ross, *Creation and Blessing: A Guide to the Study and Exposition of the Book of Genesis* (Grand Rapids: Baker, 1988), 589–93.

3. Nahum M. Sarna, *Genesis: The Traditional Hebrew Text with the New JPS Translation,* JPS Torah Commentary (Philadelphia: Jewish Publication Society, 1989), 254.

4. Claus Westermann, *Genesis 37–50,* trans. John J. Scullion, Continental Commentary (Minneapolis: Fortress, 1986), 27.

5. Wenham, *Genesis 16–50,* 344; and Derek Kidner, *Genesis: An Introduction and Commentary,* Tyndale Old Testament Commentary (Downers Grove: InterVarsity, 1967), 179–80.

6. Victor P. Hamilton, *The Book of Genesis: Chapters 18–50,* New International Commentary on the Old Testament (Grand Rapids: Eerdmans, 1995), 407–9. In the patriarchal society, everyone had a robe or cloak. Cloaks were used for a great variety of purposes and were perhaps the most expensive item an individual possessed. The nature of one's robe often indicated one's position of honor and status in the community, and sometimes also indicated one's wealth.

7. Kidner, *Genesis,* 181.

8. Harry Freedman and Maurice Simon, eds., *Midrash Rabbah,* 10 vols. (London: Soncino, 1961), 2:786.

9. Ephraim A. Speiser, *Genesis,* Anchor Bible 1 (Garden City, N.Y.: Doubleday, 1964), 291; and see the introduction to source criticism in chapter 14 below.

10. The implications of this verse for the Ishmaelite/Midianite question in Genesis 37 was observed long ago by the medieval Jewish scholar, Abraham Ibn Ezra (H. Norman Strickman and Arthur M. Silver, eds., *Ibn Ezra's Commentary on the Pentateuch: Genesis (Bereshit)* [New York: Menorah, 1988], 351).

11. Kenneth A. Kitchen, "Joseph," in *New Bible Dictionary,* ed. J. D. Douglas et al., 3rd ed. (Downers Grove/Leicester: InterVarsity, 1996), 608.

12. Kidner, *Genesis,* 181.

13. Roland de Vaux, *Ancient Israel,* trans. John McHugh, 2 vols. (New York: McGraw-Hill, 1961), 38.

14. Even from a Mosaic perspective, we should be hesitant to blame her. The patriarchal narratives contain a number of sexual relationships that are banned in the later Mosaic laws of Leviticus, which suggests the different standards of the patriarchal age. Wenham, *Genesis 16–50,* 370.

15. Title of a hymn composed by William Cowper (1731–1800), also known as "Light Shining out of Darkness." John Julian, *A Dictionary of Hymnology* (New York: Dover, 1957), 433.

16. Wenham, *Genesis 16–50,* 364.

17. The second expansion relates the two journeys of Joseph's brothers to Egypt (Gen. 42–45). Westermann, *Genesis 37–50,* 24.

18. Ibid., 60.

19. Kidner, *Genesis,* 189.

20. The NIV catches the play nicely with the contrasting expressions, "Pharaoh will lift *up* your head" and "Pharaoh will lift *off* your head" (vv. 13 and 19).

21. Westermann, *Genesis 37–50,* 72; and Wenham, *Genesis 16–50,* 385.

22. Wenham, *Genesis 16–50,* 399.

Chapter 12: *Joseph over Egypt*

1. See discussion of the context of the Joseph narrative in chapter 11.

2. Talmud, *Berakhot* 16b.

3. T. Desmond Alexander, *From Paradise to the Promised Land: An Introduction to the Main Themes of the Pentateuch* (Grand Rapids: Baker, 1998), 6–15.

4. David J. A. Clines, *The Theme of the Pentateuch,* Journal for the Study of the Old Testament—Supplement Series 10 (Sheffield: JSOT, 1978), 29.

5. Gordon J. Wenham, *Genesis 16–50,* Word Biblical Commentary 2 (Dallas: Word, 1994), 358.

6. Claus Westermann, *Genesis 37–50,* trans. John J. Scullion, Continental Commentary (Minneapolis: Fortress, 1986), 24.

7. Joseph's brothers would have been using an early Canaanite dialect that eventually became Hebrew.

8. Especially since Judah's speech had made it quite obvious that Jacob was still living. Nahum M. Sarna, *Genesis: The Traditional Hebrew Text with the New JPS Translation,* JPS Torah Commentary (Philadelphia: Jewish Publication Society, 1989), 308; and Derek Kidner, *Genesis: An Introduction and Commentary,* Tyndale Old Testament Commentary (Downers Grove: InterVarsity, 1967), 206.

9. Victor P. Hamilton, *The Book of Genesis: Chapters 18–50,* New International Commentary on the Old Testament (Grand Rapids: Eerdmans, 1995), 575.

10. Kidner, *Genesis,* 207.

11. Joyce G. Baldwin, *The Message of Genesis 12–50,* The Bible Speaks Today (Downers Grove/Leicester: InterVarsity, 1986), 189.

12. Westermann, *Genesis 37–50,* 211–13.

13. Walter Brueggemann, *Genesis,* Interpretation (Atlanta: John Knox, 1982), 352.

14. Kenneth A. Kitchen, "Goshen," in *New Bible Dictionary,* ed. J. D. Douglas et al., 3rd ed. (Downers Grove/Leicester: InterVarsity, 1996), 425; William A. Ward, "Goshen," in *Anchor Bible Dictionary,* ed. David Noel Freedman, 6 vols. (New York: Doubleday, 1992), 2:1076–77.

15. Hamilton, *Genesis 18–50,* 618–19; and Wenham, *Genesis 16–50,* 452.

16. Wenham, *Genesis 16–50,* 459.

17. Hamilton, *Genesis 18–50,* 636.

18. Joseph's parting words in Genesis 50:25 are difficult to compare to the patriarchal blessings of Isaac (Gen. 27:27–29, 39–40; 28:1–4) and Jacob.

19. For more on this pattern

throughout the Pentateuch, see John H. Sailhamer, *The Pentateuch as Narrative: A Biblical-Theological Commentary* (Grand Rapids: Zondervan, 1992), 35–36, 233.

20. On this point, see Robert E. Longacre, *Joseph: A Story of Divine Providence—A Text Theoretical and Textlinguistic Analysis of Genesis 37 and 39–48* (Winona Lake, Ind.: Eisenbrauns, 1989), 54.

21. Gerhard von Rad, *Genesis: A Commentary,* trans. John H. Marks, rev. ed., Old Testament Library (Philadelphia, Westminster, 1972), 432.

22. Similarly so with Abraham (Genesis 24:1–7), Isaac (Genesis 28:1–4), and Jacob (Genesis 47:29–31).

23. Sarna, *Genesis,* 351.

Chapter 13: *Evidence for Authorship*

1. The best book to read on the relationship of Genesis to the rest of the Bible is R. W. L. Moberly, *The Old Testament of the Old Testament: Patriarchal Narratives and Mosaic Yahwism,* Overtures to Biblical Theology (Minneapolis: Fortress, 1992). We shall consider the relationship more carefully in chapter 15, below.

2. Specifically the covenant text of Deuteronomy 5–26, plus the blessings and curses of chapters 27–28. See Eugene H. Merrill, *Deuteronomy,* New American Commentary 4 (Nashville: Broadman, 1994), 398–99; Peter C. Craigie, *The Book of Deuteronomy,* New International Commentary on the Old Testament (Grand Rapids: Eerdmans, 1976), 370; and Jeffrey H. Tigay, *Deuteronomy: The Traditional Hebrew Text with the New JPS Translation,* JPS Torah Commentary (Philadelphia: Jewish Publication Society, 1996), 248, 291.

3. See, for example, Joshua 1:7–8; 8:31–32; 1 Kings 2:3; 2 Kings 14:6; 21:8; Ezra 6:18; Nehemiah 13:1; Daniel 9:11, 13; Malachi 4:4; and others.

4. As in the Talmud (*Sanhedrin* 21b–22a).

5. And many others: Mark 12:26; John 5:46–47; Acts 3:22; Romans 10:5, etc.

6. Francis I. Andersen and A. Dean Forbes, *Spelling in the Hebrew Bible* (Rome: Biblical Institute Press, 1986), 312–13.

7. Vowel markers known as *matres lectionis.*

8. Michael O'Connor, "Writing Systems, Native Speaker Analyses, and the Earliest Stages of Northwest Semitic Orthography," in *The Word of the Lord Shall Go Forth: Essays in Honor of David Noel Freedman in Celebration of His Sixtieth Birthday,* ed. Carol L. Meyers and Michael O'Connor (Winona Lake, Ind.: Eisenbrauns, 1983), 446–51; and Andersen and Forbes, *Spelling,* 31–33.

9. This evidence also shows, however, that the grammatical revisioning of the text occurred no later than the exilic and postexilic periods, since the Old Testament does not have the more luxuriant use of the *matres lectionis* present in later rabbinic times. For a complete history of these developments, see Andersen and Forbes, *Spelling,* 66–70 and 309–28. See also Frank Moore Cross, Jr. and David Noel Freedman, *Early Hebrew Orthography: A Study of the Epigraphic Evidence* (New Haven, Conn.: American Oriental Society, 1952), 1–10 and 58–60; and Werner Weinberg, "The History of Hebrew Plene Spelling," *Hebrew Union College Annual* 46 (1975), 457–60.

10. Ronald J. Williams, *Hebrew Syntax: An Outline,* 2nd ed. (Toronto: University of Toronto Press, 1976), 25 paragraph 129, 76 paragraph 462; W. Randall Garr, *Dialect Geography of Syria-Palestine, 1000–586 B.C.E.* (Philadelphia: University of Pennsylvania Press, 1985), 85–87; and Zellig S. Harris, *Development of the Canaanite Dialects: An Investigation in Linguistic History,* American Oriental Series 16 (New Haven, Conn.: American Oriental Society, 1939), 70 paragraph 47.

11. Scholars have carefully defined a "holistic historico-geographical comparative method," which is quite helpful in making general observations about the way literature was produced in ancient Israel. See particularly Shemaryahu Talmon, "The 'Comparative Method' in Biblical Interpretation—Principles and Problems," in *Congress Volume: Göttingen, 1977,* ed. J. A. Emerton, Vetus Testamentum, Supplements 29 (Leiden: E. J. Brill, 1978), 320–56; William W. Hallo, "Biblical History in Its Near Eastern Setting: The Contextual Approach," in *Scripture in Context: Essays on the Comparative*

Method, ed. Carl D. Evans, William W. Hallo, and John B. White, Pittsburgh Theological Monograph Series 34 (Pittsburgh: Pickwick, 1980), 1–26; and *The Biblical Canon in Comparative Perspective,* ed. K. Lawson Younger Jr., William W. Hallo, and Bernard F. Batto, Ancient Near Eastern Texts and Studies 11 (Lewiston, N.Y./Queenston/Lampeter: Edwin Mellen, 1991).

12. For more details on what follows, see Bill T. Arnold, "What Has Nebuchadnezzar to Do with David? On the Neo-Babylonian Period and Early Israel," in *Syria-Mesopotamia and the Bible,* ed. Mark W. Chavalas and K. Lawson Younger Jr. (Sheffield: Sheffield Academic Press, forthcoming).

13. For example, the role of Ashurbanipal in creating the great royal library of Nineveh, and Nebuchadnezzar in sponsoring a sort of renaissance of Babylonian literature. See Arnold, "What Has Nebuchadnezzar to Do with David?" forthcoming.

14. See discussion in chapter 6 above.

15. Alan R. Millard, "Methods of Studying the Patriarchal Narratives as Ancient Texts," in *Essays on the Patriarchal Narratives,* ed. Alan R. Millard and Donald J. Wiseman (Winona Lake, Ind.: Eisenbrauns, 1983), 35.

16. Bruce K. Waltke, "The Samaritan Pentateuch and the Text of the Old Testament," in *New Perspectives on the Old Testament,* ed. J. Barton Payne (Waco, Tex.: Word, 1970), 227–35; and idem, "Samaritan Pentateuch," in *Anchor Bible Dictionary,* ed. David Noel Freedman, 6 vols. (New York: Doubleday, 1992), 5:938.

17. John H. Sailhamer, *The Pentateuch as Narrative: A Biblical-Theological Commentary* (Grand Rapids: Zondervan, 1992), 141–43.

18. For what follows, see W. G. Lambert, "Babylonien und Israel," in *Theologische Realenzyklopädie* 5 (1979): 70–71, and Gordon J. Wenham, *Genesis 1–15,* Word Biblical Commentary 1 (Waco, Tex.: Word, 1987), xliv.

19. Duane A. Garrett has argued on the basis of an alienation theme in Genesis that the most reasonable time and place for the composition of the

book was the Egyptian sojourn (*Rethinking Genesis: The Sources and Authorship of the First Book of the Pentateuch* [Grand Rapids: Baker, 1991], 233–37).

20. Moberly, *Old Testament of the Old Testament*, 79–104, 195–97.

21. Ibid., 99–104.

22. The only exceptions are the place name "Kadesh" (Gen. 14:7; 16:14; 20:1) and the word "prostitute" (qĕdēšâ, Gen. 38:21).

23. Nahum M. Sarna, *Genesis: The Traditional Hebrew Text with the New JPS Translation*, JPS Torah Commentary (Philadelphia: Jewish Publication Society, 1989), xiv.

24. Moberly, *Old Testament of the Old Testament*, 92; and Sarna, *Genesis*, xiii.

25. Moberly, *Old Testament of the Old Testament*, 93.

26. William W. Hallo, "New Viewpoints on Cuneiform Literature," *Israel Exploration Journal* 12 (1962): 13–26.

27. For helpful discussion of these passages, see Craigie, *Deuteronomy*, 370–71, 373, and Merrill, *Deuteronomy*, 398–99, 404.

28. Meredith G. Kline, *Treaty of the Great King; the Covenant Structure of Deuteronomy: Studies and Commentary* (Grand Rapids: Eerdmans, 1963), 19–20.

29. We have evidence that the priesthood at Ugarit also had scribes specializing in the storage of legal material through writing. See especially the colophon for the famous Baal Cycle, Manfried Dietrich, Oswald Loretz, and J. Sanmartín, eds., *The Cuneiform Alphabetic Texts from Ugarit, Ras Ibn Hani and Other Places* (Münster: Ugarit-Verlag, 1995), 1.6 VI 54–56, page 28; and discussion in Mark S. Smith, "Mythology and Myth-making in Ugaritic and Israelite Literatures," in *Ugarit and the Bible: Proceedings of the International Symposium on Ugarit and the Bible, Manchester, September 1992*, ed. G. J. Brooke, A. H. W. Curtis, and J. F. Healey (Münster: Ugarit-Verlag, 1994), 331–32.

30. We have orthographical evidence that the legal material usually designated "priestly" was preserved independently from the rest of the Pentateuch. Such priestly legal material contains zero occurrences of the so-called Nun Paragogicum out of 412

opportunities, which is a striking contrast with other sections of the Pentateuch (J. Hoftijzer, *The Function and Use of the Imperfect Forms with Nun Paragogicum in Classical Hebrew*, Studia Semitica Neerlandica 21 [Assen, Netherlands: Van Gorcum, 1985]).

31. In the terminology of Willem A. VanGemeren, Moses was the fountainhead of Israelite prophecy, Samuel the rapids of the prophetic stream, and Elijah shaped the course of the classical prophets (*Interpreting the Prophetic Word* [Grand Rapids: Zondervan, 1990], 36).

32. Near the end of his life, William F. Albright speculated about the manner in which later Israelite laws, rules, and regulations grew up around the original Mosaic core. See William F. Albright, "Moses in Historical and Theological Perspective," in *Magnalia Dei, The Mighty Acts of God: Essays on the Bible and Archaeology in Memory of G. Ernest Wright* (Garden City, N.Y.: Doubleday, 1976), 120–31.

33. Bruce K. Waltke, "Old Testament Textual Criticism," in *Foundations for Biblical Interpretation: A Complete Library of Tools and Resources*, ed. by David S. Dockery, Kenneth A. Mathews, and Robert B. Sloan (Nashville: Broadman & Holman, 1994), 169–71.

34. William F. Albright, *From the Stone Age to Christianity: Monotheism and the Historical Process*, 2nd ed. (Garden City, N.Y.: Doubleday, 1957), 79, and see especially his comments on Hebrew scribes of the Old Testament period, p. 80.

35. Anderson and Forbes have suggested that the Pentateuch and the historical books were preserved together in the preexilic period, and that in the fifth century Ezra was the first to detach the Pentateuch, which was already by that time an ancient and venerated text. In the process, he changed the script from old Hebrew to the Aramaic block letters in use today and formally standardized the spelling. See Anderson and Forbes, *Spelling in the Hebrew Bible*, 321–22.

Chapter 14: *Interpretations of the Evidence*

1. For more on the definitions of biblical criticism and the various methodologies discussed in this chap-

ter, see Richard N. Soulen, *Handbook of Biblical Criticism*, 2nd ed. (Atlanta: John Knox, 1981).

2. *The Oxford English Dictionary* (Oxford: Clarendon, 1933), 2:1181.

3. More generally related to "hermeneutics," or the theory of interpretation. This branch of biblical scholarship seeks to establish principles and methods for interpreting the ancient written text for modern culture.

4. Of the many good sources available, see Emanuel Tov, *Textual Criticism of the Hebrew Bible* (Minneapolis/Assen, Netherlands: Fortress/Van Gorcum, 1992); and P. Kyle McCarter Jr., *Textual Criticism: Recovering the Text of the Hebrew Bible*, Guides to Biblical Scholarship (Philadelphia: Fortress, 1986).

5. R. Laird Harris, *Inspiration and Canonicity of the Bible: An Historical and Exegetical Study* (Grand Rapids: Zondervan, 1957), 88–89.

6. On the general understanding of this task as "literary criticism" and the distinctions between the two, see Carl E. Armerding, *The Old Testament and Criticism* (Grand Rapids: Eerdmans, 1983), 21–22.

7. For more on the criteria discussed here, see G. Herbert Livingston, *The Pentateuch in Its Cultural Environment* (Grand Rapids: Baker, 1974), 224–27; Duane A. Garrett, *Rethinking Genesis: The Sources and Authorship of the First Book of the Pentateuch* (Grand Rapids: Baker, 1991), 18–31; and Norman C. Habel, *Literary Criticism of the Old Testament*, Guides to Biblical Scholarship (Philadelphia: Fortress, 1971), 18–27.

8. More significant still are the seemingly contradictory statements in the flood account about chronology. See Garrett, *Rethinking Genesis*, 25–29.

9. Gene M. Tucker, *Form Criticism of the Old Testament*, Guides to Biblical Scholarship (Philadelphia: Fortress, 1971), 1; and for the principles of form criticism outlined in this paragraph, 6–9.

10. For more on the methods of form criticism, see Tucker, *Form Criticism*, 10–17; and Klaus Koch, *The Growth of the Biblical Tradition: The Form-Critical Method*, trans. S. M. Cupitt (New York: Scribner, 1969), 1–67.

11. Tradition criticism can also have a much narrower definition, in which it is understood to refer only to the history of the preliterary development of the literature. See Tucker, *Form Criticism*, 19; and Walter E. Rast, *Tradition History and the Old Testament*, Guides to Biblical Scholarship (Philadelphia: Fortress, 1972).

12. J. Maxwell Miller, *The Old Testament and the Historian*, Guides to Biblical Scholarship (Philadelphia: Fortress, 1976), especially 11–19.

13. The term was for some time used for the source critical endeavor, but is generally reserved today for the method described in this paragraph. For a brief history of this young discipline, see Paul R. House, "The Rise and Current Status of Literary Criticism of the Old Testament," in *Beyond Form Criticism: Essays in Old Testament Literary Criticism*, ed. Paul R. House (Winona Lake, Ind.: Eisenbrauns, 1992), 3–22; and Tremper Longman III, *Literary Approaches to Biblical Interpretation* (Grand Rapids: Zondervan, 1987).

14. James A. Sanders, *Canon and Community: A Guide to Canonical Criticism* (Philadelphia: Fortress, 1984). Though Brevard S. Childs rejects the use of the designation "canonical criticism" for his approach, most consider his work also in this category. See especially *Introduction to the Old Testament as Scripture* (Philadelphia: Fortress, 1979).

15. For a thorough treatment of what follows here, see R. K. Harrison, *Introduction to the Old Testament* (Grand Rapids: Eerdmans, 1969), 1–82. Among the many briefer surveys of this material, I recommend Armerding, *Old Testament and Criticism*; Joseph Blenkinsopp, *The Pentateuch: An Introduction to the First Five Books of the Bible*, Anchor Bible Reference Library (New York: Doubleday, 1992), 1–30; Eugene Carpenter, "Pentateuch," in *International Standard Bible Encyclopedia*, ed. Geoffrey W. Bromiley, 4 vols. (Grand Rapids: Eerdmans, 1979–88), 3:742–53; Ronald E. Clements, *One Hundred Years of Old Testament Interpretation* (Philadelphia: Westminster, 1976), 1–30; R. Norman Whybray, *Introduction to the Pentateuch* (Grand Rapids: Eerdmans, 1995), 12–28.

16. J was used to designate the Jehovistic author, otherwise known as the Yahwist since the Hebrew word is Yahweh.

17. Conservative scholars have frequently emphasized that the nineteenth-century documentary theories were based on a now defunct and disproved philosophy, and that those documentary theories should no longer be considered since Hegel's Idealism can no longer be sustained. There is certainly a degree of truth in this argument, since Vatke, Wellhausen, and others were dependent on Hegel in many ways, as we shall see. Nonetheless, their dependence on Hegel has often been overstated, and in any case, such dependence in itself did not predetermine Wellhausen's methods or conclusions. Blenkinsopp, *Pentateuch*, 8–11.

18. Julius Wellhausen, *Prolegomena to the History of Israel*, trans. J. Sutherland Black and Allan Menzies (Atlanta: Scholars, 1994 [1885]), 13.

19. Wellhausen published articles detailing his source critical approach in 1876 and 1877, and these were published twelve years later as *Die Composition des Hexateuchs und der historischen Bücher des Alten Testaments* (Berlin: de Gruyter, 1963 [1889]).

20. For further philosophical implications in Wellhausen, see Blenkinsopp, *Pentateuch*, 11.

21. Kenneth A. Kitchen, *Ancient Orient and Old Testament* (Downers Grove: InterVarsity, 1966), 15–28.

22. Ibid., 25–28.

23. Note in particular his work entitled *Monument Facts and Higher Critical Fancies* (London: Religious Tract Society, 1904).

24. Wellhausen's fundamental assumption is that pentateuchal law appeared at the beginning of the *Jewish* state (that is, in the postexilic period) rather than at the beginning of *Israelite* history. Wellhausen, *Prolegomena*, 1–4.

25. We now have enough Hittite literature to warrant an extended research project, giving fruition to the multivolume *Chicago Hittite Dictionary*, ed. Hans G. Güterbock and Harry A. Hoffner Jr. (Chicago: Oriental Institute, 1990–).

26. John Bright, "Modern Study of Old Testament Literature," in *The Bible and the Ancient Near East: Essays in Honor of William Foxwell Albright*, ed. G. Ernest Wright (Winona Lake, Ind.: Eisenbrauns, 1979 [1961]), 13.

27. His first volume covered the opening chapters of Genesis in 1895 (*Schöpfung und Chaos in Urzeit und Endzeit*), followed by more detailed treatments in a commentary and a volume on Genesis as a collection of sagas, both of which appeared in 1901.

28. Garrett, *Rethinking Genesis*, 41–42.

29. John Van Seters, *Abraham in History and Tradition* (New Haven, Conn.: Yale University Press, 1975), 131–48.

30. *Historicity of the Patriarchal Narratives: The Quest for the Historical Abraham*, Beihefte zur Zeitschrift für die alttestamentliche Wissenschaft 133 (Berlin: de Gruyter, 1974).

31. Van Seters, *Abraham in History and Tradition*.

32. *Das überlieferungsgeschichtliche Problem des Pentateuch*, Beihefte zur Zeitschrift für die alttestamentliche Wissenschaft 147 (Berlin: de Gruyter, 1977), and available in English as *The Problem of the Process of Transmission in the Pentateuch*, trans. John J. Scullion, Journal for the Study of the Old Testament—Supplement Series 89 (Sheffield: JSOT, 1990).

33. Longman, *Literary Approaches*, 21–24.

34. *The Redaction of Genesis* (Winona Lake, Ind.: Eisenbrauns, 1986), 99–106.

35. Garrett, *Rethinking Genesis*, and Harrison, *Introduction* are only two of many examples.

36. See, for example, the excellent commentary by Gordon J. Wenham, *Genesis 1–15*, Word Biblical Commentary 1 (Waco, Tex.: Word, 1987), and *Genesis 16–50*, Word Biblical Commentary 2 (Dallas: Word, 1994). Wenham views Genesis as a J or proto-J edition from as early as the thirteenth century to as late as the tenth century B.C. (*Genesis 1–15*, xliv–xlv).

37. William J. Abraham, *Divine Revelation and the Limits of Historical Criticism* (New York/Oxford: Oxford University Press, 1982), especially 187–89.

Conclusion: *Genesis and Beyond*

1. David J. A. Clines, "Theme in Genesis 1–11," in *"I Studied Inscriptions from before the Flood:" Ancient Near*

Eastern, Literary, and Linguistic Approaches to Genesis 1–11, ed. Richard S. Hess and David Toshio Tsumura (Winona Lake, Ind.: Eisenbrauns, 1994), 285–309; and idem, *The Theme of the Pentateuch,* Journal for the Study of the Old Testament—Supplement Series 10 (Sheffield: JSOT, 1978).

2. R. W. L. Moberly, "Christ as the Key to Scripture: Genesis 22 Reconsidered," in *He Swore an Oath: Biblical Themes from Genesis 12–50,* ed. Richard S. Hess, Philip E. Satterthwaite, and Gordon J. Wenham (Cambridge: Tyndale, 1993), 156.

3. For more on what follows, see the important book by R. W. L. Moberly, *The Old Testament of the Old Testament: Patriarchal Narratives and Mosaic Yahwism,* Overtures to Biblical Theology (Minneapolis: Fortress, 1992).

4. Read the excellent cautions about Moberly's approach in J. Gerald Janzen, *Abraham and All the Families of the Earth: A Commentary on the Book of Genesis 12–50,* International Theological Commentary (Grand Rapids: Eerdmans, 1993), 6–12.

5. David L. Baker, *Two Testaments, One Bible: A Study of the Theological Relationship between the Old and New Testaments,* 2nd ed. (Downers Grove: InterVarsity, 1991), 36.

6. Janzen, *Genesis 12–50,* 11.

7. The use of the patriarchal promises in the intercessory prayer of Moses also reveals the role of the relationship with Abraham in the heart of God (Exod. 32:13).

8. Moberly, *Old Testament,* 204–5. For the profound implications of this for Jewish-Christian dialogue, see his pp. 147–75.

9. T. Desmond Alexander, "Abraham Re-assessed Theologically: The Abraham Narrative and the New Testament Understanding of Justification by Faith," in *He Swore an Oath: Biblical Themes from Genesis 12–50,* ed. Richard S. Hess, Philip E. Satterthwaite, and Gordon J. Wenham (Cambridge: Tyndale, 1993), 7–28.

Select Bibliography of Sources Consulted

Abraham, William J. *Divine Revelation and the Limits of Historical Criticism.* New York/Oxford: Oxford University Press, 1982.

Aharoni, Yohanan. *The Land of the Bible: A Historical Geography.* Trans. Anson F. Rainey. London: Burns & Oates, 1979.

Albright, William F. *Archaeology and the Religion of Israel.* Baltimore: Johns Hopkins, 1942.

———. *From the Stone Age to Christianity: Monotheism and the Historical Process.* 2nd ed. Garden City, N.Y.: Doubleday, 1957.

———. *Yahweh and the Gods of Canaan: An Historical Analysis of Two Contrasting Faiths.* Winona Lake, Ind.: Eisenbrauns, 1990 (1968).

Alexander, T. Desmond. *From Paradise to the Promised Land: An Introduction to the Main Themes of the Pentateuch.* Grand Rapids: Baker, 1998.

Armerding, Carl E. *The Old Testament and Criticism.* Grand Rapids: Eerdmans, 1983.

Arnold, Bill T., and Bryan E. Beyer. *Encountering the Old Testament: A Christian Survey.* Grand Rapids: Baker, 1998.

———, eds. *Readings from the Ancient Near East: Primary Sources for Old Testament Study.* Grand Rapids: Baker, 2002.

Baker, David L. *Two Testaments, One Bible: A Study of the Theological Relationship between the Old and New Testaments.* 2nd ed. Downers Grove: InterVarsity, 1991.

Baldwin, Joyce G. *The Message of Genesis 12–50.* The Bible Speaks Today. Downers Grove/Leicester: InterVarsity, 1986.

Barth, Christoph. *God with Us: A Theological Introduction to the Old Testament.* Ed. Geoffrey W. Bromiley. Grand Rapids: Eerdmans, 1991.

Blenkinsopp, Joseph. *The Pentateuch: An Introduction to the First Five Books of the Bible.* Anchor Bible Reference Library. New York: Doubleday, 1992.

Bright, John. *A History of Israel.* 3rd edition. Philadelphia: Westminster, 1981.

Brueggemann, Walter. *Genesis.* Interpretation. Atlanta: John Knox, 1982.

Childs, Brevard S. *Introduction to the Old Testament as Scripture.* Philadelphia: Fortress, 1979.

Clements, Ronald E. *One Hundred Years of Old Testament Interpretation.* Philadelphia: Westminster, 1976.

Clines, David J. A. *The Theme of the Pentateuch.* Journal for the Study of the Old Testament—Supplement Series 10. Sheffield: JSOT, 1978.

Coats, George W. *Genesis, with an Introduction to Narrative Literature.* Forms of the Old Testament Literature 1. Grand Rapids: Eerdmans, 1983.

Garrett, Duane A. *Rethinking Genesis: The Sources and Authorship of the First Book of the Pentateuch.* Grand Rapids: Baker, 1991.

Gordon, Cyrus H. *Introduction to Old Testament Times.* Ventnor, N.J.: Ventnor, 1953.

Habel, Norman C. *Literary Criticism of the Old Testament.* Guides to Biblical Scholarship. Philadelphia: Fortress, 1971.

Hamilton, Victor P. *Handbook on the Pentateuch: Genesis, Exodus, Leviticus, Numbers, Deuteronomy.* Grand Rapids: Baker, 1982.

———. *The Book of Genesis: Chapters 1–17.* New International Commentary on the Old Testament. Grand Rapids: Eerdmans, 1990.

———. *The Book of Genesis: Chapters 18–50.* New International Commentary on the Old Testament. Grand Rapids: Eerdmans, 1995.

Harris, R. Laird. *Inspiration and Canonicity of the Bible: An Historical and Exegetical Study.* Grand Rapids: Zondervan, 1957.

Harrison, R. K. *Introduction to the Old Testament.* Grand Rapids: Eerdmans, 1969.

Hess, Richard S. *Studies in the Personal Names of Genesis 1–11.* Alter Orient und Altes Testament 234. Kevelaer/Neukirchen-Vluyn: Butzon & Bercker/Neukirchener, 1993.

Hoerth, Alfred J., Gerald L. Mattingly, and Edwin M. Yamauchi, eds. *Peoples of the Old Testament World.* Grand Rapids: Baker, 1994.

Janzen, J. Gerald. *Abraham and All the Families of the Earth: A Commentary on the Book of Genesis 12–50.* International Theological Commentary. Grand Rapids: Eerdmans, 1993.

Kaufmann, Yehezkel. *The Religion of Israel: From Its Beginnings to the Babylonian Exile.* Trans. Moshe Greenberg. New York: Schocken, 1972 (1960).

Keil, Carl Friedrich, and Franz Delitzsch, *Commentary on the Old Testament.* 10 vols. Grand Rapids: Eerdmans, 1978 (n.d.).

Kidner, Derek. *Genesis: An Introduction and Commentary.* Tyndale Old Testament Commentary. Downers Grove: InterVarsity, 1967.

Kikawada, Isaac M., and Arthur Quinn. *Before Abraham Was: The Unity of Genesis 1–11.* Nashville: Abingdon, 1985.

Kitchen, Kenneth A. *Ancient Orient and Old Testament.* Downers Grove: InterVarsity, 1966.

Kline, Meredith G. *Treaty of the Great King; the Covenant Structure of Deuteronomy: Studies and Commentary.* Grand Rapids: Eerdmans, 1963.

Koch, Klaus. *The Growth of the Biblical Tradition: The Form-Critical Method.* Trans. S. M. Cupitt. New York: Scribner, 1969.

Lambert, W. G., and Alan R. Millard. *Atra-hasis: The Babylonian Story of the Flood.* Oxford: Clarendon, 1969.

Livingston, G. Herbert. *The Pentateuch in Its Cultural Environment,* 2nd ed. Grand Rapids: Baker, 1987.

Longacre, Robert E. *Joseph: A Story of Divine Providence—A Text Theoretical and Textlinguistic Analysis of Genesis 37 and 39–48*. Winona Lake, Ind.: Eisenbrauns, 1989.

Longman, Tremper III. *Literary Approaches to Biblical Interpretation*. Grand Rapids: Zondervan, 1987.

McCarter, P. Kyle Jr., *Textual Criticism: Recovering the Text of the Hebrew Bible*. Guides to Biblical Scholarship. Philadelphia: Fortress, 1986.

Mathews, Kenneth A. *Genesis 1–11:26*. New American Commentary 1A. Nashville: Broadman, 1996.

Merrill, Eugene H. *Kingdom of Priests: A History of Old Testament Israel*. Grand Rapids: Baker, 1987.

Millard, Alan R., and Donald J. Wiseman, eds. *Essays on the Patriarchal Narratives*. Winona Lake, Ind.: Eisenbrauns, 1983.

Miller, J. Maxwell. *The Old Testament and the Historian*. Guides to Biblical Scholarship. Philadelphia: Fortress, 1976.

Moberly, R. W. L. *The Old Testament of the Old Testament: Patriarchal Narratives and Mosaic Yahwism*. Overtures to Biblical Theology. Minneapolis: Fortress, 1992.

Rad, Gerhard von. *Genesis: A Commentary*. Trans. John H. Marks. Old Testament Library. Philadelphia: Westminster, 1972.

Rast, Walter E. *Tradition History and the Old Testament*. Guides to Biblical Scholarship. Philadelphia: Fortress, 1972.

Rendsburg, Gary A. *The Redaction of Genesis*. Winona Lake, Ind.: Eisenbrauns, 1986.

Rendtorff, Rolf. *The Problem of the Process of Transmission in the Pentateuch*. Trans. John J. Scullion. Journal for the Study of the Old

Testament—Supplement Series 89. Sheffield: JSOT, 1990.

Ross, Allen P. *Creation and Blessing: A Guide to the Study and Exposition of the Book of Genesis*. Grand Rapids: Baker 1988.

Sailhamer, John H. *The Pentateuch as Narrative: A Biblical-Theological Commentary*. Grand Rapids: Zondervan, 1992.

Sanders, James A. *Canon and Community: A Guide to Canonical Criticism*. Philadelphia: Fortress, 1984.

Sarna, Nahum M. *Understanding Genesis*. New York: Schocken, 1970 (1966).

———. *Genesis: The Traditional Hebrew Text with the New JPS Translation*. JPS Torah Commentary. Philadelphia: Jewish Publication Society, 1989.

Soulen, Richard N. *Handbook of Biblical Criticism*. 2nd ed. Atlanta: John Knox, 1981.

Speiser, Ephraim A. *Genesis*. Anchor Bible 1. Garden City, N.Y.: Doubleday, 1964.

Thompson, Thomas L. *Historicity of the Patriarchal Narratives: The Quest for the Historical Abraham*. Beihefte zur Zeitschrift für die alttestamentliche Wissenschaft 133. Berlin: de Gruyter, 1974.

Tov, Emanuel. *Textual Criticism of the Hebrew Bible*. Minneapolis/Assen, Netherlands: Fortress/Van Gorcum, 1992.

Tsumura, David Toshio. *The Earth and the Waters in Genesis 1 and 2: A Linguistic Investigation*. Journal for the Study of the Old Testament—Supplement Series 83. Sheffield: JSOT, 1989.

Tucker, Gene M. *Form Criticism of the Old Testament*. Guides to Biblical Scholarship. Philadelphia: Fortress, 1971.

Van Seters, John A. *Abraham in History and Tradition*. New Haven, Conn.: Yale University Press, 1975.

Vaux, Roland de. *The Early History of Israel*. Trans. David Smith. Philadelphia: Westminster, 1978.

———. *Ancient Israel*. Trans. John McHugh. 2 vols. New York: McGraw-Hill, 1961.

Walton, John H. *Ancient Israelite Literature in Its Cultural Context: A Survey of Parallels between Biblical and Ancient Near Eastern Texts*. Grand Rapids: Zondervan, 1989.

———. *Covenant: God's Purpose, God's Plan*. Grand Rapids: Zondervan, 1994.

Wellhausen, Julius. *Prolegomena to the History of Israel*. Trans. J. Sutherland Black and Allan Menzies. Atlanta: Scholars, 1994.

Wenham, Gordon J. *Genesis 1–15*. Word Biblical Commentary 1. Waco, Tex.: Word, 1987.

———. *Genesis 16–50*. Word Biblical Commentary 2. Dallas: Word, 1994.

Westermann, Claus. *Genesis 1–11*. Trans. John J. Scullion. Continental Commentary. Minneapolis: Fortress, 1984.

———. *Genesis 12–36*. Trans. John J. Scullion. Continental Commentary. Minneapolis: Fortress, 1985.

———. *Genesis 37–50*. Trans. John J. Scullion. Continental Commentary. Minneapolis: Fortress, 1986.

Whybray, R. Norman. *Introduction to the Pentateuch*. Grand Rapids: Eerdmans, 1995.

Williams, Ronald J. *Hebrew Syntax: An Outline*. 2nd ed. Toronto: University of Toronto Press, 1976.

Wiseman, P. J. *Ancient Records and the Structure of Genesis: A Case for Literary Unity*. Ed. Donald J. Wiseman. Nashville: Thomas Nelson, 1985.

Glossary

Autograph
Term in biblical studies referring to the original copy of an author's work. No autographs of biblical books have survived to the present day. The task of textual criticism is to reconstruct as completely as possible the original wording of the text based on the existing manuscript copies (see "Lower Criticism"). A few fragmentary manuscripts from the Dead Sea Scrolls appear to be within less than a century of autographs of certain Old Testament books, such as Daniel.

Babylonian Exile
After Jerusalem fell to Nebuchadnezzar in 586 B.C., most of the leaders were taken into exile to Babylonia. The exile officially ended in October 539 B.C., when Babylonia was captured by the Persians and the Jews were released and permitted to return to the ruins of Jerusalem. Scholars have often speculated about the role these exilic and postexilic communities might have played in the production of the literature of the Old Testament.

Canon
Term referring to the authoritative collection of biblical books that have been accepted as the rule of faith and practice (Greek *kanōn*).

Canonical Criticism
Term referring to a number of relatively new approaches in biblical studies sharing a similar interest in the nature, function, and authority of the biblical canon. Canonical criticism attempts to study the received form of the Old Testament and to expose its theological message. It is less concerned with particular editorial levels, and more interested in the final product. Canonical critics are less concerned with how the text arrived, and more concerned with the internal and theological message of the canon.

Cosmogony
An account or theory concerning the origin of the universe.

Cosmology
A philosophy or theory concerning the nature and principles of the universe as a whole and its various parts.

Covenant
Term (Hebrew *běrît*) describing binding relationships between human partners, or between God and humans. The concept has a legal background and describes an agreement between two parties, where no such agreement existed by nature. Such agreements had binding obligations on both parties. This is a rich theological concept in the Bible, since God commits himself to covenant relationships with humans in which he accepts obligations. This concept is behind the English word "testament" in the labels "Old Testament" and "New Testament."

Creatio Ex Nihilo
Latin phrase meaning "creation out of nothing." The early church confronted certain heresies that taught God had created the world with preexistent, uncreated matter as his raw material. But the biblical evidence led to the conviction that God created the universe from nothing and did so effortlessly (Ps 33:6, 9; Heb 11:3).

Criticism, Biblical
The search for truth through the application of the laws of reason to an investigation of the biblical text. Biblical criticism is not a negative or distasteful enterprise, as its name might imply. The primary meaning of "criticism" in this case is the act of scientifically dealing with a text, asking questions of character, composition, and origin of literary documents. As such, it is a strictly neutral term, neither negative nor positive. It is impossible to read the biblical text without also considering questions of authorship and date of composition. *See* "Lower Criticism" and "Higher Criticism."

Cuneiform
The writing system invented by the Sumerians around 3100 B.C. Wedgelike shapes were pressed into wet clay, or incised on stone or metals to represent words. The system could be easily adapted to represent many languages of the ancient Near East.

Early Bronze Age
Term used by archaeologists and historians of the ancient Near East to refer to the third millennium B.C., also called, in Palestine, the Canaanite Age (about 3300–2000 B.C.). This was an age of major new developments across the ancient Near East. In Syria–Palestine, the Early Bronze Age witnessed a sudden flourishing of population and urbanization. There was rapid transition from life in unwalled villages to fortifications at a number of sites. In Egypt and Mesopotamia, the Early Bronze Age marked the rise and fall of humankind's first great empires: Old Kingdom Egypt and the Sumero-Akkadian empires in Mesopotamia.

Eschatology, Eschatological
Term for that part of theology that deals with the doctrine of the last things. As such, eschatology is concerned with death, judgment, heaven, hell, resurrection, Jesus' second coming, and so on.

Etiology
A study of causes. The Bible often uses an ancient story to explain how a person or place was named, or to explain how some custom known to the author became accepted in the society. Such stories offer explanations about why things are the way they are now. Modern scholars often assume that the presence of etiology in a narrative means it cannot be historically accurate. But this method is not necessary and does an injustice to the traditions.

Exile. See "Babylonian Exile."

Fiat
Latin term meaning "let it be done" and referring to God's method of cre-

ation by decree in Genesis 1. On the six successive days of creation, God created by divine order or command: "Let there be light," "Let there be an expanse between the waters," and so on.

Form Criticism
The analysis and interpretation of the literature of the Old Testament through a study of its literary types or genres. This approach assumes that ancient literature usually began as oral tradition, and Old Testament form criticism likewise starts by assuming that most of Israelite literature arose as folk literature, which went through a long oral prehistory. Each genre or form is believed to have originated in a particular historical setting (*see "Sitz im Leben"*) in the history of the Israelite people. The form critic believes this original setting can be recovered through a study of the form itself. The form critic's methodology traditionally has four steps, involving the form's structure, genre, setting, and intention. *See "Genre."*

Genre
Term used by Bible scholars to refer to a literary form or type (French "kind, sort, type"). Form critics group texts in the same genre if they share distinguishing characteristics.

Hebrews
Term the Bible uses to describe Abraham and his descendants through Isaac and Jacob. The origin of the term is not known. One possibility is that the Hebrews of the Old Testament may be identified at least in part with the Habiru of Middle and Late Bronze Age texts from the ancient Near East. This was probably a social designation for seminomadic Semites. The Hebrews could have been intended by some of the ancient references to Habiru. But the latter term does not have an ethnic significance and has a much wider range of meaning.

Heilsgeschichte
Compound German word (from the words for "salvation" and "history") with several English equivalents: redemptive history, salvation history, sacred history, and so on. It denotes a theological principle that interprets the Bible as describing God's actions

of salvation in history. The events of salvation history are supernatural divine revelations in time and space, which are recorded in Scripture to promote faith.

Henotheism
The belief in one god as the deity of a particular race, tribe or other group, without claiming he or she is the only god.

Hexateuch
Name (meaning "six scrolls") given to the first six books of the Bible (Genesis, Exodus, Leviticus, Numbers, Deuteronomy, and Joshua) as a literary unit. Some scholars have argued that this unit was edited as one work.

Hieroglyphs, Hieroglyphic
Term for the earliest Egyptian writing system (Greek *hieros*, "sacred," and *glyphē*, "carving"). It was pictographic, relying on representations of common objects and geometric symbols. Hieroglyphs were eventually replaced by a less cumbersome cursive writing system, demotic.

Higher Criticism
Modern biblical criticism has developed rules for investigating the text, which have in turn led to the development of several distinct methodologies. These have sometimes been subdivided into "lower criticism" and "higher criticism," though these terms are not as common as they once were because of their derogatory implications. Higher criticism refers to all forms of biblical criticism, which seek to answer questions regarding the Bible's composition and origins. Since the Enlightenment (seventeenth and eighteenth centuries A.D.), biblical criticism has given rise to a number of distinguishable but interconnected methodologies. *See "Criticism," and "Lower Criticism."*

Historical Criticism
Sometimes this designation is used for the methodology that seeks to combine the results of all the other critical approaches in an attempt to reconstruct a chronology of the history of Israelite literature. This endeavor deals with the historical setting of a document, including its date and place of composition. Historical criti-

cism attempts a chronological narrative of events related to the composition of Israel's literature within the total picture of Israel's history in general. Its distinction from the other methods is one of emphasis, since historical criticism is interested in the history of Israel in general, including the history of the production of Israelite literature. *See "Criticism, Biblical," "Higher Criticism," "Form Criticism," "Source Criticism."*

Imago Dei
Latin expression for "image of God," referring particularly to the climax of God's creation when he made humankind in his "image" (*ṣelem*) and in his "likeness" (*dĕmût*, Gn 1:26–27).

Iron Age
Term used by archaeologists and historians of the ancient Near East for the period in which iron displaced bronze as the metal used for tools and weaponry (about 1200–332 B.C.). This period is marked by the rise of the first genuinely world empires, all from a Mesopotamian base: Assyria, Babylonia, and Persia. The Iron Age is commonly subdivided into three periods: Iron Age I (1200–930 B.C.), Iron Age II (930–539 B.C.), and Iron Age III (539–332 B.C.). This was the period of Israel's monarchy, exile, and restoration.

Late Bronze Age
Term used by archaeologists and historians for the period of internationalism and communication in the ancient Near East, dated about 1550–1200 B.C. The Late Bronze Age is marked by Egypt's powerful New Kingdom, which exerted considerable influence on the coastal areas of Syria–Palestine. This was the period of Israel's exodus from Egypt, wilderness wanderings, and conquest of Canaan.

Levant
The eastern coast of the Mediterranean Sea, which forms the western boundary of Syria–Palestine. The Levant extends for four hundred miles, and became the crossroads for all trade and travel in the ancient world.

Levirate Marriage
A law of the Old Testament providing children for a deceased family member (Dt 25:5–6). When an Israelite died without sons, his nearest relative was to marry the widow and continue the family of the deceased through the firstborn son of the new marriage, who was to carry the name and inheritance of the first husband. Levirate marriage is an important element in Genesis 38.

Literary Criticism
This recent methodology in biblical studies seeks to analyze a biblical text not in light of who composed it or when it was written. Rather, the literary critic is interested in the innate meaning of the text, and the way in which the text creates meaning through the various component elements of the structure of the text. Thus the literary critic begins not with the who and when, but with the why and how of a text. Many literary critics have challenged the findings of the older and more established conclusions of source and form criticism.

Lower Criticism
Modern biblical criticism has developed rules for investigating the text, which have in turn led to the development of several distinct methodologies. These have sometimes been subdivided into "lower criticism" and "higher criticism," though these terms are not as common as they once were because of their derogatory implications. Lower criticism refers to textual criticism, which seeks to reconstruct the original wording of the texts from the various manuscripts currently available. *See* "Higher Criticism" and "Criticism."

Magic
When used in biblical studies, this term does not refer to sleight-of-hand tricks as it does in modern parlance. Rather, it designates the use of formulaic recitations and imitative acts, which ancient peoples believed could manipulate and exploit the powers of the divine and natural realms. Through these means, the ancients believed they could make nature and the gods subservient to supernatural forces beyond the control of the deities. Israel's monotheism and con-

cept of transcendence meant magic was forbidden. The creator God is not subservient to any supernatural force beyond his control, and cannot be manipulated under any circumstances.

Messiah
Hebrew word meaning "Anointed One." The Greek word "Christ" (*Christos*) translates Messiah, though it does not contain the same connotations of Messiah, that is, one invested by God with power and authority for mission.

Middle Bronze Age
Term used by archaeologists and historians for the period of Amorite incursions across the ancient Near East, initiating a new era (about 2000–1550 B.C.). After an initial period of decline in Syria–Palestine, the Amorite culture brought a resurgence of sedentary life and the development of new urban centers. New Amorite kingdoms in Babylonia of this period were to play a major role in ancient Near Eastern history. This was also Israel's patriarchal period.

Monotheism
The theological and philosophical position that there is only one God. Such a view was not the accepted belief of ancient peoples, who were polytheists and henotheists.

Myth, Mythology
In modern English, this term usually refers to something untrue and imaginative. But in ancient Near Eastern studies, scholars use it in a more classical sense, though there is no consensus on definition. Myth is the literary instrument by which ancient peoples ordered their world. Myths explained how the world began and provided norms for human behavior. As expressions of theological convictions, these ancient myths occurred outside time and space, and were linked to the nature religions. Ancient Israel, however, "historicized" mythology by referring not to a time distinct from world time, but to the history of Israel itself. The Israelite God, Yahweh, was creator and established the norms for human behavior himself through divine revelation to the nation.

History became the instrument for expressing theology, not myth.

Negeb
The Hebrew term for the desert south of Judah. Also means simply "the South."

Omnipotence
The belief that God has all the power and strength necessary to effect whatever purposes he chooses in the way in which he chooses. Omnipotence is the idea that God is free to do whatever he wills in whatever way he wants (Mk 14:36; Lk 1:37). *See* "Sovereignty."

Patriarchs
Traditional term used to refer to our ancestors in faith. The term can sometimes refer to all the great figures of faith in the Old Testament. But following Old Testament precedent and early Jewish custom, the term is usually limited to the three ancestors of Genesis 12–36, Abraham, Isaac, and Jacob.

Pentateuch
Term referring to the first five books of the Bible (from Greek *pente*, five, and *teuchos*, scroll). The biblical evidence supports the view that Genesis, Exodus, Leviticus, Numbers, and Deuteronomy belong together as a literary unit. The Old Testament probably refers to the Pentateuch when it uses phrases like the "Book of the Law of Moses" (2 Kgs 14:6) and the "Book of the Law" (Jos 1:8), while the New Testament refers to these books as "law" in the expression "the law and the prophets" (Lk 16:16). Thus, we should not necessarily view the Pentateuch as five separate books. The Pentateuch spans history from the beginning of time down to, but not including, Israel's conquest of the Promised Land. The Jewish designation for these books is the Hebrew word "Torah" or "law." Together these five books establish the historical and theological foundations for the rest of the Bible.

Polytheism
The belief in more than one god. Polytheism is usually linked to fertility religions and nature religions of antiquity.

Primeval History
Prehistory, or the earliest phases of human activity, which occurred before history was recorded.

Redaction Criticism
Related to source criticism, the term "redaction" refers to the editorial activity in which received materials have been arranged in a definite literary form. The tasks of the redaction critic are sometimes defined differently, but they usually involve analyzing the manner in which the sources were edited together, in which case it assumes the results of source criticism and agrees with its findings. Redaction critics also attempt to uncover the theological perspectives of the individual editors of biblical sources by analyzing the editorial techniques and choices used in shaping and framing the available written sources. They study the literary tapestry of a text in order to learn about the ancient editor who created it. *See* "Criticism" and "Source Criticism."

Salvation History. See "Heilsgeschichte."

Sea Peoples
Newcomers into the ancient Near East around 1200 B.C. Presumably fleeing from the mainland of Greece after the fall of Troy, these peoples fled along the coasts of the Mediterranean, disrupting all the major powers of the day, notably Egypt and the Hittites. One group of these Sea Peoples was the Philistines, who settled on the southwestern coast of Syria–Palestine and played a major role in Old Testament times.

Semites/Semitic
A large group of peoples related ethnically and linguistically. The term is taken from the list of nations in Genesis 10, which describes these groups as the sons of "Shem," hence our term "Semitic." In the east, many various Semitic groups lived in Mesopotamia, most prominent among them the Akkadians, Amorites, Arameans, and Arabs. The Canaanites and Arameans occupied the west. The Hebrews were a subgroup of the Canaanites.

Septuagint
Latin name (meaning "seventy") of the earliest Greek translation of the Old Testament. According to tradition, the translating was done by seventy (or seventy-two) Jewish scholars at the order of Ptolemy II in Alexandria, Egypt, in the third century B.C. It became the early church's favored translation of the Old Testament. In most biblical studies, the Septuagint is designated by the Roman numerals for 70, LXX.

Sitz im Leben
German expression (meaning "setting in life") that denotes the historical and sociological setting in which a specific literary genre or form first took shape.

Source Criticism
This approach seeks to discover the literary patterns of the Old Testament text. These patterns in turn enable the critic to speculate about, and possibly to isolate, various sources used in the composition of the text. Often the source critic relies on a combination of several types of criteria to distinguish the sources. In pentateuchal studies, these include the different names for God, repetition or parallel accounts of single events, apparent contradictions, style, and theology.

Sovereignty
The biblical portrayal of God as king, or supreme ruler of the entire universe. The concept finds its origins in creation itself (Ps 103:19), but is expressed more specifically in God's comprehensive plan for world history (Eph 1:11). God's gracious work of redemption displays his sovereignty, since Jesus's ministry was always about "the kingdom of God" (Mk 1:15; Acts 1:3).

Syncretism
The attempt to unite or reconcile opposing beliefs or practices. Proponents of one religion will sometimes adapt or otherwise identify its deities or creeds with those of another religion in order to gain adherents.

Tetrateuch
Name (meaning "four scrolls") given to the first four books of the Bible—Genesis, Exodus, Leviticus, and Numbers—as a literary unit. Some scholars have argued that this unit was edited as one work consisting of the JEP sources. In this view, Deuteronomy was added much later.

Textual Criticism. See "Lower Criticism."

Theogony
Speculation about the birth of the gods. Ancient Near Eastern authors were interested in the beginning of the universe, including the birth and ancestry of the deities.

Theophany
Greek term for a manifestation of God. These sudden and unexpected appearances of God occur in perceptible forms (hearing and seeing) at decisive points in Israel's history: patriarchal promises (Gn 17; 18; 28), the call of Moses (Ex 3), the Sinai covenant (Ex 19), and so on.

Tradition Criticism
A methodology that generally attempts a comprehensive analysis of the way biblical literature originated and developed. It brings together the results of both source criticism and form criticism in order to construct a history of Old Testament literature through both its preliterary and literary stages. It assumes that both oral and written traditions played a role in the final shape of Old Testament literature. In a sense, tradition criticism lies between form criticism and redaction criticism. It is interested in all the steps, from the beginning of the oral traditions (form criticism) to the last stages of the editing (redaction criticism).

Vulgate
Name (Latin "common, popular") of the Latin translation of the Bible recognized by the medieval church. The Council of Trent (1546) declared the Vulgate to be the official Bible of the Roman Church. Most of the books of this version came from Jerome (ca. 340–420).

Subject Index

Scripture Index